SMALL CLAIMS AND SIMPLIFIED PROCEDURE LITIGATION

Fourth Edition

JOSEPH F. KENKEL
B.A. (HONS.), LL.B., of the Ontario Bar

WILLIAM S. CHALMERS
B.A., LL.B., of the Ontario Bar

Butterworths
A Member of the LexisNexis Group

Small Claims and Simplified Procedure Litigation, Fourth Edition
© Butterworths Canada Ltd. 2002
November 2002

All rights reserved. No part of this publication may be reproduced, stored in any material form (including photocopying or storing it in any medium by electronic means and whether or not transiently or incidentally to some other use of this publication) without the written permission of the copyright holder except in accordance with the provisions of the Copyright Act. Applications for the copyright holder's written permission to reproduce any part of this publication should be addressed to the publisher.

Warning: The doing of an unauthorized act in relation to a copyrighted work may result in both a civil claim for damages and criminal prosecution.

The Butterworth Group of Companies

Canada:
Butterworths Canada Ltd.
75 Clegg Road, MARKHAM, Ontario L6G 1A1
and
1732-808 Nelson St., Box 12148, VANCOUVER, B.C. V6Z 2H2
Australia:
Butterworths Pty Ltd., SYDNEY
Ireland:
Butterworth (Ireland) Ltd., DUBLIN
Malaysia:
Malayan Law Journal Sdn Bhd, KUALA LUMPUR
New Zealand:
Butterworths (New Zealand) Ltd., WELLINGTON
Singapore:
Butterworths Asia, SINGAPORE
South Africa:
Butterworth Publishers (Pty.) Ltd., DURBAN
United Kingdom:
Butterworth & Co. (Publishers) Ltd., LONDON
United States:
LEXIS Publishing, CHARLOTTESVILLE, Virginia

National Library of Canada Cataloguing in Publication

Kenkel, Joseph F.
  Small claims and simplified procedure litigation / Joseph F. Kenkel, William S. Chalmers — 4th ed.

First-2nd. eds. published under title: Small claims litigation.
Includes bibliographical references and index.
ISBN 0-433-43951-3

1. Small claims court — Ontario. 2. Civil procedure — Ontario. 3. Actions and defenses — Ontario. I. Chalmers, Williams S. II. Title. III. Title: Small claims litigation.

KEO1090.K46 2002   347.713'04   C2002-904737-4
KF8769.K46 2002

Printed and bound in Canada.

To

William and Hudson

W.S.C.

Preface

The purpose of this book is to provide a brief overview of litigation practice from the initial interview to collection procedures and appeals in the context of a claim where the amount in issue is less than $50,000. The book deals with both the Small Claims Court for claims which are less than $10,000 and the simplified procedure for claims which are more than $10,000 and less than $50,000. Given the broad range of the topics covered, commentary is necessarily limited. Reference should be made to actual rules and case law.

This book is intended to be a practitioner's guide, with numerous divisions in the text for fast and easy reference. It was written in a manner which should be accessible to persons with different levels of legal training, including lawyers, students, agents and the parties themselves. It is hoped that this book is a readable and reliable guide to the litigation of relatively modest claims in Ontario, and will prove useful to the persons who find themselves involved in a small claims court or simplified procedures action.

William S. Chalmers
July 2002

Acknowledgments

I am indebted to the lawyers and staff of Hughes, Amys for their contributions to this book. In particular, I wish to thank my partner, Albert Conforzi, who reviewed the text and provided his helpful comments. I also thank our librarian, Penny Sheehan, and our student, Michelle Arzaga, who assisted with the annotations. I am particularly grateful to my assistant, Tricia Huggins, who typed and retyped the manuscript. Finally, I would like to thank my co-author, Joseph Kenkel, for the opportunity to be involved in this project.

Table of Contents

Preface v
Acknowledgments vii
Table of Cases xv

Chapter 1: Introduction 1
    1.1   Introduction 1
    1.2   Small Claims Court 2
    1.3   Rules of Simplified Procedure 3

Chapter 2: Meeting Your Client 5
    2.1   The First Interview 5
    2.2   Counsel's Opinion 6
    2.3   Costs and Retainer 6
    2.4   A Professional Relationship 6

Chapter 3: Getting Started 9
    3.1   Whether to Sue — Alternatives to Litigation 9
    3.2   When to Sue — Limitation Periods 9
        (a)   Notice Requirements 10
        (b)   Substantive Limits 10
        (c)   Procedural Limits 11
    3.3   Who Can Sue or Be Sued — The Parties 12
        (a)   Parties Under Disability 12
            (i)   Bringing the Action on Behalf of a Party Under Disability 12
            (ii)   Defending the Action on Behalf of a Party Under Disability 14
            (iii)   Settling the Action Where a Party Is Under Disability 15
        (b)   Partnerships 15
        (c)   Corporations 15
        (d)   Sole Proprietors 16
    3.4   Where to Sue — Monetary and Territorial Jurisdiction 16
        (a)   Jurisdiction 16
            (i)   Small Claims Court 16
            (ii)   Simplified Procedure 17
        (b)   Cost Consequences 19
            (i)   Small Claims Court 19
            (ii)   Simplified Procedure 20
        (c)   Territorial Jurisdiction 21
            (i)   Small Claims Court 21
            (ii)   Simplified Procedure 21
        (d)   Transfers Between Courts 21

Chapter 4: Pleading Your Case ... 23
- 4.1 Drafting Pleadings ... 23
- 4.2 Small Claims Court ... 24
  - (a) The Claim ... 24
    - (i) Issuing the Claim ... 24
    - (ii) Serving the Claim ... 25
  - (b) Defence ... 26
  - (c) Defendant's Claim ... 26
  - (d) Defence to Defendant's Claim ... 28
- 4.3 Simplified Procedure ... 28
  - (a) Statement of Claim ... 28
    - (i) Issuing the Statement of Claim ... 28
    - (ii) Serving the Statement of Claim ... 29
  - (b) Statement of Defence ... 29
  - (c) Counterclaim ... 30
  - (d) Crossclaim ... 31
  - (e) Third Party Claim ... 31
  - (f) Reply ... 32
  - (g) Jury Notice ... 33
- 4.4 Amendment of Pleadings ... 33

Chapter 5: Resolving the Action After Pleadings ... 35
- 5.1 Small Claims Court ... 35
  - (a) Default Judgment ... 35
  - (b) Striking a Pleading ... 36
- 5.2 Simplified Procedure ... 37
  - (a) Dismissal by Registrar ... 37
  - (b) Default Judgment ... 37
  - (c) Striking a Pleading ... 39
  - (d) Summary Judgment ... 40
    - (i) Notice of Motion for Summary Judgment ... 40
    - (ii) Evidence on Motion for Summary Judgment ... 40
    - (iii) Motion Record ... 40
    - (iv) Hearing of the Motion ... 41
    - (v) Test for Summary Judgment ... 41
    - (vi) Dismissal of Motion for Summary Judgment ... 42
    - (vii) Appeal of Summary Judgment ... 43

Chapter 6: Settling the Action ... 45
- 6.1 Why Settle the Case? ... 45
- 6.2 Preparing for Settlement ... 46
- 6.3 Settlement Conferences ... 46
  - (a) Private Settlement Meetings ... 46
  - (b) Simplified Procedure — Settlement Discussion and Documentary Disclosure (Rule 76.08) ... 46
- 6.4 Alternative Dispute Resolution ... 47
  - (a) Private Mediation ... 47
  - (b) Simplified Procedure — Mandatory Mediation ... 48

6.5	Offers to Settle	49
6.6	Cost Consequences of Offers to Settle	49
	(a) Small Claims Court	50
	(b) Simplified Procedure	50
6.7	Concluding Settlement	50
	(a) Small Claims Court	51
	(b) Simplified Procedure	51

Chapter 7: Discovering the Case: Pre-Trial Proceedings 53

7.1	Discovery of Documents	53
	(a) Small Claims Court	53
	(b) Simplified Procedure	54
7.2	Oral Examinations for Discovery	55
7.3	Demand for Particulars	55
	(a) Small Claims Court	55
	(b) Simplified Procedure	55
7.4	Request to Admit	56
	(a) Small Claims Court	56
	(b) Simplified Procedure	56
7.5	Medical Examinations	57
	(a) Small Claims Court	57
	(b) Simplified Procedure	57
7.6	Interlocutory Motions	58
	(a) Small Claims Court	58
	(b) Simplified Procedure	60
	(i) Motions	60
	(ii) Appeals of Interlocutory Orders	61
	1. Appeal of Master's Order	61
	2. Appeal of Judge's Order	62
7.7	Pre-Trial Conferences	63
	(a) Small Claims Court	63
	(i) Request for Pre-Trial Conference	63
	(ii) Pre-Trial Conference	64
	(iii) Notice of Trial	65
	(b) Simplified Procedure	65
	(i) Readiness for Pre-Trial Conference	65
	(ii) Pre-Trial Conference	65
	(iii) Setting Action Down for Trial	66

Chapter 8: Preparing for Trial 69

8.1	File Organization	69
8.2	Trial Brief	69
8.3	Theory of the Case	70
8.4	Preparation of Evidence	70
	(a) Small Claims Court	70
	(i) General	70
	(ii) Documents	71
	(iii) Witnesses	72

		(iv)	Visiting the Scene	73
	(b)	Simplified Procedure		73
		(i)	General	73
		(ii)	Documents	74
		(iii)	Witnesses	74

Chapter 9: Conducting the Trial 77

9.1	Planning and Preparation			77
9.2	Preliminaries			78
	(a)	Settlement		78
	(b)	Adjournments		78
		(i)	Small Claims Court	78
		(ii)	Simplified Procedure	78
	(c)	Failure of the Parties to Attend		79
	(d)	Failure of Witnesses to Attend		79
9.3	The Trial			80
	(a)	The Courtroom		80
	(b)	Opening Statements		80
	(c)	Direct Examinations		81
	(d)	Cross-Examinations		81
	(e)	Objections		83
	(f)	Closing Arguments		83
9.4	Summary Trial			84
	(a)	Trial Record		84
	(b)	Conduct of the Summary Trial		85
	(c)	Appeal of Judgment Following Summary Trial		86
9.5	The Judgment			86
	(a)	Pre-Judgment Interest		86
	(b)	Post-Judgment Interest		87
	(c)	Costs		87
		(i)	Small Claims Court	87
		(ii)	Simplified Procedure	88

Chapter 10: Enforcing Judgment 91

10.1	Collection			91
10.2	Small Claims Court			91
	(a)	Jurisdiction		91
	(b)	Examination of Debtor		92
	(c)	Writ of Delivery of Personal Property		94
	(d)	Writ of Seizure and Sale		95
		(i)	Personal Property	95
		(ii)	Sale of Land	96
	(e)	Garnishment		96
	(f)	Consolidation Orders		98
10.3	Simplified Procedure			99
	(a)	Examination of Debtor		99
	(b)	Writ of Delivery		99
	(c)	Writ of Seizure and Sale		100

		(i) Personal Property	100
		(ii) Sale of Land	101
	(d)	Garnishment	101
10.4	Other Remedies		102
10.5	Costs of Enforcement		103

Chapter 11: Appealing the Judgment 105

11.1	The Decision to Appeal	105
11.2	Motion for New Trial — Small Claims Court	105
11.3	Where to Appeal	107
11.4	How to Appeal	107
	(a) Commencing the Appeal	107
	(i) Notice of Appeal	107
	(ii) Certificate Respecting Evidence	108
	(iii) Ordering Transcripts	109
	(b) Perfecting the Appeal	109
	(i) Appeal Book	109
	(ii) Factums and Books of Authorities	110
	(iii) Compendium of Evidence	112
	(iv) Certificate of Perfection	112
11.5	Appeal Hearing	113

Appendix 1: Conduct of an Action in the Small Claims Court 115
Appendix 2: Conduct of an Appeal from a Decision of the Small Claims Court 117
Appendix 3: Conduct of an Action Under the Simplified Procedure 119
Appendix 4: Conduct of an Appeal from a Decision Under the Simplified Procedure 121
Appendix 5: Courts of Justice Act 123
Appendix 6: Small Claims Court Rules 133
Appendix 7: Rule 76 Simplified Procedure 193
Appendix 8: Small Claims Court Forms 213
Appendix 9: Simplified Procedure Court Forms 255
Appendix 10: Court Fees 289
Appendix 11: Costs Grid 291

Index 293

Table of Cases

322262 B.C. Ltd. v. Mark's Work Wearhouse Ltd., [1999] O.J. No. 1471 (Gen. Div.) 203
394705 Ontario Ltd. v. Moerenhout (1983), 41 O.R. (2d) 637, 35 C.P.C. 258 (Co. Ct.) 172
667801 Ontario Ltd. v. Moir (1990), 1 W.D.C.P. (2d) 266 (Ont. Prov. Ct.) 186
720659 Ontario Inc. v. Wells, [2001] O.J. No. 3666 (S.C.J.) 185
777812 Ontario Inc. v. Windup Corp., [2002] O.J. No. 1102 (S.C.J.) 127

A

Adekunte v. 1211531 Ontario Ltd., [2002] O.J. No. 509 (S.C.J.) 168
Adelaide Capital Corp. v. Stinziani, [2001] O.J. No. 1465 (S.C.J.) 160
Alcox v. Woolley, [1997] O.J. 2821 (Gen. Div.) 195, 199
American Express Canada Inc. v. Engel (1982), 39 O.R. (2d) 600 (Div. Ct.) 154, 159
Applewood Holdings Inc. v. Maximum Sales Corp., [1999] O.J. No. 5387 (Gen. Div.)................ 196
Associates Financial Services of Canada Ltd. v. Campbell, [1998] O.J. No. 5612 (Gen. Div.)....... 124
Avco Financial Services Canada Ltd. v. Bowe; Steenbakkers Lumber Ltd., Garnishee
  (1979), 23 O.R. (2d) 264, 97 D.L.R. (3d) 748 (Div. Ct.) 186
Avco Financial Services Canada Ltd. v. Wall, [2000] O.J. No. 194 (S.C.J.) 147
Azulev, S.A. v. Tilerama Ltd., [1999] O.J. No. 2765 (Gen. Div.) 210

B

Babineau v. Babineau (1983), 32 C.P.C. 229 (Ont. M.C.) 151
Bain v. Rosen and Erie Meat Markets Ltd., Garnishee (1984), 45 O.R. (2d) 672, 3 O.A.C. 37,
  7 D.L.R. (4th) 505 (H.C.J.) 186
Bank of N.S. v. Cameron; Inco Ltd., Garnishee (1985), 1 W.D.C.P. 483
  (Ont. Prov. Ct. (Civ. Div.)) 186
Bank of Nova Scotia v. Pelletier (January 9, 1997), Doc. 98844/96 (Ont. Gen. Div.) 203
Baron v. Glowe, [1999] O.J. No. 4192 (S.C.J.) 167
Baslik v. Ontario Teachers Federation, [2000] O.J. No. 1460 (S.C.J.) 124
Beardsley v. Baecker (1993), 125 N.S.R. (2d) 61, 349 A.P.R. 61, 20 C.P.C. (3d)
  235 (S.C.) 16, 124
Beardsley v. Ontario Provincial Police (2000), 50 O.R. (3d) 491 (S.C.J.), revg in part
  (2001), 57 O.R. (3d) 1, 17 C.P.C. (5th) 94 (C.A.) 39
Bell Canada v. Olympia & York Developments Ltd. (1988), 30 C.P.C. (2d) 155 (Ont. C.A.),
  affg (1988), 26 C.P.C. (2d) 113 (Ont. H.C.J.) 32
Bernier v. LFD Industries Ltd. (1994), 48 A.C.W.S. (3d) 80 (B.C.S.C.) 144
Bird v. Kehrig (1990), 85 Sask. R. 216, 43 C.P.C. (2d) 97 (Q.B.) 172
Bissoondatt v. Arzaclon, [1992] O.J. 2312 (Gen. Div.) 128
Bois v. Majestech Corp. Canada, [2001] O.J. No. 3762 (S.C.J.) 209
Bonneville v. IITC Holdings Ltd., [1999] O.J. No. 428 (Gen. Div.) 195
Bonus Finance Ltd. v. Smith; Crown Trust Co., Garnishee, [1971] 3 O.R. 732 (H.C.J.) 186
Bradley-Kelly Construction Ltd. v. Ottawa-Carleton Regional Transit Commission
  (1996), 30 O.R. (3d) 301 (Gen. Div.) 204
Brockman v. Sinclair (1980), 31 O.R. (2d) 436, 119 D.L.R. (3d) 148, 19 C.P.C. 51
  (Div. Ct.), affg (1979), 26 O.R. (2d) 276 (Dist. Ct.) 168
Bussineau v. Roberts (1982), 15 A.C.W.S. (2d) 367 (Ont. Sm. Claims Ct.) 192

C

CAD-FM Micro Systems v. Coldmatic Refrigeration of Canada Ltd. (1994), 5 W.D.C.P. (2d)
250 (Ont. Gen. Div.) 129
Campbell v. Maritime Engine Specialist Ltd. (October 11, 1995), Doc. AD-0607 (P.E.I.C.A.) 170
Can.-Dom. Leasing Corp. v. Corpex Ltd., [1963] 2 O.R. 497 (M.C.) 150
Canada (Attorney General) v. Khimani (1985), 50 O.R. (2d) 476, 8 O.A.C. 359
(Div. Ct.) 125
Canada Mortgage and Housing Corp. v. Apostolou (1995), 22 O.R. (3d) 190
(Gen. Div.) 185
Canada Trust Mastercard v. Nowick (1981), 27 C.P.C. 183 (Ont. Small Cl. Ct.) 143
Canadian Imperial Bank of Commerce v. Glackin, [1999] O.J. No. 842 (Gen. Div.) 198
Canadian Shareholders Assn. v. Osiel, [2001] O.J. No. 3662 (S.C.J.) 160
Caringi v. Porco (1989), 17 W.D.C.P. 21 (Ont. Prov. Ct.) 176
Catalanotto v. Nina D'Aversa Bakery Ltd., [2001] O.J. No. 4450 (S.C.J.) 176
Central Burner Service Inc. v. Texaco Co. (1989), 36 O.A.C. 239 (Div. Ct.) 127
Chakie v. Elton, [1996] O.J. No. 4447 (Gen. Div.) 85, 207
Charlebois v. Leadbeater (1993), 4 W.D.C.P. (2d) 195 (Ont. Gen. Div.) 165
Chrich Holdings & Buildings Ltd. and David Hall v. Eugene Madore o/a Absolute
Office Furniture Services, Garnishee (December 20, 1994), Doc. 633/94, Searle Dep. J.
(Ont. Sm. Claims Ct.) 186
Clearnet Inc. v. Blue Line Distribution Ltd., [1999] O.J. No. 1064 (Gen. Div.) 129
Conestoga Tire & Rim Inc. v. Sisson, [1997] O.J. 1993 (Gen. Div.) 203
Consumers Gas Co. v. Ferreira (1990), 1 W.D.C.P. (2d) 257 (Ont. Prov. Ct.) 191
Consumers Glass Co. v. Foundation Company of Canada Ltd., (1985), 51 O.R. (2d) 385,
9 O.A.C. 193, 20 D.L.R. (4th) 126 (C.A.) 11
Cox v. Robert Simpson Co. (1973), 1 O.R. (2d) 333 (C.A.) 145
Craig Gilchrist Equipment Rental Ltd. v. Robertson (1997), 10 C.P.C. (4th) 372
(Ont. Gen. Div.) 42, 203

D

Dacon Corp. v. Treats Ontario Inc. (1995), 6 W.D.C.P. (2d) 174 (Ont. Gen. Div.) 185
Dainard v. Dainard (1981), 22 C.P.C. 283 (Ont. Prov. Ct.) 189
Danson v. Ontario (Attorney General), [1990] 2 S.C.R. 1086, 74 O.R. (2d) 763n,
41 O.A.C. 250, affg (1987), 60 O.R. (2d) 676, 22 O.A.C. 38, 41 D.L.R. (4th) 129 (C.A.),
revg (1986), 55 O.R. (2d) 1, 16 O.A.C. 246, 27 D.L.R. (4th) 758 (Div. Ct.), affg (1985), 51
O.R. (2d) 405, 20 D.L.R. (4th) 285, 18 C.R.R. 278 (H.C.J.) (sub nom. R. v. Danson) 135
Decoration J.M. Laflamme Inc. v. Arra Chemicals Inc. (1993), 44 A.C.W.S. (3d) 226
(Ont. Div. Ct.) 161
DeCorte v. Methot (1981), 11 A.C.W.S. (2d) 101 (Ont. Sm. Claims Ct.) 178
Diefenbacher v. Young (1995), 22 O.R. (3d) 641, 123 D.L.R. (4th) 641 (C.A.),
revg in part (1991), 1 B.L.R. (2d) 161 (Ont. Gen. Div.) 167
DiMenna v. Colborne Auctions (1993), 4 W.D.C.P. (2d) 137 (Ont. Sm. Claims Ct.) 171
Dimovski v. Director of Support & Custody (1991), 5 O.R. (3d) 499, 85 D.L.R.
(4th) 375, 3 C.P.C. (3d) 206 (Div. Ct.), revg (1989), 29 R.F.L. (3d) 104 (Ont. Dist. Ct.),
revg (1988), 17 R.F.L. (3d) 445 (Ont. Prov. Ct.) (sub nom. Director of Support &
Custody Enforcement v. Jones.) 186
Director of Support & Custody Enforcement v. Jones. *See* Dimovski v. Director of
Support & Custody
Dorman Estate v. Korean Air Lines Co., [1995] O.J. 1805 (Ont. Div. Ct.) 143
Dowe-Salter v. Pickering (Town), [2000] O.J. No. 3818 (S.C.J.) 210
Dronshek v. Martchenkov, [2000] O.J. No. 5193 (S.C.J.) 210

Dusto v. Hooper- Holmes Canada Ltd., [2002] O.J. No. 1289 (S.C.J.) 19, 194
Dyce v. Aquarius Management Inc. (1995), 65 B.C.A.C. 316, 106 W.A.C. 316 (C.A.) 137

E

Eades v. Kootnikoff (1995), 13 B.C.L.R. (3d) 182, [1996] 1 W.W.R. 730, 42 C.P.C.
(3d) 182 (B.C.S.C.) 158
Elguindy v. Core Laboratories Can. Ltd. (1987), 8 W.D.C.P. 216 (Ont. Div. Ct.) 143

F

Fanaken v. Bell, Temple (1985), 49 C.P.C. 212 (Ont. Assess. Ct.) 177
Field v. Menuck (1985), 2 W.D.C.P.219 (Ont. Pro. Ct. (Civ. Div.)) 172
Fossil Fuel Dev. Ltd. v. Tudex Petroleums Ltd. (1987), 6 A.C.W.S. (3d) 66 (Sask. C.A.) 178
Fuss v. Fidelity Electronics of Canada Ltd. (1996), 7 W.D.C.P. (2d) 66 (Ont. Gen. Div.) 178

G

G.B.V.S. Inc. v. DiPaola (1989), 16 A.C.W.S. (3d) 107 (Ont. Div. Ct.) 128
Garson v. Braithwaite [1994] O.J. 1662 (Gen. Div.) 177
Gasparini v. Waterfront Tennis and Squash Club Ltd., [1997] O.J. No. 785 (Gen. Div.) 198
Geilinger v. Gibbs, [1897] 1 Ch. 479 13
George v. Wagenhoffer (1995), 129 Sask. R. 214 (Q.B.) 171
Giroux v. Security National Insurance Co., [2002] O.J. No. 2665 (S.C.J.) 144
Grieco v. Marquis (1998), 38 O.R. (3d) 314 (Gen. Div.) 39, 201
Grossinger v. Olympia Business Machines Canada Ltd., [2001] O.J. No. 1108 (S.C.J.) 209
Guarantee Co. of North America v. Witts, [1997] O.J. 1657 (Gen. Div.) 203

H

Helsberg v. Allison, [2000] O.J. No. 3618 (S.C.J.), affd [2002] O.J. No. 1529 (C.A.) 211
Holden Day Wilson v. Ashton (1993), 14 O.R. (3d) 306, 104 D.L.R. (4th) 266 (Div. Ct.) 158
Holovaci v. Zsoldos, [2000] O.J. No. 1633 (S.C.J.) 128
Howard v. Canadian National Express (1980), 23 C.P.C. 77 (Ont. Small Cl. Ct.) 174
Hudon v. Colliers Macaulay Nicolls Inc. (c.o.b. Colliers International), [2001] O.J. No. 1588
(Div. Ct.) 200

I

Ingersoll Press Automation & Machinery Inc. v. Tom Saab Ind., [1994] O.J. 446
(Sm. Claims Ct.) 143
Interamerican Transport Systems Inc. v. Grand Trunk Western Railroad (1985),
51 O.R. (2d) 568, 10 O.A.C. 185 (Div. Ct.) 143
Itravel2000.com Inc. v. Contestix.com Corp., [2002] O.J. No. 2462 (S.C.J.) 202

J

James Sturino Realty Ltd. v. Andrew Michaels Group Ltd. (1988), 64 O.R. (2d)
410, 28 O.A.C. 354 (Div. Ct.) (sub nom. Sturino (James) Realty Ltd. v.
Michaels (Andrew) Group Ltd.) 160

K

K. & R. Painting v. Abraham J. Green Ltd., unreported Nov 12, 1996 (Ont. Gen. Div.) 204
Khokhar v. Blackburn (1993), 13 Alta. L.R. (3d) 223, [1994] 2 W.W.R. 202, 20 C.P.C.
　(3d) 313 (Q.B.) 178
King v. Royal Ins. Co. (1987), 10 W.D.C.P. 126 (Ont. Prov. Ct.) 168
Krackovitch v. Scherer Leasing Inc., [2001] O.J. No. 3349 (S.C.J.) 176

L

Lachowski and Federated Mutual Insurance Co., Re (1980), 29 O.R. (2d) 273, 113
　D.L.R. (3d) 202, 19 C.P.C. 126 (Div. Ct.) 170, 178
Lagadin v. King (1985), 2 W.D.C.P. 259 (Ont. Prov. Ct.) 192
Lamont v. Nieuwenhuis, [1988] O.J. 2625 (Prov. Ct.) 178
Landry, Re (1973), 1 O.R. (2d) 107 (Sm. Claims Ct.) 189
Lechier-Kimel v. Friedlander, [1999] O.J. No. 1614 (Gen. Div.) 195
LeMoine v. LeMoine (1990), 80 Nfld. & P.E.I.R. 339, 249 A.P.R. 339 (Nfld. T.D.) 16
Lenskis v. Roncaioli (1996), 45 C.P.C. (3d) 57 (Ont. C.A.), affg (1992), 11 C.P.C. (3d) 99
　(Ont. Gen. Div.) 39
Leo (Litigation guardian of) v. Hamilton-Wentworth Roman Catholic Separate School Board,
　[2000] O.J. No. 1803 (S.C.J.) 208
Lillie v. Bisson, [1999] O.J. No. 1008 (C.A.) 194, 195
Livingstone v. Tomen, [2000] O.J. No. 1462 (S.C.J.) 142
Luo v. Canada (Attorney General) (1997), 33 O.R. (3d) 300, 145 D.L.R. (4th) 457,
　28 C.C.E.L. (2d) 304 (Div. Ct.) 16, 124
Luo v. Canada (Attorney General) (March 7, 1995), Doc. Toronto T5681/1994
　(Ont. Sm. Claims Ct.) 148

M

MacDonald v. Porter (1993), 127 N.S.R. (2d) 79, 355 A.P.R. 79, 20 C.P.C. (3d) 355
　(S.C.) 171
MacInnes v. Leaman (1976), 8 N.R. 297 (S.C.C.) 170
Mandel v. Permanent, (The) (1985), 7 O.A.C. 365 (Div. Ct.) 126
Maple Lodge Farms Ltd. v. Penny Lane Fruit Market Inc., [1997] O.J. No. 4401 (Gen. Div.) 144
Marion Community Homes Corp. v. Kingston (City), [2000] O.J. No. 1329 (S.C.J.) 211
McEvenue v. Robin Hood Multifoods Inc. (1997), 33 O.R. (3d) 315 (Gen. Div.) 193, 195
McIntosh v. C.T.F. Supply Ltd., [2001] O.J. No. 5062 (S.C.J.) 194
Metropolitan Toronto Condominium Corp. No.706 v. Bardmore Developments Ltd. (1991),
　3 O.R. (3d) 278, 49 O.A.C. 1 (C.A.) 36
Miller v. York Downs Craft & Garden Centre Ltd. (1987), 17 C.P.C. (2d) 142
　(Ont. Prov. Ct.) 176, 180
Milligan, Re (1991), 1 C.P.C. (3d) 12 (Ont. Gen. Div.) 126
Mills v. MacFarlane, [2000] O.J. No. 2874 (S.C.J.) 198
Milton and O.M.B., Re (1978), 20 O.R. (2d) 257 (H.C.J.) 153
Minnesota Mining & Mfg. Co. v. Dahm, [1957] O.W.N. 100 (H.C.J.) 15
Minto Management Ltd. v. Solomonescu (1986), 5 W.D.C.P. 262 (Ont. Prov. Ct.) 174
Moffatt & Powell Ltd. v. Armour Steel Supply Ltd., [2002] O.J. No. 1475 (S.C.J.) 194
Moore v. Canadian Newspapers Co. (1989), 69 O.R. (2d) 262, 34 O.A.C. 328, 60 D.L.R.
　(4th) 113 (Div. Ct.) 124
Moshiri v. 1142682 Ontario Ltd., [1997] O.J. 2592 (Gen. Div.) 208
Mount Royal Painting & Decorating Inc. v. Central Interiors Inc., [1995] O.J. 4031
　(Gen. Div.) 135, 160, 170

Table of Cases   xix

Munro v. Thompson, Tooze, McLean, Rollo & Elkin, [1998] O.J. No. 3839 (Gen. Div.) 18, 196
Murday v. Schmidt (1992), 8 O.R. (3d) 231, 6 C.P.C. (3d) 389 (Gen. Div.) 2
Murphy v. Welsh, [1993] 2 S.C.R. 1069, 14 O.R. (3d) 799n, 106 D.L.R. (4th) 404,
  revg in part (1991), 3 O.R. (3d) 182, 81 D.L.R. (4th) 475, 4 C.P.C. (3d) 301 (C.A.),
  revg (1987), 62 O.R. (2d) 159n, 44 D.L.R. (4th) 192n, 31 C.P.C. (2d) 209 (Div. Ct.),
  affg (1986), 57 O.R. (2d) 622, 33 D.L.R. (4th) 762, 15 C.P.C. (2d) 173 (H.C.J.)
  (sub nom. Stoddard v. Watson) 11

N

Naffouj v. D.E. Wilson Management Co. (1991), 5 O.R. (3d) 424 (Gen. Div.) 2
Nagle v. Rosman (1986), 6 W.D.C.P. 58 (Ont. Prov. Ct. (Civ. Div.)) 161
Newcourt Credit Group Inc. v. Hummel Pharmacy Ltd. (1998), 38 O.R. (3d) 82, 18 C.P.C.
  (4th) 319 (Div. Ct.) 41
Newlove Estate v. Petrie (June 29, 1995), Doc. Toronto 39122/89 (Ont. Gen. Div.) 164
Niagara Structural Steel (St. Catharines) Ltd. v. W.D. Laflamme Ltd. (1987),
  58 O.R. (2d) 773, 19 O.A.C. 142, 19 C.P.C. (2d) 163 (C.A.) 168
Nunez-de-Cela v. May Co. (1973), 1 O.R. (2d) 217 (C.A.) 186

O

O'Connell v. Custom Kitchen & Vanity (1986), 56 O.R. (2d) 57, 17 O.A.C. 157,
  11 C.P.C. (2d) 303 (Div. Ct.) 127, 174
Ontario (Attorney General) v. Pembina Exploration Canada Ltd., [1989] 1 S.C.R. 206,
  33 O.A.C. 321, 57 D.L.R. (4th) 710 (sub nom. Siddall (William) & Sons Fisheries
  v. Pembina Exploration Canada Ltd., William Siddall & Sons Fisheries v.
  Pembina Exploration Canada Ltd.) 16, 124
Orion Group R.E. Services Ltd. v. D'Souza, [2002] O.J. No. 1107 (S.C.J.) 171
Osadca v. Cadillac Fairview Corp., [2000] O.J. No. 3314 (S.C.J.) 123
Osan Financial Corp. v. Bhatti, [2000] O.J. No. 4104 (S.C.J.) 210

P

Parente v. Van Holland (1988), 24 C.P.C. (2d) 233 (Ont. Dist. Ct.) 167
Paul v. Rodgers (1989), 15 W.D.C.P. 158 (Ont. Dist. Ct.) 124
Peixeiro v. Haberman, [1997] 3 S.C.R. 549, 151 D.L.R. (4th) 429, 217 N.R. 371, 12 C.P.C. (4th)
  255, 30 M.V.R. (3d) 41, affg (1995), 25 O.R. (3d) 1, 127 D.L.R. (4th) 475, 42 C.P.C.
  (3d) 37, 16 M.V.R. (3d) 46 (C.A.) 11
Pizza Pizza Ltd. v. Boyack (1995), 38 C.P.C. (3d) 306 (Ont. Gen. Div.) 142
Polish National Union of Canada Inc. v. Dopke (No. 2) (2001), 55 O.R. (3d) 728 (S.C.J.) 210
Purcell v. Taylor (1994), 120 D.L.R. (4th) 161 (Ont. Gen. Div.) 177

Q

Queensway Lincoln Mercury Sales (1980) Ltd. v. 409918 Ontario Ltd. (1981), 34 O.R.
  (2d) 568, 25 C.P.C. 186 (S.C.) 136

R

R. v. Danson. See Danson v. Ontario (Attorney General)
Realffe v. Abow-Assaf, [1996] O.J. 3066 (Gen. Div.) 208
Rizzi v. Great Atlantic and Pacific Co. of Canada (1999), 46 O.R. (3d) 509 (S.C.J.) 194
Roberts v. Dresser Industries Can. Ltd. (1988), 9 A.C.W.S. (3d) 290 (Ont. Dist. Ct.) 167

Robertson v. Ball (1996), 31 O.R. (3d) 30 (Gen. Div.) 41, 42, 204
Royal Bank of Canada v. Mancuso, [1999] O.J. No. 5055 (S.C.J.) 203

S

S & A Strasser Ltd. v. Richmond Hill (Town) (1991), 1 O.R. (3d) 243, 45 O.A.C.
    394, 49 C.P.C. (2d) 234 (C.A.) 50
Sahota v. Beauchamp; Firstline Trust Co. (Third Party), [1994] O.J. 1483 (Sm. Claims Ct.) 135, 144
Saldanha v. Eastville Hldgs. Ltd. (1985), 2 W.D.C.P. 223 (Ont. Prov. Ct.) 172
San Fransisco Pizza Ltd. v. Granata, [1995] O.J. 1408 (Gen. Div.) 177
Sears Canada Inc. v. Scott (1994), 51 A.C.W.S. (3d) 1232 (Ont. Sm. Claims Ct.) 106, 171
Seltzer-Soberano v. Kogut (c.o.b. Majestic Home Inspection), [2001] O.J. No. 9 (S.C.J.) 209
Serodio v. White, [1995] O.J. 464 (Sm. Claims Ct.) 177
Shannon v. Shannon (1995), 6 W.D.C.P. (2d) 534 (Ont. Gen. Div.) 165
Shaw v. Auto Caravan Corp. (1989), 15 W.D.C.P. 161 (Ont. Prov. Ct.) 143
Shibley v. Harris, [1995] B.C.J. 2069 (S.C.) 177
Shoppers Mortgage & Loan Corp. v. Health First Wellington Square Ltd. (1995),
    23 O.R. (3d) 362, 124 D.L.R. (4th) 440, 38 C.P.C. (3d) 8 (C.A.); supp. reasons
    25 O.R. (3d) 95n, 38 C.P.C. (3d) 18 (C.A.) 171
Shoppers Trust Co. v. Mann Taxi Management Ltd. (1993), 16 O.R. (3d) 192, 19 C.P.C.
    (3d) 7 (Gen. Div.) 22, 125
Siddall (William) & Sons Fisheries v. Pembina Exploration Canada Ltd. *See* Ontario
    (Attorney General) v. Pembina Exploration Canada Ltd.
Siemon v. Kuepfer, [1973] 3 O.R. 375 (C.A.) 146
Smith v. Galin, [1956] O.W.N. 432 (C.A.) 126, 136
Snider v. Salerno, [2002] O.J. No. 1004 (S.C.J.) 209
Sona Computer Inc. v. Carnegie (March 7, 1995), Doc. Ottawa 596/94 (Ont. Gen. Div.) 165
St. Mary's Credit Union Ltd. v. General Doors Inc. (1990), 85 Sask. R. 78, 42 C.P.C.
    (2d) 115 (Q.B.) 172
Stapley v. Intermap Technologies Ltd., [1999] O.J. No. 1411 (Gen. Div.) 195
Stoddard v. Watson. *See* Murphy v. Welsh
Sturino (James) Realty Ltd. v. Michaels (Andrew) Group Ltd. *See* James Sturino Realty Ltd.
    v. Andrew Michaels Group Ltd.
Stylecraft Dress Co. v. Gotlin, [1946] O.W.N. 114 (H.C.J.) 56
Suedfeld v. Lancia, [1993] O.J. 1693 (Gen. Div.) 135
Svajlenko v. Appco Paving Ltd. (1985), 3 W.D.C.P. 34 (Ont. Prov. Ct. (Civ. Div.)) 172
Swadron v. North York (1985), 8 O.A.C. 204 (Div. Ct.) 170

T

Teitel and Theriault, Re (1983), 44 O.R. (2d) 127 (Div. Ct.) 124
Terra Cotta Cookie Co. v. Dek Packaging Ltd., [1997] O.J. 995 (Gen. Div.) 204
Todd v. Canada (Solicitor General), [1993] O.J. 3410 (Gen. Div.) 124, 148
Tomarelli v. Co-Operators, [2002] O.J. No. 946 (S.C.J.) 175
Tope v. Stratford (City) (1994), 52 A.C.W.S. (3d) 783 (Ont. Gen. Div.) 144
Torstar Electronic Publishing Ltd. v. Asian Television Network Inc., [2000] O.J. No.
    2748 (S.C.J.) 203
Traditional Air Systems Inc. v. Custom Gas Heating Ltd. (1995), 86 O.A.C. 72
    (Div. Ct.) 144
Trans Canada Credit Corp. v. Wheeler (May 22, 1997), Doc. 96-CU-112524 (Ont. Gen. Div.) 203
Travel Machine Ltd. v. Madore (1983), 143 D.L.R. (3d) 94 (Ont. H.C.J.) 126
Trento Motors v. McKinney (1992), 39 M.V.R. (2d) 142 (Ont. Div. Ct.) 174

Tummillo v. Prouty (1990), 42 C.P.C. (2d) 308 (Ont. Dist. Ct.) 146
Turgeon v. Border Supply (EMO) Ltd. (1977), 16 O.R. (2d) 43 (Div. Ct.) 161

V

Von Felix v. Enterprise Rent-A-Car, [2002] O.J. No. 1109 (S.C.J.) 123

W

W.B. Knox & Son Ltd. v. St. Amand (1986), 5 W.D.C.P. 333 (Ont. Prov. Ct. (Civ. Div.)) 143
W.J. Realty Management Ltd. v. Price (1973), 1 O.R. (2d) 501 (C.A.).. 161
Wabi Iron Works Ltd. v. Patricia Syndicate (1923), 54 O.L.R. 640, [1924] 3 D.L.R.
  363 (C.A.)... 15
Watson v. Crystal Mountain Resources Ltd. (1988), f9 A.C.W.S. (3d) 238 (B.C.C.A.) 160
Weiss v. Prentice Hall Canada Inc. (1995), 66 C.P.R. (3d) 417, 7 W.D.C.P. (2d)
  99 (Ont. Small Cl. Ct.) 135, 177
William Siddall & Sons Fisheries v. Pembina Exploration Canada Ltd. *See*
  Ontario (Attorney General) v. Pembina Exploration Canada Ltd.
Willis v. Ontario, [1999] O.J. No. 3656 (S.C.J.) 197
Wright v. Bell Canada (1988), 13 W.D.C.P. 228 (Ont. Div. Ct.) 172

X

Xerox Canada Inc. v. Neary (1984), 47 O.R. (2d) 776, 43 C.P.C. 274 (Prov. Ct.) 143

Y

Yee v. Tight Spot Rentals Ltd. (1995), 11 B.C.L.R. (3d) 291 (B.C.S.C.) 177
York v. TV Guide Inc. (1984), 5 O.A.C. 330 (Div. Ct.) 170
Young, Re (1973), 4 O.R. (2d) 390 (Sm. Claims Ct.) 189

CHAPTER 1

Introduction

1.1 INTRODUCTION

Litigation can be an expensive and time-consuming way to resolve civil disputes. In 1997, the average lawyers' fees charged for a two-day trial was $8,575 per party. If the matter was appealed the average cost was over $17,000[1] for the trial and appeal. The costs to litigate actions in the Superior Court of Justice have continued to increase since 1997. In addition to the excessive cost of litigation, the average lawsuit takes over two years to get to trial.

In response to the cost and delay in bringing an action to trial in the Superior Court of Justice, the Government of Ontario has implemented a number of court reforms. In 2001, the monetary jurisdiction of the Small Claims Court was increased to $10,000 throughout Ontario.[2] As of January 2, 2002, the simplified procedure rules applied to all cases between $10,000 (the small claims jurisdiction) and $50,000, excluding interest and costs.

Each year in Ontario thousands of civil actions are commenced in the Superior Court of Justice and the Small Claims Court. The vast majority of those actions involve disputes over fairly modest amounts of money or property. Of the over 132,000 new civil actions (excluding divorce) commenced in Ontario in 2000, 82,000 (or 62%) were commenced in the Small Claims Court.[3] Of the actions commenced in the Superior Court, more than 50% will result in a judgment of less than $50,000.[4] Therefore, over 80% of all civil actions in Ontario fall within the jurisdiction of the Small Claims Court or the Rules of Simplified Procedure.

---

[1] "The 1997 National Fee Survey", The Canadian Lawyer, September 1917, at 23.
[2] O. Reg. 626/00, effective April 2, 2001.
[3] *Court Statistics Annual Report — Fiscal Year 1999/2000* (Toronto: Ministry of the Attorney General, 2001).
[4] *Civil Justice Review 1995* (Toronto: Ministry of the Attorney General, 1995), at 146.

1.2   SMALL CLAIMS COURT

The current Small Claims Court is part of a long tradition in Ontario of a court with special procedures to deal with civil disputes involving relatively modest sums of money. The origins of the Court date back to the beginning of government in Ontario.

The Court of Requests was established by the first Parliament of Upper Canada to deal with small claims.[5] The preamble of the Act provided that the Court of Requests was "to continue to the convenience of the inhabitants of the Province an easy and speedy method of recovering small debts". The Court of Requests was reformed in 1841, and became known as the Division Court.[6]

The monetary jurisdiction of the Division Court was gradually increased during its history, and by 1967 the monetary jurisdiction was $400 in the counties and $800 in the districts. By 1967, the Division Courts were trying all matters in their monetary jurisdiction except those actions involving title to land, estates, libel and slander, suits against justices of the peace and actions for prerogative remedies.

The 1968 *Report of the Royal Commission Inquiry into Civil Rights*, commonly known as the McRuer Report, resulted in a re-evaluation of the Ontario courts system.[7] In 1968, the Magistrates Court became the Provincial Court (Criminal Division) and the Juvenile and Family Courts became the Provincial Court (Family Division). The Division Court was reformed in 1970, and was renamed the Small Claims Court of Ontario. The monetary jurisdiction of the Court was increased to $1,000 across the province. In 1979, an experimental Small Claims Court was established in Metropolitan Toronto.[8] It was named the Provincial Court (Civil Division) and had monetary jurisdiction of $3,000. The Court was presided over by the Provincial Court judges or deputy judges. The experimental court became permanent in 1982 and the Small Claims Courts across the province became known as the Provincial Court (Civil Division). The monetary jurisdiction outside Metropolitan Toronto remained at $1,000.

In 1991 and 1992, there was some concern that the regulation which allowed for different monetary limits in Metropolitan Toronto and the rest of the province was unconstitutional and offended the Charter of Rights.[9] This issue was resolved in 1993 when the monetary jurisdiction of the Small Claims Court was

---

[5] 32 Geo. III, c. 6.
[6] "The Law and Practice of the Upper Canada Division Courts" (1861), 7 U.C.L.J. 34, at 35.
[7] *Report of the Royal Commission Inquiry into Civil Rights*, Hon. J.C. McRuer (Toronto: Queen's Printer, 1968).
[8] *Provincial Court (Civil Division) Project Act*, 1979, S.O. 1979, c. 67.
[9] *Canadian Charter of Rights and Freedoms*, Part I of the *Constitution Act*, 1982, being Schedule B to the *Canada Act 1982* (U.K.), 1982, c. 11. See *Naffouj v. D.E. Wilson Management Co.* (1991), 5 O.R. (3d) 424 (Gen. Div.); *Murday v. Schmidt* (1992), 8 O.R. (3d) 231 (Gen. Div.).

increased to $6,000 throughout the province,[10] and increased again in 2001 to $10,000.

The current rules of the Small Claims Court provide for a simple streamlined procedure. The rules are intended to allow the court to process a large number of claims efficiently and at a relatively reasonable cost.

The summary procedures in the Small Claims Court benefit those litigants who represent themselves, as well as the lawyers, students-at-law, paralegals, and agents involved in small claims practice. Pleadings require little technical drafting and are designed to be set out entirely on a single page. Discoveries are dispensed with and motions and other interlocutory proceedings are rare. A formal pre-trial conference encourages settlement negotiations between the parties.

While some of the procedures in the Small Claims Court are simplified, the rules also provide certain safeguards to ensure that each litigant before the court is treated fairly and justly. At the Small Claims Court trial, the parties are entitled to counsel, and have the same right to call evidence and cross-examine witnesses as in the Superior Court of Justice.

The Small Claims Court of Ontario has evolved into a forum which approximates the popular notion of a "people's court". It balances the simple, inexpensive procedures necessary for the litigation of claims involving modest sums, with rules that ensure that all cases are resolved fairly.

1.3 RULES OF SIMPLIFIED PROCEDURE

The simplified procedure rules are a fairly recent development in Ontario. They began as a pilot project which was initially in effect for a period of four years, from March 11, 1996 to March 11, 2000.[11] The simplified procedure rules became a permanent part of litigation in Ontario when the amendments came into effect as of January 2, 2002. Like the Small Claims Court rules, the simplified procedure rules allow for the prompt and efficient litigation of claims that involve between $10,000 and $50,000.

The rules are intended to reduce the cost of litigation by limiting the pre-trial discovery process. Discoveries have been eliminated. If motions are brought, cross-examinations on the supporting affidavits are not permitted. In addition, the parties are not required to prepare extensive pre-trial conference memoranda.

Although some of the more expensive pre-trial procedures have been eliminated, an attempt was made to ensure that the parties will continue to have sufficient notice of the other party's case. The parties are required to deliver an affidavit of documents which includes not only a list of all relevant documents but also the names and addresses of all witnesses.

---

[10] O. Reg. 92/93.
[11] *Rules of Civil Procedure*, R.R.O. 1990, Reg. 194, Rule 76.01.

The simplified procedure rules are also intended to reduce the time required to litigate actions. The rules provide for greater opportunities to either settle or try the action at an earlier date. The parties are required to conduct a settlement conference within 60 days after the close of pleadings. In the appropriate case, the action may be resolved at a summary trial in which the introduction of evidence is by affidavit, with strict time limits for cross-examination and argument.

Like the Small Claims Court rules, the simplified rules do not sacrifice fairness and justice; they satisfy the need to provide for the economic and efficient resolution of claims which, otherwise, may be too expensive to litigate.

CHAPTER 2

Meeting Your Client

2.1 THE FIRST INTERVIEW

The interview with the client is the beginning of the litigation process. In the initial meeting with the client you review together the facts of the problem, discuss any legal issues raised and agree on how best to reach a solution.

The initial interview should be conducted in a manner that encourages the client to provide a full and frank explanation of the problem that has brought him or her to your office, and the relief that is sought. How you do that is a matter of individual style, but each interview should include:

(i) a thorough review of the facts;
(ii) identification of any legal issues raised;
(iii) consideration of any relevant limitation periods;
(iv) discussion of possible solutions;
(v) mutual agreement on specific instructions as to how to proceed;
(vi) discussion of fee arrangements.

Once the general nature of the problem is established, the facts should be arranged in a chronological manner. The chronological review should organize the client's story into a logical and detailed sequence of facts. As the client reviews the facts, counsel should use leading questions to focus attention on important areas and obtain necessary details. For example: "You said you were taken to the General Hospital, did you see a doctor?"; "What was his or her name?"; "Did he or she fill out a medical report?" Counsel should also use questions to explore and test the facts related to the theory of the case. Any deficiencies in the available evidence should be discussed with the client to determine the best way to obtain further information.

At the initial meeting the client should complete authorization forms to allow counsel to obtain certain documents. For example, in a personal injury action, authorizations and directions should be completed to allow counsel to obtain the clinical notes of the treating physicians, the hospital records and the client's employment file.

2.2 COUNSEL'S OPINION

Once the problem has been analyzed, the client will want your opinion. Counsel will be expected to provide an indication of the issues raised and what legal procedures might be taken to deal with them. If there are problems that require legal research or further consideration, advise the client when he or she might expect a final opinion.

After providing a preliminary indication of the legal issues, explain the procedures and remedies available in the court which will apply to this particular case. There should be a discussion of the costs of litigating the dispute and the non-legal alternatives to resolve the problem. When a final decision is made, the client and advocate should construct a plan to achieve the client's goal — one that specifies the responsibilities of each person, and the dates by which tasks should be completed.

In most cases it is appropriate to provide your opinion in writing to the client. A written opinion may avoid any misunderstanding between lawyer and client. The opinion is also of assistance to counsel, in that the opinion will set out a summary of the facts, the issues and the applicable law, and can be referred to throughout the conduct of the action. It is good practice to have the client confirm receipt of the opinion and provide his or her instructions to the lawyer in writing.

2.3 COSTS AND RETAINER

The issue of legal costs is often at the top of the client's interview agenda. A lawyer is under a professional obligation to give the client a fair estimate of fees and disbursements and to explain the basis for the charges.[1] A frank discussion of fees in the initial interview will introduce the client to the financial reality of litigation and prevent disappointment or conflict at a later date. The fee arrangement with the client should be confirmed in writing.

In some cases, it may be necessary to obtain an up front payment of fees to cover the initial preparation and disbursements. Taking a retainer may be useful not only to protect fees, but also to remind the client that a legal action is an expensive and serious matter and should not be entered into lightly.

2.4 A PROFESSIONAL RELATIONSHIP

The client's understanding and participation in the conduct of the case is essential to the success of the action. The process of informing the client begins in the initial interview as you explain the litigation process and, together with the client, formulate a plan of action. Following the interview, provide the client with a

---

[1] Law Society of Upper Canada, *Rules of Professional Conduct*, January 30, 1987, Rule 9, Commentary 5. See also Rule 9 generally.

list of tasks he or she can perform to assist with the litigation, and a timetable of further proceedings if known. Before the client leaves your office, introduce him or her to secretaries, students and any others with whom he or she may be in contact over the course of the action.

One of the most frequent complaints to the Law Society is that the lawyer has not kept the client advised of the status of the action. As the action progresses, the client should be updated on all developments. If the client telephones, the lawyer or someone knowledgeable with the file should immediately speak with the client or at least return the telephone call the same day. If a written request for an update is received, the lawyer should ensure that a status report is delivered as soon as possible.

CHAPTER 3

Getting Started

3.1 WHETHER TO SUE — ALTERNATIVES TO LITIGATION

The first question to be considered in any dispute is whether a lawsuit is the best method of resolving the matter. Many cases can be resolved without incurring the time or expense of a legal action. For example, in some commercial disputes there are agencies specifically designed to bring the parties together to resolve the matter before litigation. For example, apartment buildings have tenant associations which represent the tenant in a dispute with the landlord. In disputes involving a government agency, complaints may be made to an ombudsperson.

In several communities, mediation services are available. Mediation is a process whereby the parties to the dispute meet with an impartial mediator to discuss the resolution of the matter. In many cases the parties can create their own settlement at mediation, rather than have a resolution imposed upon them by the court system. A "win-win" settlement created by the parties themselves will be ultimately more satisfying and more likely to be enforced than the "winner-take-all" resolution which can be ordered by the court.[1]

3.2 WHEN TO SUE — LIMITATION PERIODS

The question of limitations must be considered during or immediately after the first interview; even before any steps are taken to settle the action. The expiration of a time limit can bar a plaintiff's action or it may provide an important defence. The expiry of a limitation period is one of the few errors in litigation that cannot be corrected.

Given the importance of time limits, lawyers are required to keep a limitation reminder or "tickler" system. The most effective "tickler" system is to determine the limitation date on the very first interview and note that date in a calendar. All tickler dates must be reviewed daily. As the limitation date approaches, reminders must be sent to the responsible lawyer.

Limitations present a major difficulty to the advocate. Due to the confusion which can be caused by the seemingly arbitrary limitation periods, the Ontario

---

[1] See Chapter 6.4, Alternative Dispute Resolution.

government has proposed a standard limitation period of six years for virtually all actions, with an ultimate limitation period of 10 years from the date the cause of action arose.[2] At the present time, the legislation has not been passed, and, therefore, we are left with a wide range of limitation periods.

The fact that there is no logical scheme of limitations is a constant source of anxiety to the litigation practitioner. One approach to this problem is to review a publication such as *Ontario Limitation Periods*[3] and become familiar with the types of parties and actions to which special time limits will apply. The actual legislation should always be reviewed to confirm the time limits. The examples of notice requirements and limitation periods provided below are meant only to illustrate the variety of notices and limits and not to act as a guide for practice.

(a) Notice Requirements

Some statutes require notice to be given prior to commencing an action:

(i) Notice in writing of a claim for failure to keep a highway or bridge in repair must be given to a county or township within 10 days or to an urban municipality within seven days.[4]
(ii) Notice of certain proceedings against the Crown must be served upon the Crown within 10 days after the claim arose.[5]
(iii) Notice of loss due to lightning must be given within 30 days.[6]
(iv) Notice in writing within six weeks after the claim arose must be given to the defendant in an action for libel in a newspaper or broadcast.[7]

(b) Substantive Limits

The *Limitations Act*[8] sets out a number of general time limits for bringing actions:

contracts	6 years
torts	6 years
assault, battery	4 years
slander	2 years
lawyers	6 years
action on a judgment	20 years

---

[2] *Limitations Act, 2002* (Bill 10).
[3] (Toronto: Butterworths, 1978).
[4] *Municipal Act*, R.S.O. 1990, c. M.45, s. 284(5).
[5] *Proceedings Against the Crown Act*, R.S.O. 1990, c. P.27, s. 7(3).
[6] *Lightning Rods Act*, R.S.O. 1990, c. L.14, s. 13(2).
[7] *Libel and Slander Act*, R.S.O. 1990, c. L.12, s. 5(1).
[8] R.S.O. 1990, c. L.15, s. 45.

Getting Started 11

The *Limitations Act* also provides that the time for bringing actions may be specifically limited by statute.[9] Numerous statutes contain particular restrictions:

(i) Action for recovery of damages occasioned by a motor vehicle, two years.[10]
(ii) Action for damages occasioned by default of the duty to repair a highway bridge, three months.[11]
(iii) Action involving public officers, 10 years.[12]
(iv) Action involving public authorities, six months.[13]
(v) Action for loss by lightning must be after 60 days from loss, but before one year.[14]
(vi) Action against a hospital or nurse, two years from when the patient is discharged or ceases to receive treatment.[15]
(vii) Action against insurance companies for loss by fire or theft, one year from the date the damage or loss occurred.[16]
(viii) Action against health professionals, including doctors, one year after the date the person knew or ought to have known the facts of negligence.[17]

The point at which the limitation period commences is usually set out in the Act creating the limit. In most cases, the limitation period begins to run when the plaintiff knew or ought to have known of the facts which gave rise to the claim.[18] In actions involving persons under a disability, the limitation period does not run while the party is under a disability. For example, in the case of minors the limitation period does not begin to run until after the child has reached the age of majority.[19]

(c) Procedural Limits

Aside from the substantive limits discussed above, the rules contain a number of procedural limitations governing the conduct of an action in the small claims court or pursuant to the simplified procedure. Unlike the substantive limitations,

---

[9] *Ibid.*, s. 45(2).
[10] *Highway Traffic Act*, R.S.O. 1990, c. H.8, s. 206(1).
[11] *Municipal Act*, R.S.O. 1990, c. M.45, s. 284(2).
[12] *Public Officers Act*, R.S.O. 1990, c. P.45, s. 12.
[13] *Public Authorities Protection Act*, R.S.O. 1990, c. P.38, s. 7(1).
[14] *Lightning Rods Act, supra*, note 6, s. 13(2).
[15] *Public Hospitals Act*, R.S.O. 1990, c. P.40, s. 31.
[16] *Insurance Act*, R.S.O. 1990, c. I.8, s. 148, Stat. Cond. 14.
[17] *Regulated Health Professionals Act, 1991*, S.O. 1991, c. 18, s. 89.
[18] *Consumers Glass Co. v. Foundation Co. of Canada Ltd.* (1985), 51 O.R. (2d) 385 (C.A.); *Peixeiro v. Haberman*, [1997] 3 S.C.R. 549.
[19] *Limitations Act, supra*, note 8, s. 47; *Murphy v. Welsh*, [1993] 2 S.C.R. 1069.

failure to comply with the rules is an irregularity and does not render a proceeding or a step in a proceeding a nullity.[20]

If a procedural limit is missed however, the party in default must take action to set aside the default either with the consent of the opposite party or with leave of the court. Although procedural limits can generally be corrected, the ability to do so becomes more difficult with the passage of time.

In both the Small Claims Court and simplified procedure, the general rule is that the procedural limit will be extended if the party seeking the extension is able to satisfy the court that there was a valid reason for failing to comply with the limit and the opposite party will not be prejudiced as a result of the extension of time.[21]

3.3   WHO CAN SUE OR BE SUED — THE PARTIES

(a) Parties Under Disability

Under both the small claims and simplified procedure, the term "disability" means:

(i)   a minor,
(ii) mentally incompetent or incapable of managing his or her affairs, whether or not so declared by a court, or
(iii) an absentee within the meaning of the *Absentees Act*.[22]

The general rule is that a party under disability is represented by a litigation guardian who attends to the interests of the person under disability and takes all steps necessary to protect those interests.[23] The exception to the general rule is that a minor may bring an action in the Small Claims Court for any sum not exceeding $500 as if the minor were of full age.[24]

(i)   BRINGING THE ACTION ON BEHALF OF A PARTY UNDER DISABILITY

In the Small Claims Court, a consent of the litigation guardian must be filed at the time the claim is issued. In the consent the litigation guardian must do the following:

(i)   state the nature of the disability;
(ii) if the plaintiff is a minor, state the plaintiff's birthdate;
(iii) identify the relationship, if any, to the party under a disability;

---

[20] *Small Claims Court Rules*, O. Reg. 258/98, Rule 2.01 (hereinafter *S.C.C.R.*); *Rules of Civil Procedure*, R.R.O. 1990, Reg. 194, Rule 2.01 (hereinafter *R.C.P.*).
[21] *S.C.C.R.*, Rule 3.02; *R.C.P.*, Rule 3.02.
[22] *S.C.C.R.*, Rule 1.02; *R.C.P.*, Rule 1.03.
[23] *S.C.C.R.*, Rules 4.01, 4.02, 4.03 and 4.04; *R.C.P.*, Rule 7.01.
[24] *S.C.C.R.*, Rule 4.01(2).

(iv) confirm that the litigation guardian has no interest adverse to the party under disability;
(v) acknowledge that the litigation guardian is personally liable for costs awarded against the party under disability;
(vi) if represented by an agent or lawyer, confirm that the agent or lawyer has written authority to act.[25]

In the simplified procedure, the procedure is similar; however, the information contained above must be set out in an affidavit sworn by the litigation guardian, rather than in a consent. In addition the affidavit must also provide the following:

(i) confirmation that the litigation guardian consents to act as such in the proceeding;
(ii) in the case of a minor, the minor's birth date;
(iii) statement whether the litigation guardian and the party under disability are ordinarily resident in Ontario.[26]

Where the Children's Lawyer or Public Guardian and Trustee acts as litigation guardian, it is not necessary to file the consent or affidavit.[27]

In both the Small Claims Court and under simplified procedure, the style of cause should be as follows:

(*Name of person under disability*) by his or her litigation guardian, (*name of litigation guardian*).

Where the litigation guardian is not the Public Guardian and Trustee or Children's Lawyer and the litigation guardian also has a claim for damages or out-of-pocket expenses, the style of cause should be as follows:

(*Name of person under disability*) by his or her litigation guardian, (*name of litigation guardian*), and (*name of litigation guardian*) personally.

Anyone capable of bringing an action in Ontario may act as a litigation guardian unless that person has an interest adverse to that of the party under disability or resides outside the jurisdiction. If an action is commenced without a litigation guardian, the solicitor commencing the action may be liable to the defendant for costs.[28]

---

[25] *Ibid.*, Rule 4.01(3); see Form 4A Consent to Act as Plaintiff's Litigation Guardian in Appendix 8.
[26] R.C.P., Rule 7.02(2) [am. O. Reg. 69/95, ss. 19, 20].
[27] S.C.C.R., Rule 4.04(2); R.C.P., Rule 7.02(2) [am. O. Reg. 69/95, ss. 19, 20].
[28] *Geilinger v. Gibbs*, [1897] 1 Ch. 479.

(ii) DEFENDING THE ACTION ON BEHALF OF A PARTY UNDER DISABILITY

A claim against a person under disability must be defended by the defendant's litigation guardian.[29]

In the Small Claims Court, the defendant's parent may act as litigation guardian by filing a consent[30] when filing the statement of defence. The consent is similar to the consent filed on behalf of a plaintiff under disability and provides the following information:

(i) sets out the nature of the disability;
(ii) sets out the relationship of the litigation guardian to the defendant under disability;
(iii) states that the litigation guardian has no interest in the proceeding adverse to the party under disability.[31]

In most actions which are subject to the simplified procedure, the litigation guardian for the defendant must be appointed by the court.[32] The person who wishes to act as litigation guardian for the defendant must bring a motion before a Master or Judge. The motion must include an affidavit which sets out the following information:

(i) nature of the proceeding;
(ii) the date the cause of action arose, and the date the proceeding was commenced;
(iii) regarding the service of the proceeding on the party under disability;
(iv) the nature of the disability;
(v) if a minor, the minor's date of birth;
(vi) whether the person under disability is ordinarily resident in Ontario;
(vii) the relationship, if any, of the proposed litigation guardian and the person under disability;
(viii) that the proposed litigation guardian is ordinarily resident in Ontario;
(ix) that the proposed litigation guardian:
    (a) consents to act;
    (b) is a proper person to be appointed;
    (c) has no interest in the proceedings adverse to the party under disability; and
    (d) acknowledges having been informed that he or she may be responsible for costs not recovered from another party.[33]

---

[29] S.C.C.R., Rule 4.02(1); R.C.P., Rule 7.03.
[30] See Form 4B Consent to Act as Defendant's Litigation Guardian in Appendix 8.
[31] S.C.C.R., Rule 4.02(2).
[32] R.C.P., Rule 7.03(1).
[33] Ibid., Rule 7.03(10) [am. O. Reg. 59/95, ss. 19, 20].

(iii) Settling the Action Where a Party Is Under Disability

A claim by or against a party under disability may not be settled without the approval of the court.[34] Once settlement is reached it is necessary to either attend in court or file a motion for the court approval of the settlement. The judge will consider whether the proposed settlement is in the best interests of the party under disability. If so, the judge will grant judgment in the terms of the settlement. The judgment will include an order regarding payment of the settlement funds. In most circumstances the funds will be paid into court for the benefit of the person under disability.[35] In the case of minors, the settlement funds will be paid into court, to be paid out to the plaintiff when he or she reaches the age of 18.

(b) Partnerships

A proceeding by or against two or more persons as partners may be commenced by using the firm name of the partnership.[36] Where proceedings are commenced against a partnership, the partners should not be added as individual parties.[37]

Certain partnerships are required to file a declaration of information.[38] Failure to file the declaration means that the firm and members thereof are not capable of maintaining an action or other proceeding in an Ontario court in respect of any contract made in connection with the business carried on by the partnership.[39] A proceeding brought by a partnership not complying with the Act is stayed until the required declaration is registered.

When proceeding against a partnership, an order may be enforced not only against the property of a partnership but also (where the order so provides) against a person as a partner.[40] If you seek to enforce an order against a person as a partner, the partner must be served with the claim as well as a notice to the alleged partner.[41] The notice states that the person was a partner at the relevant time.

(c) Corporations

"A corporation has the capacity and the rights, powers and privileges of a natural person."[42] Since the company itself is the party to litigation, it must sue and be sued in its corporate name.

---

[34] *S.C.C.R.*, Rule 4.07; *R.C.P.*, Rule 7.08.
[35] *S.C.C.R.*, Rule 4.08; *R.C.P.*, Rule 7.09.
[36] *S.C.C.R.*, Rule 5.01; *R.C.P.*, Rule 8.01.
[37] *Wabi Iron Works Ltd. v. Patricia Syndicate* (1923), 54 O.L.R. 640 (C.A.); *Minnesota Mining & Mfg. Co. v. Dahm*, [1957] O.W.N. 100 (H.C.J.).
[38] *Limited Partnerships Act*, R.S.O. 1990, c. L.16, s. 25.
[39] *Ibid.*, s. 28.
[40] *S.C.C.R.*, Rule 5.05(2); *R.C.P.*, Rule 8.06(2).
[41] *S.C.C.R.*, Rule 5.03; *R.C.P.*, Rule 8.03.
[42] *Business Corporations Act*, R.S.O. 1990, c. B.16, s. 15.

An Ontario corporation must file a corporate information form with the Ministry of Consumer and Commercial Relations. A corporation does not have a right to bring an action if its corporate filings are not up to date. When acting against a corporation, a corporate search in the office of the Ministry of Consumer and Commercial Relations should be conducted to obtain the correct name of the company and the location of its registered office for service. Even when acting for a corporation as plaintiff, the lawyer or agent ought to consider obtaining a corporate search to ensure that the action is being commenced by the correct corporate entity.

(d) Sole Proprietors

An unincorporated business, other than a partnership, has no legal existence apart from the individuals who operate the business. It is not a legal entity capable of suing or being sued in its own name. The individual owner of the business ought to be named. Having said that, however, proceedings in the Small Claims Court and under simplified procedure against an unincorporated business may be commenced using the business name. The rule protects the plaintiff who commences an action using a business name and applies the rules regarding partnerships, with necessary modifications, to a sole proprietor using a business name.[43]

3.4 WHERE TO SUE — MONETARY AND TERRITORIAL JURISDICTION

(a) Jurisdiction

(i) SMALL CLAIMS COURT

The Small Claims Court exercises power only to the extent expressly conferred on the court by the Legislature. Basically, all actions for monetary relief or for property within the monetary limit can be heard in the Small Claims Court.[44] For example, the courts have confirmed the court's jurisdiction to deal with shipping cases and actions against the federal Crown.[45] The court cannot, however, grant equitable relief such as injunctions. In addition, the Small Claims Court does not have jurisdiction to hear matters which are within the exclusive jurisdiction of the family courts, or landlord and tenant matters.[46]

---

[43] S.C.C.R., Rule 5.06; R.C.P., Rule 8.07(1).
[44] Courts of Justice Act, R.S.O. 1990, c. C.43, s. 23.
[45] Ontario (Attorney General) v. Pembina Exploration Can. Ltd., [1989] 1 S.C.R. 206 (inland shipping); Luo v. Canada (Attorney General) (1997), 33 O.R. (3d) 300 (Div. Ct.).
[46] LeMoine v. LeMoine (1990), 80 Nfld. & P.E.I.R. 339 (Nfld. T.D) (family law); and Beardsley v. Baecker (1993), 20 C.P.C. (3d) 235 (N.S.S.C.).

The court has jurisdiction to hear any claim for the payment of money or for the possession of property where the amount in issue, excluding interest and costs, does not exceed $10,000. This limit is in effect throughout Ontario.[47]

As mentioned earlier, the monetary jurisdiction of the Small Claims Court was increased from $6,000 to $10,000 on April 2, 2001. Claims which were filed before that date may be amended to increase the amount claimed up to $10,000.[48]

The Small Claims Court does not have the power to try actions in excess of the monetary limit, even with consent. If the plaintiff's damages exceed $10,000, the plaintiff is required to abandon the amount over $10,000. If the plaintiff is not prepared to waive the excess, the action must be commenced in the Superior Court of Justice. The plaintiff cannot divide the action into two or more actions to bring the actions within the jurisdiction of the Small Claims Court.[49]

(ii) SIMPLIFIED PROCEDURE

Although all actions involving amounts in excess of $10,000 must be started in the Superior Court of Justice, the amount in issue dictates which rules are to apply. All actions commenced after March 11, 1996, regardless of the amount in issue, may be brought under the simplified procedure. The application of the simplified procedure rules is mandatory when the amount in issue is $50,000 or less, excluding interest and costs, and is available on consent when the amount in issue is greater than $50,000. The exceptions are class proceedings, actions brought pursuant to the *Construction Lien Act*[50] or divorce proceedings, which must be brought under the ordinary procedure.[51]

The action must be commenced under the simplified procedure if the amount in issue is $50,000 or less.[52] In an action where there are multiple plaintiffs, this rule applies to each plaintiff. Except for joint claims or joint plaintiffs, the simplified procedure is mandatory if each plaintiff in the action has a claim less than $50,000.[53]

The simplified procedure rules may also apply to cases in which the amount in issue exceeds $50,000.[54] If the amount in issue is greater than $50,000 the plaintiff may commence the action under the simplified procedure rules. If a defendant does not object, the action will continue to be governed by the

---

[47] *Supra*, note 44, s. 23.
[48] O. Reg. 626/00.
[49] S.C.C.R., Rule 6.02.
[50] R.S.O. 1990, c. C.30.
[51] R.C.P., Rule 76.01(1) [clause (c) am. O. Reg. 60/96, s. 1].
[52] *Ibid.*, Rule 76.02(1) [am. O. Reg. 284/01, s. 25].
[53] *Ibid.*, Rule 76.02(2) [am. O. Reg. 284/01, s. 25].
[54] *Ibid.*, Rule 76.02(3) [am. O. Reg. 284/01, s. 25].

simplified procedure rules.[55] If the defendant objects, the plaintiff may abandon the amount in excess of $50,000 in the Reply.[56] If the excess is abandoned the action continues to be subject to the simplified procedure rules. If the plaintiff does not file a Reply, or does not specifically abandon the excess in the Reply, the action will proceed under the ordinary procedure.[57]

The rules regarding the applicability of the simplified procedure also apply to counterclaims, crossclaims and third party claims. If the defendant brings a counterclaim, crossclaim, or third party claim which is in excess of the monetary limit of $50,000 and there is an objection in the defence to those claims, the defendant must waive the excess; otherwise, the main action, counterclaim, crossclaim or third party claim must all proceed under the ordinary procedure. In other words, if one of the counterclaim, crossclaim or third party claim must proceed by way of the ordinary procedure, the main action must also proceed by way of the ordinary rules of procedure.[58]

If a third party claim has been brought by the defendant, the third party has the right to defend the third party claim, and may also defend the main action. If the plaintiff in the main action had brought a claim in excess of the monetary jurisdiction of the simplified procedure, and the defendant did not object, the action would continue under the simplified procedure. A third party, however, would have the right to object to the use of the simplified procedure in its defence to the main action. To keep the action within the simplified procedure, the plaintiff would then be required to abandon the excess in the reply to the third party defence to the main action. If the plaintiff did not abandon the excess, the main action and the third party claim would be subject to the ordinary procedure.[59]

It is important that if the defendant wishes to object to the matter proceeding in simplified procedure and the amount claimed exceeds $50,000, he or she must do so in the Statement of Defence. A court may decide not to allow an amendment at a later date, in which the defendant objects to the use of simplified procedure.[60]

If the action was commenced under simplified procedure, but was continued under ordinary procedure because of an objection by a defendant or third party, the plaintiff must deliver a Form 76A stating that the action is continued as an ordinary action.[61]

In actions commenced under the ordinary procedure, the plaintiff may later move to amend the claim to bring it within the jurisdiction of the simplified rules. The amended claim must state that the action was commenced under the ordinary procedure and has been continued under the simplified procedure. If the plaintiff brought the claim under the simplified procedure, but the defendant's

---

[55] *Ibid.*, Rule 76.02(5) [am. O. Reg. 284/01, s. 25].
[56] *Ibid.*, Rule 76.02(5) [am. O. Reg. 284/01, s. 25].
[57] *Ibid.*, Rule 76.02(5)(a) [am. O. Reg. 284/01, s. 25].
[58] *Ibid.*, Rule 76.02(5)(b) [am. O. Reg. 284/01, s. 25].
[59] *Ibid.*, Rule 76.02(5)(a) [am. O. Reg. 284/01, s. 25].
[60] *Munro v. Thompson, Tooze, McLean, Rollo & Elkin*, [1998] O.J. No. 3839 (Gen. Div.).
[61] R.C.P., Rule 76.02(6); Form 76A [am. O. Reg. 284/01, s. 25].

crossclaim, counterclaim or third party claim resulted in the claim being subject to the ordinary procedure, the defendant may move to amend its crossclaim, counterclaim or third party claim to reduce the amount claimed to bring it within the jurisdiction of the simplified procedure.

If the action which was subject to the ordinary procedure is to continue under the simplified procedure due to an amendment of the pleadings, the plaintiff is required to deliver a Form 76A stating that the action will continue under simplified procedure.[62]

If the action is commenced under the simplified procedure and is amended to increase the amount in issue above $50,000, the matter may continue under the simplified procedure if the parties consent. If the parties do not consent, the amended pleading must state that the action was commenced under the simplified procedure and has been continued under the ordinary procedure.[63] Again, the plaintiff must file a Form 76A indicating that the action is to continue in the ordinary procedure.[64]

As mentioned above, the jurisdiction of the simplified procedure was increased from $25,000 to $50,000 on January 1, 2002. Cases involving between $25,000 to $50,000 that were commenced before that date would have been subject to the ordinary procedure. Those cases must proceed by way of simplified procedure as of January 1, 2002.[65]

The solicitor ought to file a Form 76A indicating that the action will continue under simplified procedure.[66]

(b) Cost Consequences

The rules of the Small Claims Court and simplified procedure rules use the sanction of costs to compel the parties to bring the action in the appropriate court or under the proper set of rules.

(i) SMALL CLAIMS COURT

If a plaintiff commences an action in the Superior Court of Justice and obtains a judgment at trial which is less than the Small Claims Court limit of $10,000, the court may order that the plaintiff is not entitled to any costs.[67] This rule does not apply in cases where the action has been transferred to the Superior Court of Justice to be consolidated with another action.[68]

---

[62] *Ibid.*, Rule 76.02(8); Form 76A [am. O. Reg. 284/01, s. 25].
[63] *R.C.P.*, Rule 76.02(6), (7); Form 76A [am. O. Reg. 284/01, s. 25].
[64] *Ibid.*, Rule 76.02(6); Form 76A [am. O. Reg. 284/01, s. 25].
[65] See *Dusto v. Hooper-Holmes Canada Ltd.*, [2002] O.J. No. 1289 (S.C.J.).
[66] Rule 76.02(8); Form 76A.
[67] *Ibid.*, Rule 57.05(1) [am. O. Reg. 377/95, s. 4].
[68] *Courts of Justice Act*, R.S.O. 1990, c. C.43, s. 107.

(ii) SIMPLIFIED PROCEDURE

If the plaintiff commences an action under the ordinary procedure and obtains a judgment which is less than $50,000 excluding interest and costs, or obtains a judgment involving real or personal property which has a value of $50,000 or less, the plaintiff may be denied his or her costs of the action. Although there is a general prohibition against the recovery of any costs in these circumstances, there is a saving provision. The court may award the plaintiff costs if the court is satisfied that it was reasonable for the plaintiff to have brought the action under the ordinary procedure.[69]

If the action was subject to the ordinary procedure, and the plaintiff obtained a judgment which was within the exclusive jurisdiction of the simplified procedure, not only would the plaintiff be denied costs, but the plaintiff may also be required to pay all or part of the defendant's costs. These costs would be in addition to any costs the plaintiff was required to pay to the defendant because of a formal offer to settle pursuant to rule 49.10 of the ordinary procedure.[70]

The plaintiff cannot avoid the adverse cost consequences of the rule by commencing the action under the ordinary procedure and moving at the beginning of trial to bring the action within the simplified procedure. If a party amends the claim to bring the action within the simplified procedure, the amending party must pay the costs of the other parties on a substantial indemnity basis, which would not have been incurred had the action been commenced under the simplified procedure rules in the first place.[71]

The defendant may also be subject to adverse cost consequences. If the plaintiff commenced a claim for real or personal property pursuant to the simplified procedure and the defendant in its Statement of Defence objected to the use of the simplified procedure because the fair market value of the real or personal property was in excess of $50,000, and the court found that the value was in fact less than $50,000, the defendant would be responsible for the plaintiff's costs which would not have been incurred if the action had remained under the simplified procedure.[72]

All of the costs rules also apply to counterclaims, crossclaims and third party claims. For example, if, in an action brought under the ordinary procedure, the defendant brought a counterclaim and obtained a judgment within the jurisdiction of the simplified procedure rules, the defendant may be denied his or her costs of the counterclaim.[73]

---

[69] *Ibid.*, Rule 76.13(3)(b).
[70] *Ibid.*, Rule 76.13(6). See also Chapter 6.5, Offers to Settle.
[71] *R.C.P.*, Rule 76.13(1) and (2).
[72] *Ibid.*, Rule 76.13(7).
[73] *Ibid.*, Rule 76.13(9).

(c) Territorial Jurisdiction

Once the plaintiff has decided which court and under which rules the action will be commenced, he or she must then decide where the action will be commenced.

(i) SMALL CLAIMS COURT

In the Small Claims Court, the action is issued and tried in the territorial division of the court in which the cause of action arose, or in which the defendant resides or carries on business. If there are several defendants in different jurisdictions, the action may be commenced where any one of them resides or carries on business.[74]

If the defendant is being served outside the territorial division of the court where the action has been commenced, the plaintiff must file an affidavit which provides that the territorial division of the court where the action was commenced was the correct one.[75]

A defendant may bring a motion to transfer the action to a different territorial division if the balance of convenience favours holding the trial in another county. For example, the action could be transferred if most of the witnesses who will be called at trial reside in a territorial division different than the county where the action was commenced.[76]

(ii) SIMPLIFIED PROCEDURE

Actions brought in the Superior Court of Justice pursuant to simplified procedure may be commenced in any court office in the province, regardless of where the cause of action arose or where the defendant resides.

The final paragraph of the Statement of Claim in a simplified procedure action must set out the county where the plaintiff proposes the action is to be tried. The trial will usually be conducted in the county which is most convenient, in terms of the location of counsel and the witnesses. As in the case of small claims, the defendant may bring a motion to move the trial to a different county if the balance of convenience warrants.[77]

(d) Transfers Between Courts

An action commenced in the Superior Court of Justice where the amount in issue is less than $10,000 may be transferred to the Small Claims Court if all of the parties consent. In the appropriate case, the judge of the Superior Court of Justice may transfer the action to the Small Claims Court, even if not all parties

---

[74] *S.C.C.R.*, Rule 6.01(1).
[75] *Ibid.*, Rule 11.01(2).
[76] *Ibid.*, Rule 6.01(2).
[77] *R.C.P.*, Rule 46.03(2).

consent.[78] An action that has been transferred is continued in the Small Claims Court as if it had been commenced in that court and the parties are protected from any technical deficiencies arising from the transfer.[79]

Where parallel proceedings are pending in different courts, an order may be made, upon motion, transferring the small claims action to the Superior Court of Justice. The order will not be made unless the plaintiff in the Small Claims Court action consents. If the plaintiff does not consent, one of the actions will be stayed to avoid a multiplicity of proceedings.[80] The action which has not been stayed (usually the Superior Court of Justice action) will proceed to judgment and the stayed action will be bound by the findings in the action which proceeded to trial.

---

[78] *Shoppers Trust Co. v. Mann Taxi Management Ltd.* (1993), 16 O.R. (3d) 192 (Gen. Div.).
[79] *Courts of Justice Act, supra,* note 68, s. 23(2) and (3).
[80] *Ibid.,* s. 107.

CHAPTER 4

Pleading Your Case

4.1 DRAFTING PLEADINGS

The pleading is the document which sets out, in a summary way, your client's position with respect to the issues in the action. In many cases the pleadings will be the judge's first introduction to your case. Accordingly, the pleadings should be kept clear and straightforward. The allegations should be set out as concisely as possible.

When drafting pleadings, in addition to the basic requirements of the rules, the following guidelines may prove helpful:

(i) pleadings are divided into paragraphs numbered consecutively and each allegation is contained in a separate paragraph;
(ii) each party should plead a concise statement of the material facts upon which they rely, but not the evidence by which those facts are to be proved;
(iii) inconsistent allegations in a pleading should be clearly labelled as being in the alternative;
(iv) any point of law may be raised in a pleading, but conclusions of law should be pleaded only if the material facts supporting them are pleaded;
(v) if a document or conversation is material it should be pleaded as briefly as possible, and the actual words need not be pleaded unless the words themselves are material;
(vi) if fraud, misrepresentation or breach of trust is alleged, full particulars must be set out in the pleading;
(vii) where the party is relying on a statute, section numbers should be specifically pleaded;
(viii) when defending a claim, the defendant should not simply provide a blanket denial, but should plead the facts he or she intends to prove at trial; and
(ix) a defendant must specifically plead affirmative defences, such as contributory negligence, or voluntary assumption of risk.

4.2 SMALL CLAIMS COURT

(a) The Claim

(i) Issuing the Claim

An action in the Small Claims Court is commenced by the filing of a claim.[1] The plaintiff must attend at Small Claims Court and file the original with a copy of the claim for each defendant, and pay the appropriate fee for filing.[2] Upon receipt of the claim, the court clerk will issue the claim by dating it and assigning it a court file number. All further pleadings in the action will have the same court file number.[3]

The primary aim in drafting the claim is to establish a good cause of action against the defendant. To show a cause of action, the plaintiff must set out in the claim those material facts which establish the rights of the plaintiff, the breach of those rights by the defendant, and the damages suffered by the plaintiff as a result of the breach. This requires judgment on the part of counsel to include only the facts relevant to the cause of action and eliminate facts which are evidentiary or non-material. The properly drafted claim is an outline of the case to be proved at trial.

The following information must be contained in the claim:

(i) the names of the parties and capacity in which they sue or are sued;
(ii) the nature of the claim with reasonable certainty and detail;
(iii) the amount of the claim and relief requested;
(iv) the name, address, telephone and fax numbers for the lawyer or agent representing the plaintiff or, if unrepresented, the plaintiff's address, telephone and fax numbers; and
(v) the address for service of the defendant.[4]

The task of drafting the claim is simplified by the design of Form 7A which includes all necessary elements of the pleading on a single page. Where further space is needed, the "Reasons for Claim" may be annexed to the printed claim form on plain paper. A copy of the annexure should be included with each copy of the claim filed.

The plaintiff must also attach to the claim the documents which are relevant to the claim. For example, in an action based on a contract, the contract should be attached. If for some reason the document is lost or otherwise unavailable, the claim must state the reason the document is not attached.[5]

---

[1] See Form 7A Plaintiff's Claim in Appendix 8.
[2] *Small Claims Court Rules*, O. Reg. 258/98, Rule 7.01(1) (hereinafter *S.C.C.R.*).
[3] *Ibid.*, Rule 7.03.
[4] *Ibid.*, Rule 7.01(2).
[5] *Ibid.*, Rule 7.02.

If one or more defendants do not reside or carry on business in the county where the claim is issued, the plaintiff should file an Affidavit of Establishing Proper Forum at the time of filing the claim. This affidavit is sworn by either the plaintiff or his or her agent or solicitor. The affidavit sets out that the claim is properly brought in the jurisdiction because the cause of action arose in the jurisdiction.[6] The court clerk will not note in default the defendant who is outside the territorial division unless the affidavit has been filed.

(ii) SERVING THE CLAIM

In the past, the Small Claims Court would arrange for service of the claim if the plaintiff was unrepresented by counsel. At the present time, the court will not serve the claim, and all plaintiffs, even those who are unrepresented, must arrange for the service of the claim.[7] The claim must be served on the defendants within six months of its issue.[8]

The claim must be served personally or by an alternative to personal service.[9] Personal service requires the claim to be handed to the individual or if the defendant is a business, by leaving the claim with a person at the place of business who appears to be in control or management of the business.[10]

A plaintiff may find it more convenient to serve the claim by an alternative to personal service. The plaintiff may serve the defendant by mailing the claim and the supporting documents to the defendant's last known address. The envelope must show the sender's return address. Service is deemed to have taken place on the 20th day after the claim was mailed.[11]

To prove that the claim was served, the plaintiff will be required to file an Affidavit of Service.[12] The affidavit is sworn by the person who served the document and sets out upon whom the claim was served, when it was served and where it was served.[13]

If the claim has been served to the last known address, the Affidavit of Service must set out the following:

(i) the person serving the claim believes the claim was mailed to the defendant's last known address and the reason for that belief;
(ii) the claim has not been returned; and
(iii) there is no reason to believe that the defendant did not receive the claim.

---

[6] *Ibid.*, Rule 11.01(2).
[7] *S.C.C.R.*, R.R.O. 1990 Reg. 201, Rule 8.02(1) [revoked O. Reg. 132/96, s. 2].
[8] *S.C.C.R.*, O. Reg. 258/98, Rule 8.01(2).
[9] *Ibid.*, Rule 8.01(1).
[10] *Ibid.*, Rule 8.02.
[11] *Ibid.*, Rule 8.03(7) and (8).
[12] *Ibid.*, Rule 8.06.
[13] *Ibid.*, Form 8B.

In the case of service by mail to the last known address, the affidavit cannot be completed until 20 days after the claim was mailed.[14]

(b) Defence

A party may dispute the claim by filing a Defence[15] within 20 days of being served with the claim.[16] The defendant must file with the court an original Defence and a copy for each party to the action. Upon receiving the Defence, the court clerk shall place the original in the court file and mail or fax a copy to the plaintiff and all other defendants.[17]

In the Defence, the defendant must set out in concise, non-technical language the following information:

(i) the reasons why the defendant disputes the plaintiff's claim; and
(ii) the name, address and telephone number of the solicitor or agent representing the defendant, or if unrepresented the address and telephone number of the defendant.[18]

The defendant may, in some circumstances, wish to admit responsibility for all or part of the claim. If so, a **Defence may be filed in which he or she agrees with the plaintiff's claim and requests that terms of payment be arranged. If the defendant admits the claim, a hearing with a referee will be held at which time the court may make an order as to terms of payment by the defendant.**[19]

If the defendant decides to not defend the claim, the defendant will be deemed to have admitted all allegations contained in the claim, and will not receive any further notice regarding the action until judgment is issued. In certain circumstances, the Clerk may sign default judgment against the defendant.[20]

(c) Defendant's Claim

If the defendant wishes to make a claim against any other party to the action, or a non-party with respect to any claim arising out of the circumstances which are the subject matter of the plaintiff's claim, the defendant must prepare a defendant's claim,[21] and it must contain the following information:

(i) the names of the parties to the plaintiff's claim and the defendant's claim, and the capacity in which the parties are sued;

---

[14] *Ibid.*, Rule 8.03(8)(a).
[15] See Form 9A Defence in Appendix 8.
[16] *S.C.C.R.*, Rule 9.01(1).
[17] *Ibid.*, Rule 9.01(2).
[18] Rule 9.02.
[19] *Ibid.*, Rule 9.03. See Forms 9A Defence and 9C Order as to Terms of Payment in Appendix 8.
[20] See Chapter 5.1(a).
[21] *S.C.C.R.*, Rule 10.01(1) and (2); Form 10A.

(ii) the nature of the defendant's claim, setting out in non-technical language, the occurrences upon which the claim is based;
(iii) the amount of the claim and the relief sought;
(iv) the defendant's name, address, telephone and fax numbers, if applicable;
(v) if the defendant is represented by a lawyer or agent, that person's name, address, telephone and fax numbers;
(vi) the address where the defendant believes each party may be served.[22]

If the defendant's claim is based on a document, the document must be attached to the pleading.[23]

The defendant must have the defendant's claim issued by the court.[24] The claim may be issued when the defence is filed or at any time before trial or default judgment.[25]

If the defendant's claim has been issued, the defendant must serve the claim personally on every person against whom it is made.[26] Service must be completed within six months of the issuance of the claim.[27]

The defendant's claim is required if the defendant wishes to assert a claim he or she may have against the plaintiff within the jurisdiction of the court (formerly a counterclaim). The defendant's claim is subject to the same rules as the plaintiff's claim.[28] Therefore, the defendant's claim is subject to the monetary jurisdiction of $10,000. If the claim against the plaintiff exceeds the monetary jurisdiction of the Small Claims Court, the defendant will have to issue a separate action in the Superior Court of Justice. In those circumstances, one of the actions (the plaintiff's action or the defendant's claim) will be stayed pending disposition in the other.[29]

The defendant's claim is also required if the defendant is asserting a claim against a co-defendant or non-party to the action (formerly a crossclaim or third party claim). The claim is available if the co-defendant or non-party may be liable for all or part of the plaintiff's claim or if the defendant has an independent claim arising out of the same circumstances as the main action.[30] Once again, if the independent claim exceeds the jurisdiction of the Small Claims Court, the defendant will be required to issue a separate action in the Superior Court of Justice.

---

[22] *Ibid.*, Rule 10.01(4).
[23] *Ibid.*
[24] *Ibid.*, Rule 10.01(6).
[25] *Ibid.*, Rule 10.01(2).
[26] *Ibid.*, Rule 10.02.
[27] *Ibid.*, Rule 8.01(1) and (2).
[28] *Ibid.*, Rule 10.05.
[29] See Chapter 3.4(d).
[30] *S.C.C.R.*, Rule 10.01.

(d) Defence to Defendant's Claim

If the defendant to the defendant's claim wishes to dispute the claim, he or she is required to file a defence to defendant's claim within 20 days after service. As in the case of a defence, the defendant to the defendant's claim must set out the reasons why the defendant's claim is disputed, in a reasonable amount of detail.[31]

The defendant to the defendant's claim must file a defence with the court clerk, with sufficient copies for each of the parties. The clerk will then serve the defence by mail or fax.[32]

Unless there is a possibility that the defendant's claim will unduly complicate or delay the trial of the main action, the defendant's claim will be tried at the same time as the trial of the main action. If the claim causes undue prejudice, the court may order that it proceed by way of separate action.[33]

4.3   SIMPLIFIED PROCEDURE

(a) Statement of Claim

(i)   Issuing the Statement of Claim

An action in simplified procedure is commenced with the issuance of a Notice of Action or Statement of Claim.[34] The plaintiff must attend at the court office and file one copy of the Statement of Claim or Notice of Action with the appropriate filing fee.

A Notice of Action is used when there is insufficient time to prepare a Statement of Claim due to the pending expiry of a limitation period. The Notice of Action requires only a short statement of the nature of the claim and allows the plaintiff an additional 30 days to file the Statement of Claim.[35]

In actions under the simplified procedure, the title of proceedings on the Notice of Action or Statement of Claim must indicate that the action is being brought pursuant to the simplified procedure. The following words appear after the title: "THIS ACTION IS BROUGHT AGAINST YOU UNDER THE SIMPLIFIED PROCEDURE PROVIDED IN RULE 76 OF THE RULES OF CIVIL PROCEDURE."[36]

If the action was commenced in the ordinary procedure and the plaintiff amends the claim to reduce the amount claimed to less than $50,000, or if the

---

[31] *Ibid.*, Rule 9.02.
[32] *Ibid.*, Rule 10.03.
[33] *Ibid.*, Rule 10.04.
[34] *Rules of Civil Procedure*, R.R.O. 1990, Reg. 194, Rule 76.02(4) (hereinafter *R.C.P.*).
[35] *Ibid.*, Rule 14.03(2), (3) and (4).
[36] *Ibid.*, Rule 76.02(4).

parties consent to the use of simplified procedure, the plaintiff is required to deliver a notice that the action is now continued under simplified procedure.[37]

If any of the defendants do not reside in Ontario, it will also be necessary for the plaintiff to plead facts which would allow the claim to be served on a defendant outside Ontario. Generally, a claim may be served on a defendant outside Ontario if the claim deals with property located in Ontario, the contract was made in Ontario, the tort was committed in Ontario or the damage was suffered in Ontario.[38]

(ii) Serving the Statement of Claim

The Statement of Claim must be served within six months of the issuance of either the Notice of Action or the Statement of Claim. The service may be by personal service or alternative to personal service.[39]

If the Statement of Claim is being served by mail as an alternative to personal service, the claim must be mailed to the defendant with an acknowledgment of receipt card. Service is effective only if the acknowledgment of receipt card or a post office receipt signed by the defendant is received by the sender.[40]

Although the rules allow for service within six months of the commencement of the action, the practical reality is that the claim must be served more quickly. If no defence has been filed or if the proceeding has not been disposed of within 180 days of the action being commenced, the registrar may dismiss the action as abandoned.[41] Accordingly it is good practice to serve the claim as soon as it has been issued.

(b) Statement of Defence

The defendant is required to serve either a Notice of Intent to Defend or Statement of Defence within 20 days of being served with the Statement of Claim.[42] The registrar will generally allow late filing of the defence as long as the defendant has not been noted in default.

A Notice of Intent to Defend is used by the defendant when there is insufficient time to prepare a Statement of Defence. The Notice of Intent is very brief and simply states that the defendant intends to defend the action. If the Notice of Intent is served within 20 days of service of the Statement of Claim, the defendant is entitled to an additional 10 days to serve the Statement of Defence.[43]

---

[37] *Ibid.*, Rule 76.02(7) and (8), Form 76A; see Chapter 3.4(a)(ii).
[38] *R.C.P.*, Rule 17.02.
[39] *Ibid.*, Rule 16.01(1).
[40] *Ibid.*, Rule 16.03(4).
[41] *Ibid.*, Rule 77.08. See Chapter 5.2(a) Dismissal by Registrar.
[42] *R.C.P.*, Rule 18.01.
[43] *Ibid.*, Rule 18.02.

After the Statement of Defence has been served on the other parties, the defendant must file the Defence, with proof of service with the court where the action was commenced. In the Statement of Defence the defendant must set out the reasons for disputing the plaintiff's claim. The purpose of the Defence is to:

(i)   admit facts not in dispute;
(ii) indicate which allegations the defendant denies;
(iii) state the facts on which the defendant relies;
(iv) give notice of any affirmative defences;
(v)   state the relief sought.

In addition, if the amount of the claim is in excess of $50,000, the defendant may object to the use of the simplified procedure in the Statement of Defence.[44]

(c) Counterclaim

A defendant has the right to bring a counterclaim against the plaintiff for any right or claim he or she may have against the plaintiff.[45] In addition, the defendant may join as a defendant to the counterclaim any other person (whether or not that person is a party to the main action) who is a proper party to the counterclaim.[46] If joining a new party, it is necessary for the defendant to have the counterclaim issued by the court within 20 days of being served with the claim, or before the defendant has been noted in default. The counterclaim will include a notice advising the new party of the requirements regarding the defence of the counterclaim.[47]

If the counterclaim involves parties who are already parties in the main action, the Statement of Defence and Counterclaim must be delivered within 20 days of the service of the Statement of Claim, or before the defendant is noted in default. If the counterclaim is against a person who is not already a party to the main action, the counterclaim and all other pleadings in the action must be served on the new defendant by counterclaim, personally or by alternative to personal service, within 30 days of the counterclaim being issued.[48]

If a counterclaim is asserted the defendant's pleading will be titled Statement of Defence and Counterclaim. The heading will include two styles of cause: the main action and the counterclaim, which shows who the plaintiff and defendants by counterclaim are.[49]

The plaintiff, defendant by counterclaim, is required to defend the counterclaim. Where the defendant by counterclaim resides in Ontario, the defence to

---

[44] See Chapter 3.4(a)(ii).
[45] R.C.P., Rule 27.01(1).
[46] Ibid., Rule 27.01(2).
[47] Ibid., Rule 27.03.
[48] Ibid., Rule 27.04.
[49] Ibid., Rule 27.02.

the counterclaim must be served within 20 days of the service of the counterclaim, failing which the defendant may request that the registrar note the defendant by counterclaim in default.[50]

If the counterclaim is in excess of $50,000, the plaintiff, defendant by counterclaim, may object to the counterclaim proceeding in the simplified procedure. If the excess is not abandoned in the Reply to the Defence to the Counterclaim, the counterclaim and the main action will proceed pursuant to the ordinary procedure.[51]

(d) Crossclaim

A crossclaim is generally available against a co-defendant who is or may be liable for all or part of the plaintiff's claim, or may be liable to the defendant for an independent claim arising out of the same or related incidents or transactions involved in the main action.[52] The crossclaim is included in the Statement of Defence and must be served on the parties within 20 days of being served with the Statement of Claim, or at anytime before the defendant is noted in default.[53]

The defendant by crossclaim must serve a defence to crossclaim within 20 days following service of the Statement of Defence and Crossclaim. A defence to crossclaim is not required if the crossclaim is simply for contribution and indemnity for any damages the defendant bringing the crossclaim may be ordered to pay to the plaintiff, and if the defendant to the crossclaim has served a defence to the main action.[54]

If the crossclaim is in excess of $50,000, the defendant to the crossclaim may object to the simplified procedure in the defence to the crossclaim. If the excess is not abandoned, the crossclaim and main action will proceed under the ordinary procedure.[55]

(e) Third Party Claim

A third party claim is available to a defendant against a person who is not a party to the action, and who may be liable for all or part of the plaintiff's claims, or who may be liable to the defendant for an independent claim arising out of the same circumstances involved in the main action.[56]

The third party claim must be issued by the court within 10 days of the delivery of the Statement of Defence, or within 10 days of the delivery of a reply by the plaintiff.[57] The third party claim can be issued after that date with the consent

---

[50] *Ibid.*, Rule 27.05.
[51] *Ibid.*, Rule 76.02(5)(b). See Chapter 3.4(a)(ii).
[52] R.C.P., Rule 28.01.
[53] *Ibid.*, Rule 28.04.
[54] *Ibid.*, Rule 28.05.
[55] *Ibid.*, Rule 76.02(5)(b). See Chapter 3.4(a)(ii).
[56] R.C.P., Rule 29.01.
[57] *Ibid.*, Rule 29.02(1) and (1.1) [am. O. Reg. 351/94, s. 2].

of the plaintiff, or with leave of the court. Leave will generally be granted if the bringing of the third party claim will not prejudice the plaintiff.[58]

The third party claim, along with all of the pleadings in the action, must be served personally or by alternative to personal service on the third party within 30 days of the issuance of the third party claim. The third party claim must also be served on all parties to the main action within 30 days. It is not necessary to serve the parties to the main action personally.[59]

The third party must enter a defence within 20 days of the service of the third party claim.[60] Usually, the third party will defend both the third party claim and the main action. The defence to the third party claim will set out the third party's position as to why the third party is not liable to the defendant. In the defence to the main action, the third party will plead why the plaintiff is not entitled to damages from the defendant, and may raise any other defences available to the defendant. If the third party defends the main action, the third party has the same rights to participate in the main action as if a defendant. In addition, the third party will be bound by any order made in the main action as between the plaintiff and the defendant who brought the third party claim.[61]

If the main action was in excess of $50,000 and the defendant did not object to the use of the simplified procedure, the third party may object to the use of simplified procedure in his or her defence to the main action. If so, the plaintiff must abandon the excess, or else the main action and third party action will proceed under the ordinary procedure.[62]

(f) Reply

A plaintiff may respond to the allegations raised in the Statement of Defence in a reply.[63] The reply must be delivered within 10 days after the service of the Statement of Defence. If the defence included a counterclaim, the reply is combined with the defence to the counterclaim and must be delivered within 20 days of the date of service.

A reply is required if the plaintiff intends to prove a version of facts different from the facts pleaded in the defence. In addition it may be necessary to deliver a reply to respond to new issues raised by the defendant. If the plaintiff does not file a reply, the plaintiff is deemed to have denied all allegations made in the Statement of Defence.

---

[58] *Bell Canada v. Olympia & York Developments Ltd.* (1988), 30 C.P.C. (2d) 155 (Ont. C.A.).
[59] R.C.P., Rule 29.02(2) and (3).
[60] *Ibid.*, Rule 29.03.
[61] *Ibid.*, Rule 29.05.
[62] *Ibid.*, Rule 76.02(5)(a). See Chapter 3.4(a).
[63] See Form 25A Reply (sample of contract action) in Appendix 9.

If the claim was in excess of $50,000 and the defendant objected to the use of simplified procedure, the plaintiff must waive the excess in the reply or the action will proceed under the ordinary procedure in the Superior Court of Justice.[64]

If the plaintiff does not waive the excess and the action continues in the ordinary procedure, the plaintiff is required to deliver a Form 76A stating that the action is continued as an ordinary action.[65]

(g) Jury Notice

Jury trials are not available in the Small Claims Court; however, juries continue to be available in actions subject to simplified procedure.[66]

Any party to the action may require that the issues in the action be tried by a jury. The party wishing to use a jury must serve and file a Jury Notice[67] at any time before the close of pleadings.[68]

It is unlikely that many Jury Notices will be served in actions subject to the simplified procedure. These actions generally involve sums less than $50,000 and accordingly, the amounts in issue may not justify the added time and expense of a jury trial.

4.4 AMENDMENT OF PLEADINGS

In both the Small Claims Court and in actions subject to the simplified procedure, the court has wide power to amend pleadings at any stage of the action.[69]

In the Small Claims Court, the pleadings may be amended, at least 30 days before the trial, without obtaining court approval.[70] To amend the pleading, the parties must file the new pleading with the court clerk, and the new pleading must be marked "Amended." Any addition or deletion to the original pleading must be underlined or otherwise marked.[71] The amended pleading must be served on all parties by the person making the amendment.[72]

In the simplified procedure, if the pleadings are closed the amendment can be made only on consent or with leave of the court. The court is required to allow a pleading to be amended on such terms as are just, unless prejudice would result that could not be compensated for by costs or an adjournment.[73]

---

[64] See Chapter 3.4(a)(ii), *R.C.P.*, Rule 76.02(5).
[65] *R.C.P.*, Rule 76.02(6), Form 76A. See Chapter 3.4(a)(ii).
[66] *Courts of Justice Act*, R.S.O. 1990, c. C.43, s. 108.
[67] Form 47A Jury Notice.
[68] *R.C.P.*, Rule 47.01.
[69] *S.C.C.R.*, Rule 12.02; *R.C.P.*, Rule 26.01.
[70] *S.C.C.R.*, Rule 12.01.
[71] *Ibid.*, Rule 12.01.
[72] *Ibid.*, Rule 12.01(2).
[73] *R.C.P.*, Rule 26.01.

CHAPTER 5

Resolving the Action After Pleadings

5.1 SMALL CLAIMS COURT

(a) Default Judgment

The defendant must file a defence with the court within 20 days after being served with the claim or risk being noted in default. If noted in default, the defendant is deemed to have admitted all of the allegations set out in the claim. The defendant is not entitled to take any step in the proceeding unless he or she brings a motion to set aside the noting in default. In addition, a defendant in default is not entitled to notice of any step in the action.[1]

To note the defendant in default, the plaintiff must file with the clerk an affidavit of service[2] which proves that the claim was served on the defendant within the territorial jurisdiction of the court. Upon receiving proof of service the clerk may note the defendant in default.[3] If the claim was served outside the territorial division, the plaintiff must also file an affidavit that the action was properly brought in the territorial division before the clerk will note the defendant in default.[4]

In actions where the amount in issue is a fixed sum (liquidated damages), the plaintiff may request that the registrar sign judgment against a defendant who has been noted in default.[5] If the claim is for unliquidated damages, the clerk will fix a trial date for the assessment of damages. This is done at the time the defendant is noted in default.[6] The notice of trial will be sent to the plaintiff and any defendant who has not been noted in default. At the trial, the defendant who has been noted in default will be deemed to have admitted the allegations in the claim. It is therefore not necessary for the plaintiff to prove liability against that

---

[1] *Small Claims Court Rules*, O. Reg. 258/98, Rule 11.05 (hereinafter *S.C.C.R.*); *Rules of Civil Procedure*, R.R.O. 1990, Reg. 194, Rule 19.02 (hereinafter *R.C.P.*).
[2] See Form 8B Affidavit of Service in Appendix 8.
[3] *S.C.C.R.*, Rule 11.01; *R.C.P.*, Rule 19.01.
[4] *S.C.C.R.*, Rule 11.01(2).
[5] *Ibid.*, Rule 11.02; *R.C.P.*, Rule 19.04.
[6] *S.C.C.R.*, Rule 11.04(1).

defendant. The plaintiff will, however, be required to introduce evidence to prove the amount of damages.[7]

If the defendant has been noted in default or if default judgment has been granted, despite an intention to defend the action, the defendant must immediately take action to allow for the filing of a defence. The plaintiff should be contacted to determine whether the plaintiff would be prepared to consent to setting aside the noting in default or the default judgment.[8] If consent is not granted the defendant must bring a motion to set aside the default.[9]

The length of the delay is a factor which may be taken into consideration by the court in determining whether to set aside the default, and accordingly, it is important for the defendant to bring the motion as soon as possible. An affidavit will be required. The affidavit must set out the length and reasons for the delay. Generally, the court will set aside the noting in default if the delay has not been excessive and the defendant has shown an intention to defend the action.[10]

In the case of a defendant's claim, the approach is similar. If the party against whom the defendant's claim has been brought fails to defend, the defendant may file an affidavit of service with the clerk and request that the party be noted in default. However, the clerk is not permitted to enter judgment for the defendant even if the defendant's claim is for a debt or liquidated damages. Judgment may be obtained by the court only at trial or on motion.[11]

(b) Striking a Pleading

The court has broad power to strike out or amend a pleading at any stage in the action. A party may bring a motion to strike out or amend a claim or defence on the following grounds:

(i) it discloses no reasonable cause of action or defence;
(ii) it is scandalous, frivolous or vexatious;
(iii) it may prejudice, embarrass or delay the fair trial of the action; or
(iv) it is an abuse of the court's process.[12]

The motion may be used when it is clear on the face of the pleadings that the action or defence will fail. The motion may also be of assistance when responding to a confusing and poorly drafted claim or defence. The court may strike out

---

[7] *Ibid.*, Rule 11.04(2).
[8] *Ibid.*, Rule 11.06(2); *R.C.P.*, Rule 19.03(2).
[9] *S.C.C.R.*, Rule 11.06(1); *R.C.P.*, Rule 19.03(1).
[10] *Metropolitan Toronto Condominium Corp. No. 706 v. Bardmore Developments Ltd.* (1991), 3 O.R. (3d) 278 (C.A.).
[11] *S.C.C.R.*, Rule 11.03.
[12] *S.C.C.R.*, Rule 12.02(1).

the pleading or may order amendments of the pleading which narrows the issues and removes any improper or prejudicial paragraphs in the pleading.[13]

5.2 SIMPLIFIED PROCEDURE

(a) Dismissal by Registrar

If the plaintiff has not prosecuted the action in a reasonably diligent manner, the registrar may dismiss the action as abandoned. The action will be dismissed if:

(i) more than 180 days have passed since the date the originating process was issued;
(ii) no defence has been filed;
(iii) the action has not been disposed of by final order or judgment;
(iv) the action has not been set down for trial or summary trial; and
(v) the registrar has given 45 days notice that the action will be dismissed.[14]

Even if the defence has been filed, the plaintiff must continue to move the matter forward. The registrar is required to dismiss the action if:

(i) more than 150 days have passed since the filing of the defence (or the filing of the first defence in the case of multiple defendants);
(ii) the action has not been disposed of by final order or judgment;
(iii) the action has not been set down for trial or summary trial; and
(iv) the registrar has provided 45 days notice that the action will be dismissed.[15]

This rule requires the plaintiff to insist upon a delivery of a defence within a fairly short period of time. If the defence is not received the plaintiff must note the defendant in default and take steps to obtain default judgment within 180 days of issuing the claim.[16]

(b) Default Judgment

The plaintiff may commence default proceedings if the defendant fails to deliver a notice of intent to defend or statement of defence within 20 days of being served with a statement of claim. The plaintiff must file proof of service with the registrar and request that the registrar note the defendant in default. If noted in default, the defendant is deemed to have admitted the allegations made by the

---

[13] *Ibid.*, Rule 12.02(2).
[14] *R.C.P.*, Rule 76.06(1).
[15] *Ibid.*, Rule 76.06(2).
[16] See Chapter 4.3(a)(ii).

plaintiff in the Statement of Claim. The defendant is not entitled to take any additional steps in the action and is not entitled to notice of any step in the action.

To obtain default judgment, the plaintiff must file with the registrar a requisition for default judgment form, which generally sets out the fact that the claim is one in which the registrar has jurisdiction to sign default judgment. The form sets out the following information:

(i) the claim comes with the class of case for which default judgment may be signed by the registrar, *i.e.*, a debt or liquidated damages;
(ii) whether there has been partial payment of the amount claimed, and if so, the date and amount of the payment;
(iii) if prejudgment interest was claimed, the amount of the interest and how interest was calculated;
(iv) if the plaintiff is seeking post-judgment interest at a rate different from the rate set out in the *Courts of Justice Act*,[17] the rate of interest claimed and the reasons for a different rate being applied; and
(v) whether the plaintiff wishes the registrar to fix costs.[18]

The registrar will sign judgment if satisfied that the information set out in the requisition form is accurate and adequately proves that he or she has jurisdiction to sign judgment. If the registrar is uncertain he or she will not sign judgment and the plaintiff will be required to bring a motion or proceed to trial to obtain the default judgment.

If a motion for judgment is required, the plaintiff must file an affidavit which sets out sufficient evidence to support the claim. The affidavit should include all documents which provide detail regarding the damage suffered by the plaintiff. The affidavit would generally be in the name of the plaintiff personally and would include all invoices, medical reports or other documents which pertain to the plaintiff's claim.[19]

In some circumstances the judge hearing the motion may not be satisfied that the plaintiff's damages have been properly proved by way of affidavit and that oral testimony is required to make a proper determination of the issue. The motions court judge could order that the matter proceed to a trial for an assessment of damages.

In the undefended trial the plaintiff is not required to prove the liability of the defendant, but must prove the amount of damages. After hearing the oral testimony and reviewing the documentary evidence filed, the judge will assess the plaintiff's damages and grant judgment accordingly.

If the defendant has been noted in default or if default judgment has been granted, the defendant may move to set aside the default judgment.[20] As a

---

[17] R.S.O. 1990, c. C.43.
[18] *R.C.P.*, Rule 19.04(2).
[19] *Ibid.*, Rule 19.05(2).
[20] *Ibid.*, Rule 19.03; Rule 19.08.

general rule, the test for setting aside a default judgment is more onerous than that for setting aside a noting in default.

The defendant must bring the motion to set aside the default as soon as possible. The motion must include an affidavit which explains the reasons for the default. In a motion to set aside default judgment, the defendant's affidavit must also establish, to the satisfaction of the judge hearing the motion, that there is a valid defence on the merits.[21]

In establishing a valid defence on the merits the defendant, in a Simplified Rule Action, must show that the issues in the action ought not to have been resolved by way of default judgment. The defendant must meet the summary judgment test set out in Rule 76.07, namely whether issues in the action could not be decided without cross-examination or, if it would be otherwise unjust to decide the issues on a motion.[22]

(c) Striking a Pleading

After the close of pleadings, any party may bring a motion before a judge for a determination on a question of law or to strike out a pleading on the ground that it discloses no reasonable cause of action.[23] The motion must be brought promptly, after the close of pleadings.[24] No evidence is admissible on a motion to determine a question of law except with leave of the court. In the case of a motion to strike a pleading for disclosing no reasonable cause of action or defence, no evidence is permitted,[25] and the judge will look only to the pleadings to decide the issue. It is important to note that documents incorporated by reference in the Statement of Claim may be used on the motion.[26] Factums are required and must be served and filed by the parties at least two days before the motion is to be heard.[27]

The defendant may also move before a judge to dismiss the plaintiff's action on the following grounds:

(i) the court has no jurisdiction over the subject matter of the action;
(ii) the plaintiff does not have the legal capacity to bring the action;
(iii) there is another proceeding involving the same parties in another court involving the same subject matter;
(iv) the action is frivolous, vexatious or is an abuse of process.[28]

---

[21] *Lenskis v. Roncaioli* (1992), 11 C.P.C. (3d) 99 (Ont. Gen. Div.), affd (1996), 45 C.P.C. (3d) 57 (C.A.).
[22] *Grieco v. Marquis* (1998), 38 O.R. (3d) 314 (Gen. Div.).
[23] R.C.P., Rule 21.01.
[24] *Ibid.*, Rule 21.02.
[25] *Ibid.*, Rule 21.01(2).
[26] *Beardsley v. Ontario Provincial Police* (2000), 50 O.R. (3d) 491 (S.C.J.).
[27] R.C.P., Rule 21.03. For motion procedure, see Chapter 7.6, Interlocutory Motions.
[28] R.C.P., Rule 21.01(3).

The courts are generally reluctant to dispose of an action after the close of pleadings. The motion will not be granted unless it is "plain and obvious" that the claim or defence will not succeed.

(d) Summary Judgment

A party in an action under the simplified procedure may also move, after the close of pleadings, for summary judgment.

(i) NOTICE OF MOTION FOR SUMMARY JUDGMENT

The party seeking summary judgment must serve a notice of motion with supporting affidavit material. The motion will be heard in the county where the action was commenced unless the parties consent or the court orders the motion to be heard elsewhere.[29]

(ii) EVIDENCE ON MOTION FOR SUMMARY JUDGMENT

The affidavit evidence from both the moving and responding parties must clearly set out the specific facts which either support judgment or provide why judgment should not be granted. The parties cannot simply recite the allegations set out in the pleadings.[30] As a general rule the affidavit should be sworn by the parties themselves. Although the court may consider an affidavit which is based on information and belief as opposed to direct knowledge, an adverse inference may be drawn by the court from the failure to put forward an affidavit from the persons having personal knowledge of the facts.[31]

Under the simplified procedure, there is no cross-examination permitted on the affidavits filed on a motion for summary judgment. In addition, a party may not conduct an oral examination of a witness on a pending motion. If the witness' evidence is necessary for the motion, an affidavit from the witness will be required.[32]

(iii) MOTION RECORD

It is the responsibility of the moving party to prepare the motion record. The motion record must contain the following information:

(i) a table of contents which contains a list of each document, including a description of each exhibit and the date of the exhibit;
(ii) the notice of motion;

---

[29] *Ibid.*, Rule 76.07(2). See Chapter 7.7(b).
[30] *Ibid.*, Rule 76.07(4).
[31] *Ibid.*, Rule 76.07(5).
[32] *Ibid.*, Rule 76.04.

(iii) all affidavits filed by any party for use on the motion; and
(iv) all pleadings.[33]

The moving party must serve the motion record on all parties to the action. The motion record must be filed, with proof of service, in the court office where the motion is to be heard at least two days before the date fixed for the hearing of the motion.[34]

Each party on the motion is required to serve a factum, which must set out the facts and law relied on by the party. The factum must be served and filed in the court office at least two days before the motion is to be heard.[35]

(iv) Hearing of the Motion

The intent of the simplified rules is to provide a relatively streamlined and inexpensive procedure for summary judgment motions. It has been held that it is implicit in the simplified procedure rule that the motion is "intended to be short, to the point and based on a minimum of evidence that requires no cross-examination".[36]

(v) Test for Summary Judgment

The judge hearing the motion for summary judgment is required to grant judgment unless:

(i) the judge is unable to decide the issues in the action without cross-examination; or
(ii) it would be unjust to decide the issues on the motion.[37]

The test for summary judgment under the simplified procedure is a less onerous test than the test for summary judgment under the ordinary procedure. It is not necessary for the party bringing the motion to show that there is no genuine issue for trial. Accordingly, the court may grant summary judgment even if there is a genuine issue for trial, as long as the court is satisfied that there is sufficient evidence to decide the case. If the judge can make determinations as to credibility without cross-examinations, the judge is required to do so.[38]

The purpose of the summary judgment motion under the simplified procedure has been described as follows:

---

[33] *Ibid.*, Rule 76.07(7).
[34] *Ibid.*, Rule 76.07(6).
[35] *Ibid.*, Rule 76.07(8).
[36] *Robertson v. Ball* (1996), 31 O.R. (3d) 30 at 41 (Gen. Div.).
[37] R.C.P., Rule 76.07(9).
[38] *Newcourt Credit Group Inc. v. Hummel Pharmacy Ltd.* (1998), 38 O.R. (3d) 82 (Div. Ct.).

In my view, the purpose of the rule in question is to allow the parties to bring forward a relatively inexpensive application for summary judgment based on the affidavits of the parties, any supporting material that can be properly placed before the court in that manner, and perhaps, the affidavits of witnesses which, when reviewed in total, and upon applying the principles of justness and fairness, demonstrate a clear case that the judge may cut to the chase and enter judgment. In circumstances where the case is not clear or where the dictates of justice and fairness would suggest otherwise, it is appropriate for the judge to refer the matter for trial.[39]

In objecting to a motion for summary judgment, the responding party will have two main arguments — that cross-examination is required, and that it would be unfair to decide the matter on a summary judgment motion. It is not, however, appropriate for the responding party to argue that more time is needed to obtain additional evidence. The parties are expected to put forward all evidence in support of their position which is available at the time of the motion. An exception may be in the case of a reluctant non-party witness who refused to provide an affidavit for the motion.[40] In those circumstances, the responding party may argue that it would be unfair to grant judgment on the motion without the evidence of the witness.

(vi) Dismissal of Motion for Summary Judgment

In the event the judge hearing the motion is of the view that it would be unfair to grant summary judgment, the judge will dismiss the motion for summary judgment. At that time, the judge is required to determine whether the action is to be resolved by way of summary trial or an ordinary trial.[41]

There are no specific costs consequences for an unsuccessful motion. Under the ordinary procedure if the moving party does not succeed in the motion, the court may order the moving party to pay the responding party's costs on a substantial indemnity scale.[42] Those rules specifically do not apply in a summary judgment motion in simplified procedure.[43] In all likelihood, any costs awarded on a motion for summary judgment under the simplified rules will be modest, in keeping with the general intent of the rules to provide an inexpensive procedure for resolving actions.[44]

---

[39] *Robertson v. Ball*, *supra*, note 36, at 40-41.
[40] *Craig Gilchrist Equipment Rental Ltd. v. Robertson* (1997), 10 C.P.C. (4th) 372 (Ont. Gen. Div.).
[41] R.C.P., Rule 76.07(10). See Chapter 9.
[42] R.C.P., Rule 20.06.
[43] *Ibid.*, Rule 76.07(3).
[44] *Robertson v. Ball*, *supra*, note 36, at 42.

(vii) APPEAL OF SUMMARY JUDGMENT

If the motion for summary judgment is dismissed, the order would be interlocutory and the decision would be appealed to the Divisional Court with leave.[45] If the motion is successful and judgment is granted, the order would be a final order and the appeal would be to the Divisional Court (if the judgment was for less than $25,000) or to the Court of Appeal (if the judgment was for more than $25,000).[46] In the Court of Appeal, there are strict time limits for oral argument for the appeal of summary judgment. The argument is generally limited to one hour: 30 minutes for the appellant; 20 minutes for the respondent; and 10 minutes for reply.[47]

---

[45] See: Chapter 7.6(b)(ii)(2) Appeal of a Judge's Order, and see Chapter 7.6(b)(ii) Appeals of Interlocutory Orders.
[46] See Chapter 11 for appeals of final orders.
[47] Practice Direction: New Scheduling Procedures for Civil Appeals, Dec. 18/95.

CHAPTER 6

Settling the Action

6.1 WHY SETTLE THE CASE?

"Like warfare, litigation should be avoided."[1] Going to trial can be unsatisfactory because no matter who wins, both parties lose time and money in the process. From the moment you first meet with your client, the possibility of settlement should be your uppermost thought. Unlike litigation, negotiation need not produce a winner and a loser. Parties can cooperate and work together to achieve a result that is beneficial to both sides.

The first obstacle to settlement may be in obtaining instructions from the client to negotiate. Nobody likes to be told that his or her case may not be as strong as originally thought or that the court system might not provide the desired outcome. To satisfy the client's expectation of justice you must help him or her see the dispute in objective terms and advise as to the difficulties and uncertainties litigation presents. You may also have to readjust your own orientation and focus on achieving the best result for the client, including minimizing legal fees. The Law Society imposes a professional duty upon its members to advise and encourage settlement.[2]

Every case contains some opportunity for negotiation. Even where a defendant has no defence to a claim, the plaintiff may find it beneficial to discuss terms of payment. A plaintiff may well accept an immediate payment of an amount less than that claimed to avoid the delay and costs of litigation and the uncertainty of collection.

Counsel should not commence settlement negotiations without instructions from the client. The client should be informed and involved throughout the negotiation process. Start by advising the client of your assessment of the strengths and weaknesses of both sides of the dispute. Second, review the objectives established at the outset of the action and discuss various strategies to achieve those goals. The client should provide counsel with instructions to negotiate settlement which include a financial range and terms acceptable to the client. The best practice is to obtain all settlement instructions in writing. If the client

---

[1] Roger Fisher, "What About Negotiation as a Specialty?" (1983), 69 A.B.A.J. 1221.
[2] Law Society of Upper Canada, *Rules of Professional Conduct* (hereinafter *R.P.C.*), January 30, 1987, Rule 3, Commentary 5, and Rule 10, Commentary 6.

provides oral instructions, a note should be made of settlement instructions and the lawyer should send a letter to the client confirming the oral instructions. All offers received from the other side must be communicated to the client.

6.2 PREPARING FOR SETTLEMENT

The best way to negotiate is face to face, not over the telephone. Without visual feedback the risk of misunderstanding is increased. Telephone conversations also tend to be faster and more competitive than a personal meeting and thus such negotiation is more likely to fail. When scheduling a negotiation discussion, try to arrange to meet in person. If discussions must take place on the telephone, set up a specific time to discuss settlement so both sides may be fully prepared.

Negotiations should be conducted in a courteous and professional manner.[3] If your opponent is unrepresented, do not undertake to advise that person, but rather urge that he or she seek independent legal advice.[4] Where the opposite party is represented, you must communicate or negotiate directly with that person's counsel; counsel cannot deal directly with the party.

6.3 SETTLEMENT CONFERENCES

(a) Private Settlement Meetings

Settlement meetings either in person or on the telephone may be conducted at any stage of the proceeding. There is no reason why attempts cannot be made to contact the other side to discuss the resolution of the dispute even before the action has been commenced.[5]

Most counsel prepare far less for a settlement conference than for a trial. Too often negotiation is treated as an interim step and not as a possible conclusion. Successful advocacy, whether in negotiation or litigation, is based on thorough preparation.

(b) Simplified Procedure — Settlement Discussion and Documentary Disclosure (Rule 76.08)

In actions brought pursuant to the simplified procedure, the parties are required to discuss the possible resolution of the action within 60 days after the filing of

---

[3] *R.P.C.*, Rule 10, Commentary 7.
[4] *R.P.C.*, Rule 5, Commentary 14.
[5] See Chapter 3.

the first Statement of Defence or Notice of Intent to Defend. The discussion may be by way of a face-to-face meeting or by telephone call.[6]

One of the reasons for the rule is that the best time to discuss the resolution of the case occurs when the parties are required to meet at a stage of the litigation. In cases under the ordinary procedure, there is an opportunity for the parties to meet and discuss settlement at the examinations for discovery. Because there is no discovery in the simplified procedure, the rules provide for a special meeting at a relatively early stage in the proceedings to compel the parties to consider settlement.

The rule also requires the parties to consider whether all relevant documents have been produced.[7] In this way the meeting can also fulfill the same purpose as a discovery in an action subject to the ordinary procedure with respect to the disclosure and production of documents.

6.4   ALTERNATIVE DISPUTE RESOLUTION

(a) Private Mediation

In both small claims and simplified procedure actions, the parties may require the assistance of an impartial third party to bring them towards settlement. A mediation is simply a more formal settlement meeting with a third party who encourages the parties to reach a mutually satisfactory resolution.

The mediator will usually start the mediation with a brief explanation of the process. The parties are reminded that all discussions are strictly without prejudice and nothing said in the mediation can be used in the litigation if the mediation fails to result in a settlement. The mediator will then ask the parties to briefly state the issues which will have to be addressed. After the initial statements, the mediator will focus on the respective interests of the parties and lead the discussion as to what the parties really want to achieve in the litigation.

Once the interests of the parties have been established, both sides, with the assistance and encouragement of the mediator, should try to create as broad a range of options as possible. Once the options are on the table, the process of offer and response begins. Listen carefully to the offers your opponent makes. The changes in terms through successive offers may indicate the other party's areas of compromise. Offers often link concessions in one area to gains in another. By examining the linkages, you can determine the other side's true goals and the terms on which they might be prepared to settle.

If a settlement is reached on the mediation, the parties will be expected to execute minutes of settlement. The minutes of settlement represent a concluded settlement. If one party refuses to comply with the settlement, the other party

---

[6] *Rules of Civil Procedure*, R.R.O. 1990, Reg. 194, Rule 76.08 (hereinafter *R.C.P.*).
[7] See Chapter 7.

may bring a motion for judgment to enforce the terms of the settlement reached at the mediation.

(b) Simplified Procedure — Mandatory Mediation

Mediation is mandatory with respect to all simplified procedure actions commenced in Toronto and Ottawa.[8] It is expected that mandatory mediation will be phased in for the rest of the province over the next few years.

The mediation is expected to take place within 90 days after the first Statement of Defence or Notice of Intent to Defend has been filed with the court.[9] This time limit can be altered only by order of the court[10] or may be extended for up to an additional 60 days with the consent of the parties.[11]

If the date for the mediation has not been extended, the parties are required to arrange the mediation within 30 days of the first defence being filed. Within 30 days the plaintiff is required to file a notice with the court mediation co-ordinator, advising of the name of the mediator and the date scheduled for the mediation.[12]

In choosing a mediator the parties may choose either a mediator from the court approved list, or any other person, if they consent. If the mediation co-ordinator does not receive the notice of mediator within 30 days of the first defence, he or she will choose the mediator from the approved list, and fix a date for the mediation.[13]

At least seven days before the mediation date, each party is required to serve a statement of issues on the other parties, with a copy to the mediator.[14] The purpose of the statement is to set out the issues in dispute and each party's position and interests.[15] The documents the party intends to rely upon at the mediation should be attached to the statement.[16] In addition, the plaintiff is to attach a copy of the pleadings to his or her statement.[17]

All parties and their lawyers, if any, are required to attend the mediation.[18] If an insurance company is involved, and it may be required to indemnify a party, a representative of the insurer is also required to attend.[19] The parties and/or insurer with authority to settle must attend the mediation, or, if another person's authority is required, the party should have access to that person by telephone.[20]

---

[8] *R.C.P.*, Rule 24.1.04(1)(a).
[9] *Ibid.*, Rule 24.1.09.
[10] *Ibid.*, Rule 24.1.09(1).
[11] *Ibid.*, Rule 24.1.09(3).
[12] *Ibid.*, Rule 24.1.09(5); Form 24.1A.
[13] *Ibid.*, Rule 24.1.09(6) and (7).
[14] *Ibid.*, Rule 24.1.10; Form 24.1C.
[15] *Ibid.*, Rule 24.1.10(2).
[16] *Ibid.*, Rule 24.1.10(3).
[17] *Ibid.*, Rule 24.1.10(4).
[18] *Ibid.*, Rule 24.1.11(1).
[19] *Ibid.*, Rule 24.1.11(1.1).
[20] *Ibid.*, Rule 24.1.11(2).

The mediation is mandatory, and, accordingly, if any of the parties fail to comply with their obligations, the mediator may file a certificate of non-compliance. This may result in an order for the non-complying party to pay costs.[21]

Mandatory mediation has been very successful in bringing about settlements at an early stage of litigation. In simplified procedure actions where there are no examinations for discovery, the mediations also give the parties an opportunity to assess their opponent and ask questions. Accordingly, the mediation should be taken seriously, and the parties should attend the mediation thoroughly prepared.

If the mandatory mediation takes place within 60 days after the filing of the first defence, the parties could combine the requirement of the settlement discussion and documentary disclosure meeting, pursuant to Rule 76.08.[22]

6.5 OFFERS TO SETTLE

In actions pursuant to both the *Small Claims Court Rules* and simplified procedure, any party may serve an offer to settle the claim on the other parties to the action.[23] The other parties may accept the terms of the offer by accepting the offer at any time before it is withdrawn, by serving a written acceptance of the offer.[24]

The acceptance of the offer resolves the dispute between the parties. Where a party fails to comply with the accepted offer, the other party may bring a motion to the court for judgment in the terms of the accepted offer, or may proceed with the action as if the offer had not been made.[25]

6.6 COST CONSEQUENCES OF OFFERS TO SETTLE

All settlement offers are "without prejudice" discussions and must not be disclosed to the court until after there has been a determination of the matters in issue.[26] At the conclusion of the case, the trial judge will usually ask counsel for their submissions on costs. It is at this time that offers to settle should be disclosed to the court.[27]

---

[21] *Ibid.*, Rule 24.1.13.
[22] See Chapter 6.3(b).
[23] *Small Claims Court Rules*, O. Reg. 258/98, Rule 14.01 (hereinafter *S.C.C.R.*); *R.C.P.*, Rule 49.02.
[24] *S.C.C.R.*, Rule 14.05; *R.C.P.*, Rule 49.07.
[25] *S.C.C.R.*, Rule 14.06; *R.C.P.*, Rule 49.09.
[26] *S.C.C.R.*, Rule 14.04; *R.C.P.*, Rule 49.06.
[27] See Chapter 9.5(c).

(a) Small Claims Court

An offer to settle served at least seven days before the trial, which has not been accepted or withdrawn before trial, can result in cost consequences if the offer is not accepted. In Small Claims Court, the court may award up to double the normal costs if the plaintiff making the offer obtains a judgment as favourable or more favourable than the offer to settle. If the defendant makes an offer and the judgment for the plaintiff is as favourable or less favourable than the offer, the defendant may be entitled to up to double the normal costs from the date the offer was served. If the party who served the offer was not represented, the court may award up to $300 for inconvenience.[28]

(b) Simplified Procedure

In actions under the simplified procedure the rules also require the offers to be made at least seven days before trial and remain open for acceptance at the commencement of trial before the cost consequences for failing to accept the offer will apply.[29]

If the plaintiff made an offer and obtains a judgment which is as favourable or more favourable than the offer to settle, the plaintiff is entitled to partial indemnity costs to the date the offer was served and substantial indemnity costs from that date forward.[30] If the defendant made an offer and the plaintiff obtains a judgment which is as favourable or less favourable than the defendant's offer, the plaintiff is entitled to partial indemnity costs to the date of the offer, and the defendant is entitled to partial indemnity costs from that date forward. If the plaintiff's action is dismissed and the defendant had served an offer to settle which was more favourable to the plaintiff, the defendant may be entitled to payment of his or her partial indemnity costs to the date of the offer and substantial indemnity costs from the date of the offer forward.[31]

6.7 CONCLUDING SETTLEMENT

Once an agreement is reached, a letter confirming the negotiated terms should be sent immediately to the other party. The court should be contacted to alert the staff and the judge that the matter will not proceed. For settlements involving persons under disability, court approval is required.[32]

---

[28] S.C.C.R., Rule 14.07; see Chapter 9.5(c)(i) Small Claims Court.
[29] R.C.P., Rule 49.10.
[30] Ibid., Rule 49.10(1).
[31] S. & A. Strasser Ltd. v. Richmond Hill (Town) (1991), 1 O.R. (3d) 243 (C.A.).
[32] For the settlement of these claims see Chapter 3.3(a)(iii) Settling the Action Where a Party is Under Disability.

Once the action has settled, the plaintiff will usually be asked to execute a full and final release. In the release the plaintiff agrees that the claim against the defendant has been resolved with the settlement and that the plaintiff will not take any further action against the defendant or anyone who may claim against the defendant.

(a) Small Claims Court

In the Small Claims Court the parties should execute minutes of settlement and file the minutes with the court office. The filing of minutes of settlement completes the action and it is not necessary for the parties to file an order dismissing the action. If the court does not have the executed minutes of settlement by the time of trial, counsel may be required to attend in court and advise the judge of settlement.

(b) Simplified Procedure

Upon settling the action in the simplified procedure, the parties will be required to obtain an order from the court dismissing the action on a without costs basis. A consent executed by the parties or their solicitors and draft order dismissing the action without costs should be filed with the court. This material will be placed before a judge or master who will sign the consent order. Once the order has been signed and entered with the court, the action is officially concluded.

CHAPTER 7

Discovering the Case: Pre-Trial Proceedings

7.1 DISCOVERY OF DOCUMENTS

(a) Small Claims Court

A Small Claims Court action has a number of stages where the parties are required to advise the other side of the documents that are relevant to the matter in issue in the case.

The plaintiff is required to include with the claim a copy of each document on which the claim is based. For example, if the claim is based on a contract, a copy of the specific contract is to be attached to the claim and must be served on the defendants. If for some reason the document on which the claim is based is not available, the plaintiff must set out in the claim the reasons for the unavailability of the document.[1] Similarly, if the defence or the defendant's claim is based on a document, a copy of the document is to be attached to the pleading.[2]

The pre-trial conference also presents an opportunity for documentary disclosure, as one of the purposes of the pre-trial is to provide full disclosure of the relevant facts and evidence.[3] Accordingly, the parties are expected to bring all relevant documents to the pre-trial conference. If they fail to do so, the pre-trial judge may make an order with respect to the disclosure and production of relevant documents.

The rules relating to evidence at trial also encourage the parties to disclose their documents. All written statements or reports of witnesses and all documents such as medical reports, hospital records, financial reports or invoices may be served 14 days in advance of the trial date.[4] The party serving the document may simply file the document as evidence at trial rather than call the author as a witness.[5] Although this rule does not require the party to serve the

---

[1] *Small Claims Court Rules*, O. Reg. 258/98, Rule 7.01(2) (hereinafter *S.C.C.R.*). See also Chapter 4.2, Small Claims Court.
[2] *S.C.C.R.*, Rules 9.02(1) and 10.01(6).
[3] *Ibid.*, Rule 13.02(1); see Chapter 7.7(a) Small Claims Court.
[4] For further clarification, see Chapter 8.4(a)(ii) Documents.
[5] *S.C.C.R.*, Rule 18.02.

document, the advantages of being able to file the document at trial without having to call the author will generally result in parties serving their relevant documents on the other side at least 14 days in advance of the trial.

(b) Simplified Procedure

In actions subject to the simplified procedure, the parties are required to serve an affidavit of documents within 10 days after the plaintiff served a reply, or the time for serving a reply has expired. The affidavit must list all documents in the party's power, possession or control which relate to a matter in issue in the action.[6] The definition of document is very broad and includes a sound recording, videotape, film, photograph, chart, graph, map, plan, survey, book of account and information recorded or stored by means of any device, including a computer disc. A document is deemed to be in a party's power if that party is entitled to obtain the original document or a copy of it.[7]

The affidavit of documents for actions subject to simplified procedure consists of four separate schedules: (1) Schedule A which lists all relevant documents the party does not object to producing; (2) Schedule B which lists all relevant documents for which the party claims privilege along with the grounds for the claim for privilege; (3) Schedule C which lists those relevant documents which were formerly in the power, possession or control of the party, along with a reason why the documents are no longer available; and (4) Schedule D which lists the persons who may be called as witnesses at trial, along with their addresses and telephone numbers.[8]

Copies of the documents listed in Schedule A of the affidavit of documents must be served on every other party at the time the affidavit of documents is served.[9]

The list of witnesses in Schedule D of the affidavit of documents is a unique feature of the simplified procedure. If a witness is not disclosed in the affidavit of documents the party may be prevented from calling that witness at the trial of the action.[10]

In addition to the list of relevant documents and witnesses, the affidavit must also include a statement by the deponent of the affidavit that the party has never had in his or her power, possession or control any relevant document other than the documents listed in the affidavit of documents. The affidavit must also include a solicitor's certificate, in which the solicitor certifies that he or she has explained to the deponent the necessity and requirement to make full disclosure

---

[6] *Rules of Civil Procedure*, R.R.O. 1990, Reg. 194, Rule 30.03 (hereinafter *R.C.P.*).
[7] *Ibid.*, Rule 30.01.
[8] *Ibid.*, Rule 76.03(2).
[9] *Ibid.*, Rule 76.03(1)(b).
[10] *Ibid.*, Rule 76.03(3). See also Chapter 8.4(b)(iii) Witnesses.

of all relevant witnesses and to list all relevant witnesses in the affidavit of documents.[11]

7.2 ORAL EXAMINATIONS FOR DISCOVERY

There is no right of examination for discovery in either the Small Claims Court or in simplified procedure matters. This includes both oral discovery and discovery conducted by way of written questions and answers. There is no discretion on the part of the court to order a discovery under any circumstances.

7.3 DEMAND FOR PARTICULARS

In the absence of examinations for discovery, the parties may wish to use other methods to obtain the information which would otherwise have been obtained at discovery. One of the tools available is the demand for particulars.

(a) Small Claims Court

The Small Claims Court does not specifically provide for one party requesting particulars from the other. In fact, it could be argued that the Small Claims Court rules which contemplate a fairly summary approach when it comes to pleadings would not require a party to provide greater particularity. Having said that, however, a party is required to set out the nature of the claim or defence with reasonable certainty and detail[12] and, if the party fails to do so, the court could order greater detail to be provided. In addition, in a motion to strike out or amend a claim or defence for disclosing no reasonable cause of action or defence, the court may make an order requiring the party to provide greater detail or particulars.[13]

(b) Simplified Procedure

In a simplified procedure action, a party may make a demand for particulars of any allegation in the pleading of an adverse party. The particulars are required to be provided within seven days of receiving the demand for particulars.[14]

As a general rule, particulars are requested before the party is required to plead. In the case of a defendant, particulars of an allegation in the claim may be required to allow the defendant to properly prepare the statement of defence. In the case of a plaintiff, particulars of the allegations in the defence may be

---

[11] *R.C.P.*, Rule 76.03(4).
[12] *S.C.C.R.*, Rules 7.01(2) and 9.02.
[13] *Ibid.*, Rule 12.02(1); see also Chapter 5.1(b).
[14] *R.C.P.*, Rule 25.10.

required before the reply can be prepared. A court will not order particulars unless it can be proved that the particulars are required to allow the party to prepare its pleading.[15]

Many of the questions that would have been asked on an oral examination for discovery may be asked through a demand for particulars. For example, in a claim which contains a broad allegation that the defendant breached a duty of good faith, the defendant may make a demand for particulars of all facts upon which the plaintiff intends to rely upon in support of the allegation.

At least 10 days before the trial, the party who served a notice of readiness for pre-trial must serve a trial record which includes, among other things, any demand or order for particulars and the response received.[16]

7.4 REQUEST TO ADMIT

In addition to the demand for particulars, parties may wish to use the request to admit to obtain information which would otherwise have been available on an examination for discovery.

(a) Small Claims Court

As in the case of the demand for particulars, the Small Claims Court rules do not specifically provide for a request to admit. The rules with respect to the pre-trial conference allow the pre-trial judge to make recommendations to the parties regarding the admission of facts or documents without further proof.

In the appropriate case, a party may make a request of the other side to admit certain facts. If the other side does not agree to admit the facts, this can be raised on the pre-trial conference. The pre-trial judge may recommend that the party admit the facts or documents without requiring further proof at trial.[17]

(b) Simplified Procedure

In the simplified procedure, a party may serve a request to admit on any other party to admit the truth or a fact or the authenticity of a document.[18] The party receiving the request has 20 days to provide a response. In the response the party may admit the facts, refuse to admit the facts (in which case a reason for the refusal is required) or deny the fact. If the party fails to respond to the request to admit, the party is deemed to have admitted the facts set out in the request to admit.[19]

---

[15] See *Stylecraft Dress Co. v. Gotlin*, [1946] O.W.N. 114 (H.C.J.).
[16] R.C.P., Rules 48.03 and 76.11(4).
[17] S.C.C.R., Rule 13.03. See Chapter 7.7(a)(ii).
[18] R.C.P., Rule 51.02.
[19] *Ibid.*, Rule 51.03.

One of the purposes of an examination for discovery was to obtain admissions of fact. The admissions could then be used at trial to avoid the necessity of calling evidence to prove the fact. In the case of a request to admit, where a party has admitted certain facts, the request and the response may be filed as an exhibit at trial. There would then be no need to call further evidence to prove the fact admitted.

7.5 MEDICAL EXAMINATIONS

In both the Small Claims Court and in actions pursuant to the simplified procedure, the court may order a party to attend on a medical examination where the physical or mental condition of a party is in issue.[20]

The party seeking the medical examination must bring a motion before the court (master or judge). The moving party must establish to the satisfaction of the court that the other party's medical condition is an issue in the action.[21] If the court orders a medical examination, the party who is to be examined is required to answer the questions of the medical practitioner, and all answers may be admissible into evidence.[22]

(a) Small Claims Court

Although a medical examination is technically available in the Small Claims Court, such an examination will rarely be requested. The amounts in issue in the action may not justify the expense of obtaining a doctor's report.

If a party obtains an order for a medical examination, the party who is being examined (usually the plaintiff) should ask the court to order the examining party to produce a copy of the report immediately after it has been prepared.

(b) Simplified Procedure

Under the simplified procedure, a court may be more likely to grant the motion for a medical examination. Because of the prohibition against oral examinations for discovery, the medical examination will be an effective method for a party to obtain further information regarding the medical condition of the opposite party.

The party being examined must provide to the examining party all medical reports and hospital reports prepared in the course of the party's treatment. The examining party is not entitled to reports prepared in contemplation of litigation where the party to be examined undertakes not to call the author of the report at trial.[23]

---

[20] *Courts of Justice Act*, R.S.O. 1990, c. C.43, s. 105.
[21] *R.C.P.*, Rule 33.01.
[22] *Supra*, note 20, s. 105(5).
[23] *R.C.P.*, Rule 33.04(2) [am. O. Reg. 441/90, s. 8].

Once the report has been prepared by the medical practitioner, the report must be served on the party examined and the other parties to the action. The party obtaining the order has no discretion in serving the report and must serve the report even if it assists the other side.[24]

7.6 INTERLOCUTORY MOTIONS

An action that proceeds to trial will ultimately end with a final order called a "judgment". During the conduct of litigation, matters may arise which require orders to resolve but which do not involve a final disposition. Orders made during the conduct of an action are termed "interlocutory" since one "speaks between" the commencement and final disposition of an action. Requests for interlocutory orders are made by way of motion to the court.

(a) Small Claims Court

The Small Claims Court is organized to provide summary hearings in an expeditious and inexpensive manner.[25] The use of motions in this court is not generally encouraged. If you are considering bringing a motion, proceed only if the order sought is necessary to the just determination of the action or if it is necessary to enforce previous orders of the court.

Once you have decided that a motion is necessary, the first task is to contact the court and make an appointment for the motion to be heard. The court clerk will schedule a time based on the availability of a judge. It is not the practice in Small Claims Court to choose your own motion date and serve documents without first obtaining an appointment. Parties served with a notice of motion should contact the court to confirm that an appointment was in fact made and that the necessary materials were filed with the court.

Once an appointment has been scheduled, counsel for the party bringing the motion (the "moving party") must draft a notice of motion. The notice states the precise relief sought, the grounds to be argued and the documentary evidence to be relied upon.[26]

Evidence on a motion is given by affidavit.[27] The affidavit contains a sworn statement of facts in support of the motion. Where the facts are not within the personal knowledge of the deponent, they should state the source of the information or the grounds for the belief. The affidavit must provide sufficient evidence to allow the judge to make the order requested in the notice of motion. Counsel should never submit their own affidavit to a tribunal in any proceeding

---

[24] *Ibid.*, Rule 33.06.
[25] S.C.C.R., Rule 1.03(1).
[26] *Ibid.*, Form 15A Notice of Motion in Appendix 8.
[27] *Ibid.*, Form 15B Affidavit in Appendix 8.

in which they appear as advocate. The role of counsel is to submit arguments to the court, not to give testimony.[28]

The notice of motion and supporting affidavit must be served on every party to the action at least seven days before the hearing date. A motion does not require personal service.[29]

A motion in Small Claims Court is generally heard in judge's chambers, not in open court. Although the hearing may tend towards informality, counsel should be prepared to make succinct and informed submissions to the judge. The moving party begins as follows:

(i) identify yourself, the party you represent and the capacity in which you appear;
(ii) state the purpose of the motion;
(iii) provide a summary of the facts;
(iv) state the issues arising from the facts;
(v) state the arguments and authorities upon which you rely;
(vi) state the order requested.

This sequence assumes jurisdiction is not in issue. Generally, a judge of the Small Claims Court has jurisdiction to hear any motion in a proceeding before that court. The court has wide powers to make such orders on such terms as are considered just.[30]

If the opposite party ("responding party") does not wish to oppose the motion, that party should so advise the court and the moving party when served with the notice. If the responding party opposes the motion, that party may wish to file an affidavit which sets out the facts upon which the responding party will rely. On the hearing of the motion, the responding party answers by:

(i) identifying himself or herself, the party represented, and the capacity in which he or she appears;
(ii) stating any dispute with the facts as submitted by the moving party and referring to the affidavit of the responding party;
(iii) replying to the arguments and authorities cited by the moving party;
(iv) stating the arguments and authorities upon which the respondent relies; and finally
(v) concluding with the order requested.

Parties to a contested motion should plan on a maximum of five minutes each to make submissions. On the rare occasion that a motion might require more

---

[28] Law Society of Upper Canada, *Rules of Professional Conduct*, January 30, 1987, Rule 10, Commentary 16(a).
[29] S.C.C.R., Rule 15.01(2).
[30] *Ibid.*, Rules 1.03 and 1.04; *Courts of Justice Act, supra,* note 20, s. 24.

time, the court clerk should be so advised at the time the appointment is made.

Upon hearing the arguments, the judge will grant an order upon such terms as are considered just.[31] The judge delivers the order orally to the parties and writes it in the court file. No separate order need be prepared by the parties. Counsel should write down the terms of the order as they are delivered.

One disincentive to bringing a motion in Small Claims Court is the general prohibition on the awarding of costs. Costs on a motion are available only where the court is satisfied that the motion was unnecessary or was necessary because of the default of a party. In either event, costs will not exceed $50 unless there are special circumstances.[32]

An interlocutory order made in the Small Claims Court may not be appealed.

(b) Simplified Procedure

(i) Motions

Any party to an action commenced under the simplified procedure may bring a motion before a judge, or in some circumstances, a master. As a general rule, a master has jurisdiction to hear all interlocutory motions in actions pursuant to the simplified procedure.[33] In those jurisdictions where there are no masters, the motion must be brought before a judge of the Superior Court of Justice.

The motion is brought in the county where the action was commenced.[34] This is to be contrasted with motions in ordinary procedure, which must be brought where the opposing solicitor practises.

In an apparent attempt to limit the costs of bringing motions, the simplified procedure rules provide that if it is not practical, the motion may be made without a supporting affidavit. In addition, the motion may be argued in writing, facsimile or by telephone or video conference.[35]

The moving party is required to serve and file a notice of motion. If affidavit evidence is to be used, it must be served and filed with the notice of motion. After receiving the motion material, the responding party may file its own affidavit in opposition to the motion.[36]

Under the simplified procedure, cross-examination of a deponent on the affidavit is not permitted under any circumstances. In addition, a party may not conduct an oral examination of a witness on a pending motion.[37]

---

[31] *S.C.C.R.*, Rule 1.04.
[32] *Ibid.*, Rule 15.02.
[33] *R.C.P.*, Rule 37.02.
[34] *Ibid.*, Rule 76.05(2).
[35] *Ibid.*, Rule 76.05(3).
[36] *Ibid.*, Rules 37.10 and 39.02.
[37] *Ibid.*, Rule 76.04.

Following the hearing of the motion, the master or judge will make a decision as to whether the relief sought is to be granted and, if so, on what terms. As a general rule the disposition of the motion will be recorded on the motion form and no formal order will be required.[38]

(ii) APPEALS OF INTERLOCUTORY ORDERS

Appeals of interlocutory orders in the simplified procedure made by a master are made to a single judge of the Superior Court of Justice. If the motion appealed from was heard by a judge, the appeal is to the Divisional Court. In those circumstances, the party wishing to appeal must first seek leave to appeal the order.[39]

1. Appeal of Master's Order

The party seeking to appeal the interlocutory order (the appellant) must serve a notice of appeal on all parties whose interests may be affected by the appeal within seven days of the date of the order.[40] The appellant must contact the trial co-ordinator's office where the motion is to be heard to obtain a date and location for the hearing of the appeal. The notice of appeal must set out the date for the appeal and state the relief sought and the grounds for the appeal. The appeal is to be heard in the county where the solicitor for the responding party has his or her office.[41]

At least three days before the hearing of the appeal, the appellant must file the notice of appeal and proof of service in the court office. In addition, the appellant must serve on the parties affected by the appeal and file with the court office an appeal record which contains the following:

(i) a table of contents describing each document in the appeal record;
(ii) a copy of the notice of appeal;
(iii) a copy of the order appealed from, issued and entered, and the reasons, if any, as well as typed copy of the reasons if they were handwritten;
(iv) such other material as may be required for the hearing of the appeal.[42]

The appellant must also serve and file a factum no later than four days before the hearing of the appeal. The factum is to consist of consecutively numbered paragraphs which set out the facts and law to be relied upon by the appellant on the appeal.[43] The factum should be a concise argument stating the facts and law. As the factum will be read by the judge hearing the appeal, and will be referred

---

[38] *Ibid.*, Rule 76.05(6) and (7).
[39] *Ibid.*, Rule 62.01.
[40] *Ibid.*, Rule 62.01(2).
[41] *Ibid.*, Rule 62.01(4) and (6).
[42] *Ibid.*, Rule 62.01(7).
[43] *Ibid.*

to by the judge during argument, care should be taken to ensure the factum sets out the substance of your argument as accurately and persuasively as possible.

The responding party must also serve his or her factum at least four days before the hearing. Once the responding party receives the appeal record and factum, he or she must carefully review the record to determine whether all material which may be required on the appeal has been included. If the responding party wishes to put additional material before the judge, the responding party must serve and file the additional material no later than two days before the hearing. At that time the responding party must also file his or her factum.[44] As with the appellant's factum, the responding party's factum must consist of a concise statement of the facts and law which will be relied upon by the responding party on the appeal.[45]

2. Appeal of Judge's Order

Where the order appealed from was made by a judge, the appellant must bring a motion for leave to appeal before a single judge of the Divisional Court. As with a direct appeal, the notice of motion for leave to appeal must be served on the parties who would be affected by the appeal within seven days of the date of the order appealed from.[46]

As a first step, the appellant must obtain a date for the motion for leave from the registrar where the motion is to be heard. As with any other motion, the motion for leave to appeal must be brought where the action was commenced.[47]

The party seeking leave must serve and file with the court, at least three days before the hearing of the motion,[48] a motion record which contains the following:

(i) the original motion record used on the motion which is being appealed;
(ii) a supplementary motion record containing a copy of the following:
    (a) a copy of the notice of motion for leave to appeal,
    (b) the order appealed from, and
    (c) the reasons for judgment.[49]

If the reasons are handwritten, a typed copy of the reasons is required.

Each party on a motion for leave to appeal must serve and file with the court office a factum no later than two days before the hearing of the motion.[50]

There are two tests for granting leave to appeal:

---

[44] *Ibid.*, Rule 62.01(8).
[45] *Ibid.*
[46] *Ibid.*, Rule 62.02(2).
[47] *Ibid.*, Rule 76.07(2).
[48] *Ibid.*, Rule 37.10(1).
[49] *Ibid.*, Rule 62.02(5).
[50] *Ibid.*, Rule 62.02(6).

(i) there is a conflicting decision by another judge on the issue, and it is desirable that leave to appeal be granted, or
(ii) there is good reason to doubt the correctness of the order in question and the issues to be appealed involve matters of such importance that leave should be granted.[51]

If leave is granted, the moving party must, within seven days, serve a notice of appeal on the parties who may be affected by the appeal.

7.7 PRE-TRIAL CONFERENCES

In both small claims and simplified procedure actions, the pre-trial conference is the key stage in the proceedings where the counsel for the parties may discuss settlement as well as the merits of the case and obtain orders from the pre-trial judge or master with respect to the conduct of the action. The meeting of the parties and a frank discussion of the strengths and weaknesses of the case will greatly increase the chances of settling the action. Accordingly, the pre-trial conference is one of the best opportunities to resolve the case.

The pre-trial conference is a meeting between counsel (or the parties themselves, if unrepresented) before a judge, or in the case of the Small Claims Court, a deputy judge or referee. All discussions are confidential and the parties are encouraged to freely discuss the merits of their case.[52] The primary objective of the pre-trial conference is to settle the action, and the judge will usually provide his or her comments regarding the respective strengths and weaknesses of each party's case and encourage the parties to take a realistic approach to the settlement of the action. The judge who conducted the pre-trial conference is prohibited from presiding at the trial except with the consent of all parties.[53]

(a) Small Claims Court

(i) Request for Pre-Trial Conference

Currently, a pre-trial conference will be scheduled in the Small Claims Court on the court's own initiative or upon the request of a party.[54] While the court office is scheduling more pre-trial conferences, not all cases will be automatically pre-tried. Should you require a pre-trial conference, you must ensure that you file a request for pre-trial conference with the court office.

You should always consider whether a pre-trial conference would be of assistance in your particular case. Because of the value of the pre-trial in terms

---

[51] *Ibid.*, Rule 62.02(4).
[52] S.C.C.R., Rule 13.02(2); R.C.P., Rule 50.01.
[53] S.C.C.R., Rule 13.04; R.C.P., Rule 50.04.
[54] S.C.C.R., Rule 13.01(1). See Form 13A Request for Pre-Trial Conference in Appendix 8.

of increased likelihood of settlement, a narrowing of the issues and trial preparation, the pre-trial conference should be requested in virtually every action.

In completing the request for pre-trial, you must set out the facts which support your request. It is sufficient to indicate on the form that you require the pre-trial for the following reasons:

(a) to resolve or narrow the issues in an action;
(b) to expedite the disposition of the action;
(c) to facilitate settlement of the action;
(d) to assist the parties in effective preparation for trial; and
(e) to provide full disclosure between the parties of the relevant facts and evidence.[55]

The court will fix the time and place of the conference and will notify the parties by issuing a notice of pre-trial conference.[56]

(ii) PRE-TRIAL CONFERENCE

Each party is expected to attend at the pre-trial prepared for a full discussion of the action with all relevant documents. The greater the preparation and organization, the more receptive the pre-trial judge will be to your arguments. A positive comment from the judge as to the merits of your case will greatly assist in achieving a beneficial settlement. Where a party attends the pre-trial inadequately prepared such that the purpose of the pre-trial is frustrated, the judge may order costs of the pre-trial against that party. The costs are not expected to exceed $50.[57]

In some circumstances, it may be beneficial to have your client attend the pre-trial. In this way the client is exposed to the other side's argument, as well as the judge's comments. This may result in the client taking a more reasonable approach when discussing the settlement of the action. In addition, the presence of the client will allow you to immediately obtain instructions regarding settlement.

At the conclusion of the pre-trial, the judge may make recommendations to the parties regarding the simplification of the issues, the elimination of unsupported claims or defences and the admission of certain facts.[58] The judge may also make orders regarding the conduct of the action.[59] The judge may prepare a memorandum of the matters agreed upon at the pre-trial, along with any other information regarding scheduling.[60]

---

[55] *Ibid.*, Rule 13.02(1) and Form 13A.
[56] *Ibid.*, Rule 13.01(2).
[57] *Ibid.*, Rule 13.01(5) and (6).
[58] *Ibid.*, Rule 13.03(1).
[59] *Ibid.*, Rule 13.03(2).
[60] *Ibid.*, Rule 13.03(5).

(iii) Notice of Trial

If the matter does not settle at the pre-trial, the court clerk shall advise the parties that they must request a trial date.[61] The request for the trial must be made to the court clerk. In actions which do not have a pre-trial conference, the clerk will fix a date for trial and send a notice of trial to each party.[62]

(b) Simplified Procedure

(i) Readiness for Pre-Trial Conference

The plaintiff is required to set the action down for trial within 90 days after the first Statement of Defence or Notice of Intent to defend has been filed. The action is set down by serving a notice of readiness for pre-trial conference on all parties and filing the notice with the court.[63] If the plaintiff fails to set the action down for trial, any other party may do so by serving the notice of readiness. If no party sets the action down for trial and 150 days have passed since the filing of the first Statement of Defence, the registrar is required to make an order dismissing the action as abandoned.[64]

The party who serves the notice of readiness is required to certify that the settlement discussion and documentary disclosure meeting required pursuant to Rule 76.08 took place.

After the notice of readiness has been filed with the court office, the registrar will schedule the pre-trial conference. The parties will receive at least 45 days notice of the pre-trial date.[65]

(ii) Pre-Trial Conference

A unique feature of pre-trial conferences in simplified procedure actions is the requirement that the parties personally attend the pre-trial with their counsel, if represented. If a personal attendance would require undue time or expense, the party could attend by telephone or video conference.[66] The presence of the parties is expected to improve the opportunity to settle the action since all decision-makers will be present at the pre-trial conference.

As soon as the lawyer receives the date of the pre-trial conference, the client ought to be advised of the date and the requirement for the party to personally attend. At that time, the lawyer should ensure that the party has sufficient authority to settle the claim at the pre-trial and, if another person is required for

---

[61] *Ibid.*, Rule 13.01(7).
[62] *Ibid.*, Rule 16.01; Form 16A.
[63] *R.C.P.*, Rule 76.09(1); Form 76C.
[64] *Ibid.*, Rule 76.06(2).
[65] *Ibid.*, Rule 76.10(1).
[66] *Ibid.*, Rule 76.10(2).

approval before settlement, arrangements ought to be made to have the person available by telephone during the pre-trial.[67]

At least five days before the pre-trial conference, each party is required to deliver a two-page statement that sets out the issues and the party's position with respect to the issues. The pre-trial conference statement will be similar to the mediation statement in those cases subject to mandatory mediation.[68]

At the time the pre-trial statement is delivered, each party must also deliver a trial management checklist, which requires each party to advise as to the issues outstanding, as well as procedural matters that could affect the trial, such as whether there will be a request to admit or expert evidence.[69]

The parties must file the statement and checklist with the court, along with a copy of their affidavit of documents and copies of all relevant documents and any expert reports.[70]

The objectives of the pre-trial conference under the simplified rules are the same as those of the Small Claims Court: to discuss the merits of the action, simplify the issues and consider the settlement of the action.

If the action does not settle at the pre-trial, the parties will be required to discuss the mode of trial. The parties may then agree to proceed by summary trial. If they do not agree on a summary trial, the pre-trial judge may decide that summary trial is the appropriate mode of trial.[71]

(iii) SETTING ACTION DOWN FOR TRIAL

At the conclusion of the pre-trial conference, the registrar will place the action on the trial list. The manner in which trial dates are set varies depending upon the county where the trial is to be heard. Generally, the parties will receive notice that the action is to be spoken to at a trial scheduling or assignment court. The trial date will be fixed by the presiding judge or master at that time.

At least 10 days before the trial date, the party who served the notice of readiness for pre-trial conference is required to serve a trial record.[72] If the action is to proceed by way of ordinary trial, the trial record will include the following material:

(i)   a table of contents describing each document;
(ii) a copy of a jury notice, if any;
(iii) a copy of the pleadings;
(iv) a copy of any demand for particulars and the response to the demand;

---

[67] *Ibid.*, Rule 76.10(3).
[68] See Chapter 6.4(b).
[69] *R.C.P.*, Rule 76.10(4); Form 76D.
[70] *Ibid.*, Rule 76.10(4).
[71] *Ibid.*, Rule 76.10(6).
[72] *Ibid.*, Rule 76.11(2).

(v) any order respecting an agreement on special damages, or any other matter affecting the conduct of the trial;
(vi) a solicitor's certificate signed by the lawyer setting the action down for trial, confirming that the record contains all necessary documents and that the time for the delivery of pleadings has expired.[73]

If the matter is to proceed to a summary trial, the trial record will include the following material:

(i) a table of contents describing each document;
(ii) a copy of the pleadings;
(iii) a copy of any demand for particulars and the response to the demand;
(iv) a copy of any order respecting an agreement on special damages, or any other matter affecting the conduct of the trial;
(v) a copy of the affidavits served by all parties for use on the summary trial; and
(vi) a solicitor's certificate signed by the lawyer setting the action down for trial, confirming that the record contains all necessary documents.[74]

---

[73] *Ibid.*, Rule 48.03(1).
[74] *Ibid.*, Rule 76.11(4); see Chapter 9.4(a).

CHAPTER 8

Preparing for Trial

8.1 FILE ORGANIZATION

Running an efficient litigation practice requires organization in the structure and contents of your files. Every file, from Small Claims Court to Superior Court of Justice, should be organized in a standard and easily understandable manner so documents can be located quickly and with the minimum of anxiety.

File organization need not be complicated or expensive. The simplest system involves one expansion file folder and a number of different coloured folders. The expansion folder is divided into separate folders. The following divisions are suggested:

(i)   correspondence;
(ii) pleadings and proceedings;
(iii) investigation;
(iv) medical reports and/or property damage documentation; and
(v)   trial brief.

This simple system may be adjusted to suit particular requirements and individual preferences. It is not important how the file is organized, only that some system be used.

8.2 TRIAL BRIEF

The trial brief is a way to organize your file to ensure a smooth, well-prepared presentation of your case at trial. The trial brief contains, in an organized form, everything that will be required at the trial. Like the organization of the file, the trial brief is a flexible system and should be arranged in a way with which you are comfortable.

One method of organization is to keep all the necessary materials in a three-ring binder and tab each section. This keeps all of the material organized and easily referenced at trial.

The actual contents of the trial brief will depend upon the nature of the case and the individual preferences of the lawyer. Every trial brief, however, should contain the following sections:

(i)   theory of the case;
(ii) a summary of the elements of the case which must be proved to be successful at trial and the evidence you will be relying on to prove those elements;
(iii) pre-trial motions, if any;
(iv) opening statement;
(v)   witness list;
(vi) outline of direct examination of your witnesses;
(vii) documents you intend to introduce at trial;
(viii) outline of the cross-examination of opponent's witnesses;
(ix) closing arguments;
(x)   offers to settle and notes regarding pre-judgment interest and costs.

8.3 THEORY OF THE CASE

The "theory of the case" is your strategy — your position and approach to all the evidence which will be presented by the parties at trial. The "theory of the case" has been described as follows:

> The theory of the case is the basic, underlying idea that explains not only the legal theory and factual background, but also ties as much of the evidence as possible into a coherent and credible whole. Whether it is simple and unadorned or subtle and sophisticated, the theory of the case is a product of the advocate. It is the basic concept around which everything else revolves.[1]

The development of the theory of the case begins with the impressions gained in the first interview, and is refined through the process of gathering information and research to produce a final explanation of the evidence which will be presented at trial. Once you have decided upon a coherent strategy, you may then organize the evidence to best advance your theory at trial.

8.4 PREPARATION OF EVIDENCE

(a) Small Claims Court

(i) GENERAL

The Small Claims Court is generally reluctant to apply the strict rules of evidence which would result in the exclusion of evidence. The Small Claims Court may admit as evidence any oral testimony and any document or other thing that the court considers relevant, including hearsay. The court may exclude evidence

---

[1] James W. McElhaney, *McElhaney's Trial Notebook*, 2nd ed. (Chicago: American Bar Association, 1987) at 48.

that is unduly repetitious. The court may not admit evidence which would be inadmissible by reason of any privilege under the laws of evidence or is inadmissible under any Act.[2]

(ii) DOCUMENTS

The evidence at trial will be in the form of either documents or oral testimony from witnesses. As a general rule, one should use documentary evidence as much as possible. As stated by Sopinka J.:

> As a matter of tactics it is preferable to avoid calling a witness if a fact can be proved otherwise. Every witness is a two-edged sword. There will usually be some negative evidence in the testimony of every witness. For this reason every counsel should be fully abreast of the special rules which render the calling of witnesses unnecessary.[3]

The *Small Claims Court Rules* assist a party in using documentary evidence at trial. The following documents may be admitted into evidence without calling a witness to identify the document:

1. The signed written statement of any witness, including the written report of an expert, to the extent that the statement relates to facts and opinions to which the witness would be permitted to testify in person.
2. Any other document, including but not limited to a hospital record or medical report made in the course of care and treatment, a financial record, a bill, documentary evidence of loss of income or property damage, and a repair estimate.[4]

The rule covers virtually all statements, experts' reports and documentary evidence one would expect to require at trial. In Small Claims Court, almost every aspect of a case may be proved through the use of documents without the need to call witnesses.

To allow you to file a statement or document at trial without calling a witness, the statement or document must be served on all parties at least 14 days before the trial date. The name and address of the witness or author must be included with the document when it is served.[5] The party served with the statement or document may wish to cross-examine the author or witness at the trial. If so, it is the responsibility of the party who wishes to cross-examine to summon the witness or author to the trial.[6]

If you neglect to serve a document 14 days before the trial, or if you discover new documents on the eve of the trial, it is still possible to have the document

---

[2] *Courts of Justice Act*, R.S.O. 1990, c. C.43, s. 27.
[3] John Sopinka, *The Trial of an Action* (Toronto: Butterworths, 1981) at 43.
[4] *Small Claims Court Rules*, O. Reg. 258/98, Rule 18.02(2) (hereinafter *S.C.C.R.*).
[5] *Ibid.*, Rule 18.02(1).
[6] *Ibid.*, Rules 18.02(4) and 18.03(1); Form 18A.

entered into evidence. The trial judge has the discretion to grant leave to allow the document to be received into evidence at trial without calling the witness.[7] If leave is not granted, it would be necessary to call the author of the document as a witness at trial and introduce the document during the witness' evidence in chief. You should be prepared to call the witness in the event the trial judge does not grant leave.

If the documentary evidence is to be introduced through a witness, it must be introduced as an exhibit. To admit an exhibit into evidence counsel should take the following steps:

(i) show the exhibit to opposing counsel;
(ii) show the exhibit to the witness;
(iii) have the witness identify the item;
(iv) establish through questioning of the witness that the exhibit is relevant; and
(v) move to have the exhibit admitted into evidence.

A document brief should be prepared if you anticipate that you will be referring to a number of documents throughout the trial. The document brief contains all of the relevant documents which will be referred to at trial. The brief could be filed at the commencement of the trial to provide the trial judge easy access and reference to the documents throughout the trial.

If you are referring to any item before calling the witness who will identify it, have the exhibit marked for identification and move for its admission into evidence when the necessary witness is called. Exhibits are numbered; exhibits for identification are given letter designations.

(iii) Witnesses

Although documentary evidence is preferable, there will usually be a need for witnesses to give oral evidence at trial. Prior to the trial the witnesses should be contacted and a witness list prepared. The witness list will include the names of the witnesses, their address for service, their home and business telephone numbers and a short summary of their evidence. The list will enable you to keep track of the different witnesses and provide easy reference to contact them.

You should meet personally with your witnesses so you may assess their demeanour and determine how they may be received by the trial judge. Should you come to the conclusion that a witness will not make a favourable impression at the trial, you may wish to consider using a different witness or file a document to prove the fact.

Preparing a witness to testify involves reviewing with that person those facts which are necessary elements of your theory of the case and making sure he or she is ready to testify to those facts. If the witness is expected to identify exhibits at trial, review the documents with the witness and explain the method re-

---

[7] *Supra*, note 2.

garding the introduction of the exhibits. Counsel must review with the witness both the plan for direct examination and the possible areas of cross-examination.

Witnesses should also be prepared to properly conduct themselves at the trial. In answering the questions, the witness should be reminded to carefully listen to the questions asked and try to make sure the answers are truthful, and as succinct and to the point as possible. The witness should be reminded to dress properly and to speak up during testimony.

Where the evidence of a particular witness is necessary to prove your case, a summons to witness should be served. Counsel will be in a better position to request an adjournment should a witness not attend the trial if the witness has been served with a summons. The summons must be served personally on the witness and not by alternative service. Appropriate attendance money must be served on the witness with the summons to witness.[8]

If the opposite side has served a document at least 14 days before trial, and intends to file the document at trial without calling the author, counsel must consider whether it will be necessary to cross-examine. If so, it will be the responsibility of the party who wishes to conduct a cross-examination to serve a summons to witness on the author of the document, along with the appropriate conduct money.[9]

Where a witness fails to attend the trial despite being properly served with a summons, the judge may order that a warrant be issued for the witness' arrest.[10] Because of this coercive power, the court may order compensation where a party has improperly summoned a witness.[11]

(iv) VISITING THE SCENE

If the location is crucial to the case, nothing replaces a visit to the scene to see for yourself the layout of the site. It is always far easier to argue about something that you have actually seen. Similarly, if the dispute involves damage to a vehicle or other property, try to view the damage first hand. In the appropriate case, a judge at trial may inspect any place or property involved in the action.[12]

(b) Simplified Procedure

(i) GENERAL

There are no special evidence rules for cases subject to the simplified procedure. The rules regarding evidence at trial are found in the *Rules of Civil Procedure*[13] and the Ontario *Evidence Act*.[14]

---

[8] *S.C.C.R.*, Rule 18.03; Form 18A.
[9] *Ibid.*, Rule 18.02(4).
[10] *Ibid.*, Rule 18.03(6); Form 18B.
[11] *Ibid.*, Rule 18.03(8).
[12] *Ibid.*, Rule 17.03.
[13] R.R.O. 1990, Reg. 194, Rule 53 (hereinafter *R.C.P.*).
[14] R.S.O. 1990, c. E.23.

In a simplified procedure action, counsel should prepare for trial in the same manner as in an action pursuant in the Small Claims Court. The documents should be organized and the witnesses interviewed and prepared for trial.

(ii) Documents

As a general rule, documents may not be admitted directly into evidence without being introduced through a witness in oral evidence. The exceptions to the rule include business records and medical reports.

If the business record is made in the usual and ordinary course of business, and the record was generated a reasonable time after the event, the record may be admitted into evidence if the party has complied with the notice requirements. The party wishing to introduce the document into evidence must give notice of the party's intention to introduce the business record at trial, at least seven days before the commencement of trial. The party providing notice must make the business record available for inspection by the other parties.[15]

A report of a medical practitioner, which includes a medical doctor, nurse, psychologist, chiropractor and physiotherapist, may be admitted directly into evidence if a written report, signed by the medical practitioner has been served on all parties to the action at least 10 days before the commencement of trial. If, after serving the report, the opposite party states his or her intention to cross-examine the medical practitioner, it is the responsibility of the party who served the report to ensure that the author of the report is in attendance at the trial.[16]

(iii) Witnesses

In an action subject to simplified procedure, the parties must provide the list of potential witnesses in their affidavit of documents.[17] If a party fails to disclose a witness in his or her affidavit of documents, that party may not call the person to give evidence at trial, except with leave of the trial judge.[18]

To compel the attendance of a witness, the party must serve a summons to witness with appropriate attendance money.[19] The summons and attendance money must be served personally and not by alternative service. Once served with the proper summons, the witness must attend at the trial and remain in attendance until his or her evidence is no longer required. If the witness fails to attend, a warrant may be issued for the witness' arrest.[20]

It is necessary for the party who wishes to serve a summons to first have the summons issued by the court. Upon request, the registrar of the court will sign,

---

[15] *Evidence Act, ibid.*, s. 35.
[16] *Ibid.*, s. 52.
[17] See Chapter 7.1(b) Simplified Procedure; *R.C.P.*, Rule 76.03.
[18] *R.C.P.*, Rule 76.03(3).
[19] *Ibid.*, Rule 53.04(1); Form 53A.
[20] *Ibid.*, Rule 53.04(7); Form 53B.

seal and issue the summons. It is not necessary to obtain separate summons for each witness. The registrar will issue a blank single summons to witness. The party (or counsel, if represented) may complete the summons and list the names of as many witnesses as required.[21]

In some cases, it may be necessary to call the opposite party as a witness. If so, the party who wants to examine the opposite party must serve the summons to witness with appropriate attendance money at least 10 days before trial. In addition, the examining party must also serve a notice of intention to call that person as a witness.[22]

If a party wishes to call an expert to give opinion evidence at trial, a copy of the expert's report, signed by the expert, setting out his or her name, address and qualifications and a synopsis of the expert's expected evidence at trial, must be served on all parties to the action not less than 90 days before the commencement of trial.[23] If a party intends to call an expert to respond to the expert witness of another party, a copy of the responding expert's report must be served on the other parties to the action not less than 60 days before trial.[24] If a party has complied with these rules and wishes to file a supplementary report from the expert, the report must be served on all the other parties not less than 30 days before the commencement of trial.[25]

---

[21] *Ibid.*, Rule 53.04(2).
[22] *Ibid.*, Rule 53.07(2).
[23] *Ibid.*, Rule 53.03(1).
[24] *Ibid.*, Rule 53.03(2).
[25] *Ibid.*, Rule 53.03(3)(b).

CHAPTER 9

Conducting the Trial

9.1 PLANNING AND PREPARATION

Part of the excitement of litigation is that it is still essentially a contest in which both parties compete to persuade a neutral arbiter. Knowing that you are about to be put to the test creates excitement about the challenge and apprehension about your ability to meet that challenge.

Much can be done to reduce the anxiety associated with trial. If you have assembled your evidence, researched the law to be argued and briefed your witnesses, you will look forward to the trial with relative calm. Leaving any of these tasks until the morning of trial is a prescription for disaster. An advocate who spends the morning of trial rushing about to find witnesses or to photocopy cases and then arrives in court late and in a state of panic has probably done more to destroy his or her own case than anything the opponent could have accomplished. Too often pre-trial anxiety is self-imposed and can easily be avoided through planning and preparation.

Having fully prepared in advance, the most important thing you can do on the morning of trial is to arrive early and allow yourself enough time to set up in a calm and unhurried manner. When you arrive at the courthouse, there are a number of administrative tasks to be done before the court convenes. Each court will post daily trial lists indicating the matters to be heard and the rooms in which they will be heard. Upon arrival, look for the lists and determine the room in which your matter will be heard and the name of the judge presiding. It is handy to make a note of the number of your matter on the trial list so that if necessary you may assist the court in locating your matter on the lists when it is spoken to. Finally, it is helpful to the court staff to notify the clerk that you have arrived and that your party is ready to proceed. In most courts it will be necessary for the student or lawyer to complete a counsel slip in which the name of the proceeding and the lawyers' names are written on a slip of paper for use by the trial judge.

If possible, arrange to meet with your client and witnesses on the morning of the trial. Many of them will never have been in a courtroom before and would appreciate a brief talk about what will happen at trial. If the courtroom is open, take your client and witnesses inside and show them the layout of the courtroom including the witness box. This brief tour is a very good way of reducing the worries most people have about appearing in court.

9.2 PRELIMINARIES

(a) Settlement

There may be an opportunity to settle the case even on the morning of the trial. A settlement is more certain than what may happen at trial and should always be considered regardless of the stage in the proceedings. It is in the best interests of your client to consider any offer which may be made by your opponent, even if the offer is made just before the start of the trial.

Some judges meet with the parties in chambers prior to trial to canvass the possibilities of settlement. Even if the issue of settlement has been thoroughly discussed, the input of the judge at this stage of the proceedings may assist the parties in coming to a settlement before the trial begins.

(b) Adjournments

(i) SMALL CLAIMS COURT

In Small Claims Court, the parties will receive a Notice of Trial from the court office advising them of the date, time and location of the trial.[1] The notice will normally be received by the parties well before the day of the trial. If it becomes apparent that you will not be able to proceed on the trial date, you should notify the court and the opposite party immediately.

Adjournments are generally granted by telephone call to the court clerk, where the parties have agreed to the adjournment. The request for an adjournment must be made at least three weeks in advance of the trial date. If the parties are unable to agree to the adjournment, it will be necessary to appear in court on the day fixed for trial and request an adjournment when the court reviews the trial list. The court may adjourn the trial on such terms as are just.[2] It should be noted that the court may require the party seeking the adjournment to compensate the other party for the inconvenience and expense caused by the adjournment.

(ii) SIMPLIFIED PROCEDURE

The trial date in the simplified procedure case will be fixed by the judge or master at the pre-trial conference.[3] The registrar shall place the action on the

---

[1] *Small Claims Court Rules*, O. Reg. 258/98, Rule 16.01 (hereinafter *S.C.C.R.*). See Form 16A Notice of Trial in Appendix 8.
[2] *S.C.C.R.*, Rule 17.02.
[3] *Rules of Civil Procedure*, R.R.O. 1990, Reg. 194, Rule 76.10(5) (hereinafter *R.C.P.*).

ordinary or summary trial list, depending on the mode of trial.[4] There may not be any notices delivered by the court office, and accordingly, counsel must ensure that they record the date in their diary immediately after the pre-trial.

Even if the parties consent to an adjournment of the trial, it may be necessary to speak to the matter before a judge. The court is generally reluctant to grant adjournments. If an adjournment is granted, the judge may impose such terms as he or she considers just.[5] The terms may include an order that the party requesting the adjournment pay the costs of the other party.

(c) Failure of the Parties to Attend

The rules relating to the failure of a party to attend the trial are the same whether the case is in Small Claims Court or under the simplified procedure. If both parties to the action fail to attend at trial, the action may be struck from the trial list.[6] If one party fails to attend, the court may make such an order as is just, including proceeding with the trial in the absence of the missing party.[7]

Where a party failed to attend the trial due to mistake, or any other reason, and judgment was granted to the other party, the party who failed to attend may bring a motion to set aside the judgment. The party who failed to attend would be required to introduce affidavit evidence which sets out the reason for the failure to attend, and that the setting aside of the judgment would not cause prejudice to the other party.[8]

(d) Failure of Witnesses to Attend

In both the Small Claims Court and simplified procedure, a witness who has been properly served with a summons to witness and appropriate attendance money must attend at trial and remain in attendance according to the terms of the summons.[9] Where a witness whose evidence is material to the conduct of an action fails to attend at trial, the judge may issue a warrant directing that the witness be apprehended and brought before the court.[10] If you anticipate problems with a vital witness, make sure that you have an affidavit of service proving that the summons to witness and attendance money was properly served on the witness.[11]

---

[4] *Ibid.*, Rule 76.11.
[5] *Ibid.*, Rule 52.02.
[6] *S.C.C.R.*, Rule 17.01; *R.C.P.*, Rule 52.01(1).
[7] *S.C.C.R.*, Rule 17.01(2); *R.C.P.*, Rule 52.01(2).
[8] *S.C.C.R.*, Rule 17.01(4); *R.C.P.*, Rule 52.01(3).
[9] *S.C.C.R.*, Rule 18.03(5); *R.C.P.*, Rule 53.04(6).
[10] *S.C.C.R.*, Rule 18.03(6); *R.C.P.*, Rule 53.04(7).
[11] *S.C.C.R.*, Rule 18.03(3); *R.C.P.*, Rule 53.04(5). See Chapter 8.4.

9.3 THE TRIAL

(a) The Courtroom

The courtroom is arranged in a traditional British pattern. The judge is seated upon a raised dais at the front and centre of the room. The witness box is located beside the dais. In front of the judge sits the court clerk and the court reporter. Counsel are seated at tables located in the well of the court, facing the dais. Members of the public are seated in the gallery separated from the main body of the court.

Common sense dictates that you will be properly attired when you appear before the court. If you seek to persuade a judge, do not begin by irritating him or her with untidy or improper dress. Counsel appearing in actions under the simplified procedure must be gowned.

When entering the court or leaving when the judge is sitting, it is customary to bow. One also bows when the judge takes his or her place on the dais or leaves it. Finally, it is customary to bow when taking your place at counsel table or when leaving it. Other traditions of etiquette include counsel standing whenever addressing the court, and referring to opposing counsel as "my friend" or Mr. or Ms., but never "he" or "she".

Address the judge as "Your Honour". If the matter is in the Small Claims Court and is being presided over by a deputy judge, the deputy judge should be addressed as "Sir" or "Madam" or "Your Worship".

In courts of law, at all levels, it is customary when counsel first rises to identify himself or herself and the party he or she represents and then to introduce the opposing counsel to the court in the same fashion. If the matter is in the Small Claims Court and an agent or student is appearing for the party, this fact must be stated to the judge.

The most common complaint heard in any court is the judge's plea for counsel or a witness to speak up. You will obviously never persuade someone who cannot hear you or your witnesses. Make sure that you speak in a voice loud enough to carry forward to the dais. When questioning a witness, try to remain in the centre of the room near the counsel table. In this position the conversation between counsel and witness will occur across the front of the dais and will be heard by the judge. If you must approach the witness box, do not converse with the witness from a position immediately beside the box away from the judge. This would require the witness to turn towards counsel, away from the judge, and the judge's interest, if not the testimony itself, may be lost.

(b) Opening Statements

It is generally useful to make an opening statement to introduce the court to the issues of the case, and provide a preview of the witnesses and evidence that will be introduced. The opening should also set out your theory of the case. In the

(c) Direct Examinations

Television trials are won when the witness breaks under a blazing cross-examination. Real life is usually not so glamorous. Most trials are won on the strength of evidence presented in chief, not by weaknesses in the opponent's case. The direct examination of your witness is generally the most important part of the trial.

The purpose of the direct examination is to elicit from the witness clear and logical testimony in a manner which will be believed by the judge. During direct testimony, the witness should be the centre of attention. Counsel should use open-ended questions (questions which generally start with who, what, where, when, why and how) which elicit general, flowing descriptions. The objective is to let the witness tell the story and to minimize the presence of counsel.

Most examinations begin with a few questions designed to relax the witness and introduce him or her to the court. It is proper for counsel to "lead" the witness (to suggest the answer in the question) through these preliminary matters which are not in dispute. It is not proper to lead the witness on any matter in dispute. Putting words into the mouth of the witness not only violates an evidence rule, but also is ineffective as a technique of persuasion.

As the witness tells his or her story, counsel should be listening carefully to the answers. Be prepared to steer the witness back on course if he or she strays, or to have the witness explain in detail important areas. When crucial areas arise, stop the witness and use specific questions to review each important detail. If the client uses technical "jargon" or other confusing terms the witness should be asked to explain the terms in plain words. Although the witness is telling the story, counsel should control what information is conveyed and how it is presented. Know exactly what you must obtain from each witness and structure each person's testimony to achieve it.

If exhibits are to be introduced through the witness, ensure that the procedural steps are properly followed.[12]

The direct examination of witnesses in a summary trial in simplified procedure is done by way of affidavit.[13]

(d) Cross-Examinations

Cross-examination provides an opportunity to elicit facts which support your theory of the case and discredit the testimony of the witness on the evidence which damages your client's case. The essential ingredient in cross-examination is, of course, preparation. If you have properly prepared for the cross-

---

[12] See Chapter 8.4(a)(ii) Documents.
[13] See Chapter 9.4.

examination, you are more likely to get the information you want from each witness.

The first question counsel should ask before cross-examining any witness is whether he or she should cross-examine at all. If the witness has said nothing to harm your case and has no information which would help your case, it may be appropriate to let that person leave the witness box before he or she does say something damaging.

Over the course of time, a few simple rules of cross-examination have evolved which, if followed, will save counsel a great deal of grief. Although the rules are not absolute, and may not apply to the particular facts of the case, the rules should be kept in mind when preparing the cross-examination:

(i) On cross-examination, you are entitled to lead the witness by putting facts to the witness and suggesting the answer. The objective at all times is to be in control. The key to control is the use of precise, leading questions which elicit "yes" or "no" responses from the witness.

(ii) Do not ask a question to which you don't know the answer. Cross-examination is not the time for curiosity; one should resist impulse and stay on safe ground. An answer which hurts your case will be all the more devastating if elicited in response to your questions during cross-examination.

(iii) Do not ask one question too many. In many cases the best cross-examination suggests the final point but does not "hammer it home". It is far more effective to let the judge draw the conclusion than for counsel to hand it to him or her during cross-examination. An appreciation of subtlety also guards against the danger of asking "one question too many". Too often that last question, meant to drive the point home, instead provides the witness with a chance to explain away inconsistencies and undoes all of the work done to that point. Once you have asked enough questions to establish the points needed in closing argument, sit down.

(iv) Listen to the witness. The last point should be obvious but is so often forgotten during the excitement of trial that it bears repeating. You cannot stick to a prepared script during cross-examination. Witnesses constantly provide unexpected and surprising answers and counsel should be in a position to respond. You should also be watching the witnesses' reactions to questions and noting the subtleties in their responses. Rather than write the questions, experienced counsel may prepare for cross-examinations by using an outline which maps out particular topics which must be covered with each witness. This allows for direct contact with the witness without the danger of missing necessary evidence.

In summary trials under simplified procedure, there are strict time limits for cross-examination. The cross-examination of all of the opposing party's witnesses are not to exceed 50 minutes in total.[14]

---

[14] See Chapter 9.4.

(e) Objections

No advocate should appear before the court without a thorough knowledge of evidence law. The true test of that knowledge occurs when counsel must decide whether to make an objection. If a question is improper, the objection must be made before the answer is given. This requires an instant assessment of the laws of evidence to determine the propriety of the question. Once the answer is given, it is too late. One cannot belatedly request that the answer be struck from the record.

Part of the secret of timely objections is to think about evidence rules as they would actually apply to trial. Counsel should learn to react to certain common words which indicate a leading question or call for a hearsay answer. In some circumstances, you may decide not to object to an improper question. One needs a sense of discretion to know which questions justify an interruption and which technical breaches are harmless and should be ignored.

Counsel should be prepared to make the following common objections, when necessary, at trial:

(i)   hearsay, where the examiner asks the witness what another person said to the witness;
(ii) leading the witness in direct examination on a critical point;
(iii) question calls for opinion or conclusion from a non-expert witness;
(iv) question is irrelevant;
(v)   question misstates evidence;
(vi) question is confusing or unintelligible; and
(vii) question has already been answered.

(f) Closing Arguments

The closing argument provides counsel with the opportunity to tie together the various themes established during the trial into a coherent logical case which compels a favourable decision from the court. This is the point at which advocacy is truly tested — counsel's last chance to persuade the judge.

In arguing your position there are certain restrictions on what can be said. Counsel must not misstate the evidence or the law. If a misstatement takes place, one can be sure that either the judge or opposing counsel will bring this to counsel's attention. Not only is a misstatement improper, but it also results in a loss of credibility with the court. In addition, counsel is not permitted to state his or her personal views on the evidence. For example, it is improper for counsel to personally vouch for the credibility of a witness.

As a general rule, the final argument must highlight the issues, the facts which relate to the issues and the applicable law. A suggested outline for a final argument is as follows:

(i) introduction;
(ii) state the issues in dispute;

(iii) highlight important evidence on each issue;
(iv) discuss the credibility of the witnesses;
(v) establish basis of liability or defence in law;
(vi) discuss damages;
(vii) conclusion and request for relief.

A closing argument should be a forceful analysis of the facts and the law. Counsel should use plain and persuasive language and speak directly to the judge. The closing argument should be as succinct as possible.

In the case of a summary trial under simplified procedure, closing statements are limited to no more than 45 minutes for each party.[15]

9.4 SUMMARY TRIAL

The summary trial procedure is unique to actions brought pursuant to the simplified procedure. Summary trials set out strict time limits for the conduct of the trial in the expectation that a simple trial can be completed in one day.

A summary trial is available if the parties consent. Even if the parties do not consent to a summary trial, the judge who heard (and dismissed) the summary judgment motion may order that the matter proceed to a summary trial.[16] The pre-trial judge is also required to determine the mode of trial and may order that the matter be tried by summary trial.[17] If the pre-trial conference judge or master has determined that the matter will proceed by summary trial, a timetable will be set at the pre-trial for the delivery of the affidavits to be used by the parties on the summary trial.[18]

(a) Trial Record

The party who set the action down for trial by serving a notice of readiness for pre-trial conference must serve a trial record on the other parties to the action. The trial record, with proof of service, must be filed with the court at least 10 days before the trial date.[19]

The trial record shall include the following:

(i) a table of contents describing each document by its nature and date;
(ii) a copy of all pleadings;
(iii) a copy of any demand or order for particulars and the response;
(iv) a copy of any order regarding the trial;

---

[15] See Chapter 9.4.
[16] R.C.P., Rule 76.07(10).
[17] Ibid., Rule 76.10(6).
[18] Ibid., Rule 76.10(7).
[19] Ibid., Rule 76.11(2).

(v) a copy of all affidavits served by the parties for use on the summary trial; and
(vi) a certificate from the solicitor filing the trial record that all documents have been included.[20]

(b) Conduct of the Summary Trial

On the summary trial, all evidence in chief is introduced by way of affidavit evidence. The affidavit evidence must set out specific facts that prove either the responding party's claim or defence.

If either party intends to cross-examine on any of the affidavits, he or she must serve a notice of intention to cross-examine at least 10 days before the commencement of trial. It is the responsibility of the party filing the affidavit to arrange for the deponent to attend the summary trial.[21]

Although the pre-trial or trial judge has the discretion to vary the order and time of the presentation of the summary trial,[22] it is expected that the procedure of the summary trial will be as follows:

(i) all evidence in chief is to be adduced by way of affidavit;
(ii) an adverse party may orally cross-examine the deponent of the affidavit;
(iii) all of the party's cross-examinations must be completed within 50 minutes;
(iv) the cross-examination may be followed by an oral re-examination of not more than 10 minutes; and
(v) at the conclusion of the evidence, each party may make an oral argument of no more than 45 minutes.[23]

The summary trial judge may extend any of the time limits set out above.[24]

It is important to note that the time limit of 50 minutes for cross-examination is for the cross-examination of all witnesses. If, for example, a party wishes to cross-examine more than one witness, he or she cannot take 50 minutes with the first witness. Accordingly, counsel must be selective in determining when to exercise the right of cross-examination.[25]

At the conclusion of the summary trial, the judge is required to grant judgment.[26]

---

[20] *Ibid.*, Rule 76.11(4).
[21] *Ibid.*, Rule 76.12(3).
[22] *Ibid.*, Rule 76.10(6) and (7).
[23] *Ibid.*, Rule 76.12(1).
[24] *Ibid.*, Rule 76.12(2).
[25] See *Chakie v. Elton*, [1996] O.J. No. 4447 (Gen. Div.).
[26] R.C.P., Rule 76.12(4).

(c) Appeal of Judgment Following Summary Trial

The judgment rendered at the conclusion of the summary trial is a final order and the appeal from it would be to the Divisional Court or the Court of Appeal, depending on the amount awarded. If the amount of the judgment was less than $25,000, the appeal would be to the Divisional Court. If the judgment was greater than $25,000, the appeal would be to the Court of Appeal.[27]

9.5 THE JUDGMENT

Following the trial, the judge will usually deliver an oral judgment on the merits in dispute. Where the issues of fact or law are particularly complex, the judge may reserve judgment and issue written reasons at a later date.

Once the judgment has been rendered, it will be necessary for the parties to address the issues of interest and costs.

(a) Pre-Judgment Interest

The successful party will generally be entitled to pre-judgment interest on the amount of the award at trial.[28] To determine the amount of interest payable, if any, the court will consider the following questions:

(i)   Is pre-judgment interest claimed?
(ii) What is the pre-judgment interest rate?
(iii) From what date is the interest payable?
(iv) Are there any factors which could reduce the interest?

Pre-judgment interest is payable only if a request for pre-judgment interest was made in the claim. The general rule is that where pre-judgment interest is not requested, it will not be allowed. Pre-judgment interest is also not awarded on punitive damages, or on an award of interest or costs.[29]

The rate of interest on general damages in an action for personal injury which arose after October 23, 1989, is the rate set out in the *Rules of Civil Procedure*. The interest rate is currently 5% per annum.[30]

The rate of interest for special damages is generally based on the bank rate established by the Bank of Canada. The applicable pre-judgment interest rate, is the bank rate (rounded to the nearest tenth) on the first day of the last month in the quarter preceding the date the claim was issued.[31] If the claim is based on a

---

[27] See Chapter 11 for appeals of final orders.
[28] *Courts of Justice Act*, R.S.O. 1990, c. C.43, s. 128(1).
[29] *Ibid.*, s. 128(4).
[30] *Courts of Justice Act, supra*, note 28, s. 128(2) [am. S.O. 1994, c. 12, s. 44]; *R.C.P.*, Rule 53.10.
[31] *Courts of Justice Act, supra*, note 28, s. 127(1).

contract which stipulates a different interest figure, the court may order that the applicable rate is the one set out in the contract.

Pre-judgment interest in actions which arise out of events that occurred after October 23, 1989 is generally calculated from the date the cause of action arose to the date of the judgment.[32] In the case of actions arising out of motor vehicle accidents, which occurred after January 1, 1996, interest is payable from the date the plaintiff provided notice of his or her intention to commence the action against the defendant.[33]

The trial judge has discretion when dealing with the issue of pre-judgment interest. At the time of rendering judgment, a judge may disallow interest, allow interest at a rate higher or lower than that provided in the statute, or allow interest for a shorter or longer period of time. In this way, a judge may penalize a plaintiff who has not diligently prosecuted the action.[34]

(b) Post-Judgment Interest

All judgments which provide for the payment of money are subject to post-judgment interest.[35] Post-judgment interest is payable on the whole of the judgment including pre-judgment interest and costs. The post-judgment interest rate is calculated from the date of the order.

The post-judgment interest rate is also based on the bank rate. The applicable rate is the bank rate at the end of the first day of the last month of the quarter preceding the date of the order, rounded to the next higher whole number, plus 1%.[36]

(c) Costs

Once the trial judge has decided liability and damages, the parties will be asked if they have any submissions on the issue of costs. It is at this point in the trial that offers to settle, if any, are to be disclosed to the court.

(i) SMALL CLAIMS COURT

Every successful party is entitled to be paid his or her reasonable disbursements by the unsuccessful party, unless the court orders otherwise. Disbursements are the out-of-pocket expenses incurred by the party in the lawsuit, and could include photocopying, postage, filing fees and witness fees.[37]

In addition to the payment of disbursements, the successful party may be entitled to a counsel fee. A counsel fee represents the cost of obtaining representa-

---

[32] *Ibid.*, s. 128(1).
[33] *Insurance Act*, R.S.O. 1990, c.I.8, s. 258.3(8).
[34] *Courts of Justice Act, supra*, note 28, s. 130(1).
[35] *Ibid.*, s. 129.
[36] *Ibid.*, s. 127(1).
[37] *S.C.C.R.*, Rule 19.01.

tion or, if unrepresented, compensation for any inconvenience caused by the proceeding. A successful party may be entitled to receive no more than $50 for the counsel fee for preparing and filing the pleadings.[38] In an action for more than $500, the successful party may receive up to $300 for a counsel fee if represented by a lawyer and up to $150 if represented by a student-at-law.[39] No counsel fee is available if the successful party is represented by an agent. In an action for more than $500, the successful party may receive up to $300 for inconvenience if unrepresented.[40]

It is important to advise the trial judge of any offers to settle which have been served at least seven days prior to trial. A represented party may be entitled to double costs, if the party obtains a judgment as favourable or more favourable than the offer to settle.[41]

As a general rule, the counsel fee is not to exceed 15% of the amount claimed or the value of property to be recovered. The judge has discretion to allow an award of costs which exceeds 15% of the amount claimed if the court considers it necessary to penalize a party, counsel or agent for unreasonable behaviour in the proceeding.[42]

(ii) SIMPLIFIED PROCEDURE

In the simplified procedure, the court may award a counsel fee based on costs calculated on a "partial indemnity" scale or on a "substantial indemnity" scale.[43] Partial indemnity costs represent a partial recovery of the party's costs of retaining their own lawyer. The substantial indemnity costs are intended to provide greater indemnification for the successful party's costs.

The costs are based on the Costs Grid (Part I of Tariff A. Solicitors' Fees and Disbursements Allowable Under Rule 58.05).[44]

It is expected that the judge will fix costs in accordance with the Costs Grid immediately after trial.[45] It is good practice for counsel to prepare a bill of costs to be provided to the other side and to the trial judge when the issue of costs is addressed.[46]

Although the Costs Grid imposes some guidelines, the judge continues to have discretion with respect to the award of costs.

In determining the appropriate amount of costs, the court may consider the following factors:

---

[38] *Ibid.*, Rule 19.03.
[39] *Ibid.*, Rule 19.04.
[40] *Ibid.*, Rule 19.05.
[41] *Ibid.*, Rule 14.07. See Chapter 6.5 Offers to Settle.
[42] *Courts of Justice Act, supra*, note 28, s. 29.
[43] R.C.P., Rule 57.01; *Courts of Justice Act, ibid.*, s. 131.
[44] See Appendix 11.
[45] R.C.P., Rule 57.01(3).
[46] *Ibid.*, Rule 57.01(5).

(i) the amount claimed and the amount recovered;
(ii) the split in liability, if any;
(iii) the complexity of the proceedings;
(iv) the importance of the issues;
(v) the conduct of the parties which tended to shorten or unnecessarily lengthen the proceedings;
(vi) whether any step in the proceeding was unnecessary;
(vii) a party denying or refusing to admit anything that should have been admitted.[47]

In addition to the factors set out above, the court will also take into consideration any offers to settle which may have been served at least seven days before trial, and which remained open for acceptance at the commencement of the trial. If the plaintiff served an offer and received a judgment which is as favourable or more favourable than the offer, the plaintiff is entitled to partial indemnity costs to the date of the offer, and substantial indemnity costs from the date of the offer to the date of judgment. If the defendant served an offer and the plaintiff obtained a judgment at trial which was as favourable or less favourable than the offer, the plaintiff would be entitled to partial indemnity costs to the date of the offer, and the defendant would be entitled to partial indemnity costs from the date of the offer to the date of the judgment.[48]

If the plaintiff in an action under the simplified procedure obtains a judgment which is less than $6,000, and is therefore within the jurisdiction of the Small Claims Court, the court may order that the plaintiff is not entitled to any costs. This provision does not apply if the action was originally commenced in the Small Claims Court but was transferred to the Superior Court of Justice to be consolidated with another action.[49]

---

[47] *R.C.P.*, Rule 57.01(1).
[48] *Ibid.*, Rule 49.10. See Chapter 6.
[49] *R.C.P.*, Rule 57.05 [am. O. Reg. 377/95, s. 4]. See also Chapter 3.4(b).

CHAPTER 10

Enforcing Judgment

10.1 COLLECTION

The client will not be satisfied with a judgment in his or her favour unless that judgment is paid by the defendant. A judgment in an action merely states the disposition of the court; it does not guarantee that the relief granted will ever be paid.

The enforcement of a judgment occurs late in the chronology of an action; yet, collection issues should be considered from the moment counsel is retained by the client. The risk of an unenforceable "paper judgment" arises at the outset of any proceeding. Every step taken beyond the initial interview is potentially a waste of effort and expense if the defendant has no means with which to satisfy judgment.

It is necessary to consider potential enforcement problems both before the action is launched and later during settlement negotiations. At each stage, the client must weigh the amount he or she is seeking to collect against the risk and cost of further proceedings. In many cases, it will make economic sense to accept an offer of immediate payment even if it is less than the amount sought.

10.2 SMALL CLAIMS COURT

One of the advantages of the small claims system is the simplified manner in which a plaintiff can obtain enforcement of a judgment. A creditor has a range of procedures available to obtain payment similar to the procedures used in the Superior Court of Justice, but in the small claims system, the creditor is assisted by the court in enforcing the judgment.

(a) Jurisdiction

The first consideration of the creditor is the location where the judgment will be enforced. The creditor may specify the territorial division in which he or she wants the certificate of judgment registered.[1] The general rule is that the judg-

---

[1] *Small Claims Court Rules*, O. Reg. 258/98, Rule 20.04(1) (hereinafter *S.C.C.R.*).

ment will be enforced in the jurisdiction where the debtor resides or carries on business.

If the debtor does not reside in the jurisdiction in which the order was made, the order must be transferred to the jurisdiction where the debtor resides or carries on business. This rule also applies to a debtor who has moved out of the court's jurisdiction prior to enforcement. To transfer an order to another court the creditor must request in writing that the order be transferred. The request for transfer should include:

(i) style of cause and action number;
(ii) date of judgment;
(iii) court and jurisdiction to which the order is to be transferred;
(iv) amount of judgment and pre-judgment interest;
(v) date and amount of any payments received;
(vi) amount still owing;
(vii) any costs awarded; and
(viii) rate of post-judgment interest.

Upon receiving the creditor's request, the clerk will prepare a certificate of judgment[2] and send it directly to the appropriate court. Once the court receives the order, the clerk of the court will advise the creditor that the order has been received and entered. The creditor may then commence enforcement proceedings in the new jurisdiction.

Where an order is obtained against two or more debtors, the procedure is somewhat different. In that case, the order is *not* transferred to another jurisdiction even if one or more of the debtors live in another jurisdiction. The court in which the order is made will prepare a certificate of judgment on written request of the creditor and will forward it to the courts where the debtors reside along with the creditor's written request for enforcement. The proceeds obtained are not distributed by the courts where the debtors reside, but are returned to the original court that made the order for distribution.

(b) Examination of Debtor

It is the responsibility of the creditor to obtain information regarding the debtor's assets to enable the creditor to decide what enforcement process would be suitable and to properly instruct the bailiff. This information is best obtained through an examination of the debtor.

The examination of a debtor allows the creditor to obtain information related to collection of the debt and also provides an opportunity for the parties and the court to consider possible ways to satisfy the order. The scope of the examination includes:

---

[2] *Ibid.* See Form 20A Certificate of Judgment in Appendix 8.

(a) the reason for nonpayment;
(b) the debtor's income and property;
(c) the debts owed to and by the debtor;
(d) the disposal the debtor has made of any property either before or after the order was made;
(e) the debtor's present, past and future means to satisfy the order;
(f) whether the debtor intends to obey the order or has any reason for not doing so; and
(g) any other matter pertinent to the enforcement of the order.[3]

To obtain an examination of the debtor, the creditor must submit a written request to the court accompanied by an affidavit. If the order was made in another jurisdiction, the creditor must also submit a certificate of judgment. The affidavit should include the following information:

(i) style of cause and action number;
(ii) date of the order;
(iii) jurisdiction in which the order was made;
(iv) amount awarded;
(v) costs awarded, if any;
(vi) date and amount of any payments received;
(vii) amount owing; and
(viii) rate of post-judgment interest.[4]

Upon receipt of the above information, the court shall issue a notice of examination. The notice must be served on the debtor at least 30 days before the date of the examination.[5] The most common method of serving the debtor is by mail to the debtor's last known address.[6]

Examinations are conducted before a Small Claims Court judge or deputy judge, and are usually held in private in the judge's chambers.[7] The questioning of the debtor is generally carried out by the judge in the presence of the creditor. The creditor may also have an opportunity to ask the debtor questions. Following the hearing, the court may make an order as to payment of the judgment.[8]

The examination process gives the creditor an early appreciation of how frustrating collection efforts can be. It can take a number of months from the date of request until the examination can be heard. If the debtor fails to attend, the examination is simply rescheduled. A debtor may be given up to several chances to attend before the debtor is ordered to attend a contempt hearing.

If the debtor ignores the notice of examination or fails to answer proper questions in the examination, the court may order the debtor to attend court for a

---

[3] S.C.C.R., Rule 20.10(4).
[4] Ibid., Rule 20.10(2).
[5] Ibid., Rules 20.10(3) and 8.01(7) and (8).
[6] Ibid., Rule 8.01(7).
[7] Ibid., Rule 20.10(6).
[8] Ibid., Rule 20.10(7).

contempt hearing.[9] The court will then deliver a notice by mail to the creditor, who will be required to serve the notice on the debtor personally.[10] In the case of an individual debtor, the notice must be served by leaving a copy of the document with him or her.[11]

At the contempt hearing, the debtor will be required to explain why he or she failed to cooperate with the examination, and why a warrant of committal ought not to be made. At the conclusion of the hearing, the court may make an order for a further examination, make an order for payment or jail the debtor for a period of not more than 40 days.[12]

If the court orders the debtor to be jailed, the clerk will issue a warrant of committal to all Ontario police officers. The warrant directs the police to take the debtor into custody, and it is in effect for 12 months; however, the creditor may bring a motion to renew the warrant for additional 12-month periods.[13]

(c) Writ of Delivery of Personal Property

Where the creditor obtains an order for the delivery of personal property, a writ of delivery may be issued upon the request of the creditor.[14] The request for a writ of delivery must be supported by an affidavit from the creditor stating:

(i)   style of cause and action number;
(ii) date of the order;
(iii) jurisdiction in which the order was made;
(iv) terms of the order for delivery of property; and
(v)   that the property was not delivered as ordered.

The writ of delivery authorizes the bailiff to seize the personal property referred to in the order. Once the property is successfully seized, the bailiff will arrange to turn it over to the creditor subject to any conditions set out in the order made by the court. If the property cannot be found or taken by the bailiff, provision is made for seizure of other personal property of the debtor, upon motion to the court.[15] It is therefore important to ask the debtor on the examination what personal property he or she owns that could be seized to satisfy the judgment.

---

[9] *Ibid.*, Rule 20.10(9).
[10] *Ibid.*, Rule 20.10(10).
[11] *Ibid.*, Rule 8.02(a).
[12] *Ibid.*, Rule 20.10(11).
[13] *Ibid.*, Rule 20.10(12), (13) and (14).
[14] *Ibid.*, Rule 20.05(1). See Form 20B Writ of Delivery in Appendix 8.
[15] *Ibid.*, Rule 20.05(2) and (3).

(d) Writ of Seizure and Sale

(i) PERSONAL PROPERTY

A writ of seizure and sale of personal property permits the bailiff to seize and then sell the personal property of the debtor if there has been default under an order for the payment of money. The writ is issued by the court clerk at the request of the creditor. The request must be supported by a written statement which sets out the following information:

(i) style of cause and action number;
(ii) date of the order;
(iii) jurisdiction in which the order was made;
(iv) costs awarded;
(v) post-judgment interest to date;
(vi) dates and amounts of any payments received; and
(vii) amount still owing.

The bailiff enforces the writ by selling property to realize the amount owing, plus post-judgment interest and the bailiff's fees and expenses.[16] The bailiff may advise the debtor of the steps being taken to enforce the writ and will deliver, on request, an inventory of property seized.[17]

A writ of seizure and sale of personal property remains in force for six months from the date of issue and upon each renewal.[18] The writ may be renewed prior to expiry by filing with the clerk of the court a written request to renew.[19] There is no provision in the rules for the bailiff to provide notice of the expiry of a writ of seizure and sale of personal property. Accordingly, counsel should diarize the expiry date of each writ to ensure successive renewals until the judgment has been satisfied.

At common law, the bailiff had the power to seize and sell almost any goods belonging to the debtor except the clothes actually being worn. Today, assets eligible under a writ of seizure and sale are limited by statute. The *Execution Act*[20] grants to the debtor a number of exemptions so that he or she will not be deprived of the basic necessities of life. Clothing of the debtor up to a value of $5,000 and household furniture and utensils up to a value of $10,000 are among the items exempt from seizure.[21] A number of other Acts, including the *Family Benefits Act*[22] and the *Workplace Safety and Insurance Act, 1997*[23] provide fur-

---

[16] *Ibid.*, Rule 20.06(1).
[17] *Ibid.*, Rule 20.06(5).
[18] *Ibid.*, Rule 20.06(2).
[19] *Ibid.*, Rule 20.06(3).
[20] R.S.O. 1990, c. E.24.
[21] *Ibid.*, s. 2 [am. S.O. 2000, c. 26, Sch. A., s. 8(2)].
[22] R.S.O. 1990, c. F.2.
[23] S.O. 1997, c. 16, Schedule A.

ther exemptions. These exemptions are significant since many of the more valuable assets held by the debtor may be exempt from seizure.

(ii) SALE OF LAND

On the examination of the debtor, the creditor may learn that the debtor owns land that could be used to satisfy the judgment. The creditor may request the clerk of the court to issue a writ of seizure and sale of land. The creditor's requisition must be supported by a written statement of the amount still owing.[24] The writ is issued to the sheriff of the county or district where the land is situated. This creates a charge upon the lands owned by the debtor registered in the registry system. To bind lands registered under the Land Titles System, the sheriff should be instructed to forward a certified copy of the writ with the land registrar.[25]

A writ of seizure and sale issued in the Small Claims Court has the same force and effect as a writ of seizure and sale in the Superior Court of Justice.[26] The writ remains in force for six years from the date of issuance and upon each renewal.[27] A writ of seizure and sale may be renewed prior to expiry by filing a request to renew with the sheriff.[28]

(e) Garnishment

Garnishment is probably the most effective collection procedure provided for under the rules. The term "garnishment" refers to a procedure by which the creditor obtains an order from the court directing persons who may owe money to the debtor to pay that money into court and ultimately to the creditor.[29] One common source of moneys owing to the debtor is the debtor's employer.

To obtain enforcement of an order by garnishment the creditor must file with the court in the jurisdiction in which the defendant resides or carries on business, an affidavit stating:

(i) style of cause and action number;
(ii) date of the order;
(iii) amount awarded;
(iv) jurisdiction in which the order was made;
(v) rate of post-judgment interest;
(vi) date and amount of any payments received;
(vii) amount owing including post-judgment interest;

---

[24] S.C.C.R., Rule 20.07(1). See Form 20D Writ of Seizure and Sale of Land in Appendix 8.
[25] *Land Titles Act*, R.S.O. 1990, c. L.5, ss. 137-39.
[26] S.C.C.R., Rule 20.07(2).
[27] *Rules of Civil Procedure*, R.R.O. 1990, Reg. 194, Rule 60.07(6) (hereinafter *R.C.P.*).
[28] *Ibid.*, Rule 60.07(8), Form 60E.
[29] S.C.C.R., Rule 20.08.

(viii) name and address of each person to whom a notice of garnishment is to be directed;
(ix) that the creditor believes that those persons are or will become indebted to the debtor and the grounds for that belief; and
(x) such particulars of the debts as are known to the creditor.[30]

A certificate of judgment must also be filed if the order was made in a different territorial jurisdiction.[31] A notice of garnishment may only be issued in the jurisdiction where the defendant resides or carries on business, *not* where he or she is employed.

Upon receiving the affidavit and certificate of judgment, if applicable, the clerk shall issue a notice of garnishment. The garnishment notice is enforceable for a period of 24 months and attaches to debts payable at the time the notice is served or arising within this period.[32] Where the full amount of the order has not been paid within 24 months and the creditor wishes to continue the garnishment process, the creditor must submit a new request along with a new amended affidavit and the process begins again.

Where there is a dispute over the garnishee's debt to the debtor or any other problem with the garnishment procedure, the creditor, garnishee, debtor or any interested person may, upon motion to the court, ask the court to review the problem. The court has wide-ranging powers to grant relief.[33]

A garnishment order against the debtor's wages is delivered to the debtor's employer. The garnishee (employer) must pay to the clerk of the court the amount set out in the notice of garnishment. If the garnishee fails to make this payment, the creditor is entitled to an order against the garnishee.[34]

Where more than one creditor has issued a notice of garnishment in the court for the same debtor, the rules require that the clerk distribute any moneys received equally among the creditors who have requested garnishment.[35]

The garnishment procedure is subject to statutory exemptions. The *Wages Act*[36] exempts 80% of an employee's wages from a garnishment order. It is important to note, however, that payments made on a contract of service to an independent contractor are not considered to be wages and therefore are not covered by the protection available to debtors in the *Wages Act*.

---

[30] *Ibid.*, Rule 20.08(3)(a).
[31] *Ibid.*, Rule 20.08(3)(b).
[32] *Ibid.*, Rule 20.08(7) and (8).
[33] *Ibid.*, Rule 20.08(15).
[34] *Ibid.*, Rule 20.08(17).
[35] *Ibid.*, Rule 20.08(10).
[36] R.S.O. 1990, c. W.1, s. 7.

(f) Consolidation Orders

Debt collection can be a very difficult chore and, on occasion, some frustrated creditors cross the line between persistent pressure and the harassment of the debtor. The Small Claims Court provides for some protection of the debtor and may assist in the resolution of a debtor's outstanding liabilities in a fashion that will benefit both debtor and creditor. The court may stay enforcement proceedings or vary the times and proportions in which money payable under an order of the court shall be paid.[37]

A debtor who has two or more outstanding unsatisfied Small Claims Court orders against him or her may make a motion to the court to request a consolidation order.[38] The notice of motion will set out the hearing date which has been obtained by the court office. The debtor must file, with the notice of motion, an affidavit stating:

(i) names and addresses of the creditors who have obtained an order for the payment of money against the debtor;
(ii) amount owed to each creditor;
(iii) amount of the debtor's income from all sources;
(iv) amount of the debtor's current financial obligations; and
(v) any other relevant fact.[39]

Copies of the notice of motion and affidavit are served on each creditor at least seven days prior to the hearing date.[40]

At the hearing both the debtor and the creditors may make submissions to the court.[41] Following the hearing the court may make a consolidation order setting out a list of unsatisfied debts and the terms of repayment by the debtor.[42] A consolidation order terminates immediately if the debtor is in default for 21 days under the order. Where the order is thus terminated, the debtor will be unable to obtain a further consolidation order for one year.[43] Any proceeds of payments under a consolidation order are shared equally among the creditors.[44] The clerk is required to distribute the money paid into the consolidation account at least once every six months.[45]

---

[37] S.C.C.R., Rule 20.02.
[38] Ibid., Rule 20.09(1).
[39] Ibid., Rule 20.09(2).
[40] Ibid., Rule 20.09(3).
[41] Ibid., Rule 20.09.
[42] Ibid., Rule 20.09(4).
[43] Ibid., Rule 20.09(10) and (11).
[44] Ibid., Rule 20.09(12).
[45] Ibid., Rule 20.09(13).

10.3 SIMPLIFIED PROCEDURE

(a) Examination of Debtor

As with the Small Claims Court, it is necessary for the creditor to conduct an examination of the debtor to obtain information regarding the debtor's assets to determine the appropriate method of enforcement. The creditor may serve on the debtor a notice of examination in aid of execution, which sets out the time and place of the examination. The notice must be served on the debtor personally or by an alternative service. The notice is not to be served on the debtor's solicitor.[46]

On the examination, the debtor may be examined with respect to the following:

(i)   reason for the nonpayment or nonperformance of the order;
(ii) debtor's income and property;
(iii) debts owed to and by the debtor;
(iv) disposal of any property of the debtor made before or after the making of the order;
(v)   debtor's past, present and future means to satisfy the order;
(vi) whether the debtor intends to obey the order; and
(vii) any other matter which is relevant to the enforcement of the order.[47]

The creditor is entitled to only one examination of the debtor in a one-year period, unless the court orders otherwise.[48] There is no limit as to the number of examinations which may be conducted, as long as in any one-year period there is no more than one.

In addition to an examination of the debtor, the court may make an order entitling the creditor to examine another person who may have knowledge of the matters relating to the nonpayment of the order.[49] As a general rule, the court will not order the examination of a party other than the debtor unless the creditor has exhausted all available means to satisfy the order.

(b) Writ of Delivery

In an action for the recovery for personal property, the creditor may enforce the order by way of a writ of delivery. The writ of delivery is issued by the registrar in the court where the proceeding was commenced, after receiving a requisition from the creditor along with a copy of the order.[50]

---

[46] *R.C.P.*, Rule 60.18(7) [am. O. Regs. 739/94, s. 6; 377/95, s. 5].
[47] *Ibid.*, Rule 60.18(2).
[48] *Ibid.*, Rule 60.18(4).
[49] *Ibid.*, Rule 60.18(6).
[50] *Ibid.*, Rule 60.04(1); Form 60D.

If the debtor fails to deliver the personal property, the creditor may make a motion to the court for a writ of sequestration.[51] The writ of sequestration directs the sheriff to seize other property of the debtor and to collect any income generated from the property to satisfy the judgment.[52]

(c) Writ of Seizure and Sale

When the creditor has obtained a money judgment, the creditor should request the court to issue a writ of seizure and sale. The writ will act as a lien and will usually prevent the debtor from disposing of his or her property.

To obtain a writ of seizure and sale, the creditor must file with the registrar in the region where the action was commenced a requisition for a writ.[53] The requisition sets out the date of any payments which have been received by the creditor and the amounts of the payments. The requisition must also set out the balance of the debt at the time of the requisition and the rate of post-judgment interest. The order must be attached to the requisition.[54]

The creditor must requisition the writ within six years of the date of the order. If more than six years has passed, the creditor must obtain leave of the court to have the writ issued.[55] The writ remains in force for a period of six years.[56] The creditor may renew the writ before the expiration by filing a request to renew with the sheriff. Each renewal of the writ remains in effect for six years.[57]

Once the writ has been issued, it must be filed with the sheriff. The filing of the writ does not mean the sheriff will enforce the writ. The creditor is obligated to provide directions to the sheriff regarding the enforcement of the writ. The creditor must file with the sheriff a direction to enforce, which contains the following information:

(i)   date of the order and the amount awarded;
(ii) rate of post-judgment interest which is payable;
(iii) costs of enforcement to which the creditor is entitled;
(iv) date and amount of any partial payment made by the debtor;
(v)   amount owing including post-judgment interest at the time of the direction.[58]

(i) PERSONAL PROPERTY

If the creditor discovers on an examination of the debtor or otherwise that the debtor has personal property which may satisfy the order, the creditor may file a

---

[51] *Ibid.*, Rule 60.09.
[52] *Ibid.*, Rule 60.09; Form 60B.
[53] *Ibid.*, Rule 60.07(1); Form 60A.
[54] *Ibid.*, Rule 60.07(1).
[55] *Ibid.*, Rule 60.07(2).
[56] *Ibid.*, Rule 60.07(6).
[57] *Ibid.*, Rule 60.07(6) and (8).
[58] *Ibid.*, Rule 60.07(13). See Form 60F.

direction to enforce which instructs the sheriff to sell the personal property. The sheriff must provide notice of the sale of the personal property to the creditor and debtor at least 10 days before the sale. In addition, the sheriff is required to publish notice of the sale in a newspaper in the place where the property is located.[59]

(ii) SALE OF LAND

If the debtor has land which could satisfy the order, the creditor may instruct the sheriff to sell the land. No steps can be taken by the creditor to sell the land until four months after the writ was filed with the sheriff. The actual sale of the land cannot take place until six months after the writ was filed.[60]

The sheriff is required to give notice of the sale to both the creditor and debtor, at least 30 days before the date of the sale. In addition, the sheriff must publish notice of the sale in the Ontario Gazette and in a newspaper in the place where the land is located. The sheriff is also required to post a notice of sale in the sheriff's office for at least 30 days before the sale.[61]

(d) Garnishment

As with actions in the Small Claims Court, garnishment may be the most effective method available to a creditor to enforce an order. The notice of garnishment is issued by the registrar in the district where the action was commenced. The creditor must file a requisition for garnishment,[62] with a copy of the entered order and an affidavit which provides the following information:

(i) date and amount of any payment received since the order was made;
(ii) amount owing including post-judgment interest;
(iii) details of the amount owing and how the post-judgment interest was calculated;
(iv) address of the debtor;
(v) name and address of each person to whom a garnishment is to be directed;
(vi) that the creditor believes that the persons to whom the garnishment is to be directed will become indebted to the debtor, and the reasons behind that belief;
(vii) particulars of the debtor's debts, as known by the creditor;
(viii) if the person to whom the garnishment is directed will in the future become indebted to the debtor, the date on which the debt will arise and the circumstances of the debt;

---

[59] *Ibid.*, Rule 60.07(16).
[60] *Ibid.*, Rule 60.07(17) and (18).
[61] *Ibid.*, Rule 60.07(19).
[62] *Ibid.*, Rule 60.08(4). See Form 60G Requisition for Garnishment.

(ix) if the person to whom the garnishment is to be directed does not reside or carry on business in Ontario, that the debtor would be entitled to sue that person in Ontario to recover the debt.[63]

The creditor is entitled to the notice of garnishment, without leave, if the notice of garnishment is issued within six years of the date of the order.[64]

A separate notice of garnishment is issued for each garnishee.[65] The creditor must serve the notice of garnishment on the debtor along with a copy of the affidavit filed with the requisition for the notice of garnishment. The creditor must also serve the notice on the garnishee along with a blank garnishee statement.[66] Service is made by mail, personal service or an alternative to personal service.[67]

The garnishee is required to make the payments set out in the notice to the sheriff. The requirement to pay is effective within 10 days of the date of service. The garnishee is entitled to deduct $10 from each payment to take into account its costs.[68]

10.4 OTHER REMEDIES

Aside from the enforcement provisions under the rules, a number of other statutes contain provisions which are useful in the collection of a debt. As an example, the *Highway Traffic Act* provides that every person who fails to satisfy a judgment rendered against him or her for damages occasioned by a motor vehicle may have his or her driver's licence suspended within 15 days from the expiry of the time for appeal.[69] The creditor must file with the Ministry of Transportation the original order, the amount which remains outstanding and an affidavit confirming that the judgment is for damage caused by a motor vehicle. The driver's licence remains suspended until the judgment has been paid.

The suspension of driving privileges is one sanction which can motivate the debtor to make arrangements to pay a debt. This remedy is available regardless of whether the judgment is made pursuant to the Small Claims Court or simplified procedure. Counsel should consider this and other remedies not provided for in the rules when seeking to enforce judgment.

---

[63] *Ibid.*, Rule 60.08(4).
[64] *Ibid.*, Rule 60.08(2).
[65] *Ibid.*, Rule 60.08(6.1); Form 60H.
[66] *Ibid.*, Rule 60.08(7); Form 60I.
[67] *Ibid.*, Rule 60.08(8).
[68] *Ibid.*, Rule 60.08(11).
[69] R.S.O. 1990, c. H.8, s. 198.

10.5 COSTS OF ENFORCEMENT

There is no specific provision in the *Small Claims Court Rules* that the creditor is entitled to the costs of enforcing the order. Actions which are subject to the simplified procedure allow for the payment of the creditor's costs of enforcing the order. The creditor is entitled to the costs of the examination in aid of execution, and for the issue, service, enforcement and renewal of a writ of execution of notice of garnishment. The amount of the costs to which the creditor is entitled is set out in the tariff.[70]

---

[70] *R.C.P.*, Rule 60.19.

CHAPTER 11

Appealing the Judgment

11.1 THE DECISION TO APPEAL

In every case, the unsuccessful party must decide whether it would be appropriate to appeal the decision. The appeal must be commenced within 30 days of the judgment, and therefore the decision to appeal must be considered immediately. In determining whether an appeal is appropriate, one must take into account the amount in issue. The appeal of a decision in cases under either the Small Claims Court (if the amount claimed is greater than $500, excluding costs) or the simplified procedure (if the amount of the judgment is less than $25,000, excluding costs) must be to the Divisional Court.[1] An appeal in the simplified procedure would be to the Court of Appeal if the amount of the judgment is in excess of $25,000, excluding costs.[2] Appeals to the Divisional Court and the Court of Appeal cannot be performed by an agent or law student and requires representation by a lawyer. As a result, the appeals can be lengthy and expensive. The benefits of a successful appeal must be balanced against the cost. In many cases the amount in issue will not justify an appeal.

The decision to appeal cannot be taken lightly. If an appeal is launched, the responding party is entitled to costs even if the appellant later abandons the appeal.[3] Due to the potential cost consequences of initiating an appeal, a lawyer must not do so unless he or she has instructions from the client.

11.2 MOTION FOR NEW TRIAL — SMALL CLAIMS COURT

A unique feature of the *Small Claims Court Rules* is the motion for a new trial. The motion for a new trial is available in all actions brought in the Small Claims Court including those claims where the amount in issue is less than $500.[4] The motion for a new trial provides an attractive alternative to an appeal to

---

[1] *Courts of Justice Act*, R.S.O. 1990, c. C.43, s. 31 (Small Claims Court appeals), s. 19(1) (simplified procedure).
[2] *Ibid.*, s. 6(1)(*b*).
[3] *Rules of Civil Procedure*, R.R.O. 1990, Reg. 194, Rule 61.14(3) (hereinafter *R.C.P.*).
[4] *Small Claims Court Rules*, O. Reg. 258/98, Rule 17.04(1) (hereinafter *S.C.C.R.*).

Divisional Court. The Small Claims Court procedure is inexpensive and simple and does not require the services of a lawyer.

A new trial is appropriate when there has been a complete failure to have a trial on the merits. A new trial may be ordered if one of three conditions is satisfied:

(i) there was an arithmetic error in determining the damages;
(ii) the party failed to attend the trial for valid reasons;
(iii) there is relevant evidence that could not have been available when the trial was conducted.

The failure of a party to correctly anticipate evidence at trial is not, however, a satisfactory ground for a motion for a new trial.

The motion for a new trial is commenced by serving a notice of motion, with supporting affidavit evidence, within 30 days of the judgment.[5] The practice for motions in the Small Claims Court applies to motions for a new trial. Before serving the motion material, the moving party must obtain a date from the court for the hearing of the motion. The motion material must be served on all parties who may be affected by the order.[6]

There is no requirement in the rules that the moving party must order the transcripts of the evidence at trial and include the transcripts in the motion material. However, if the moving party wishes to refer to the trial evidence on the motion, it is his or her responsibility to order the transcript, and serve and file it with the motion material. Generally, judges hearing this motion want to see the transcripts so they can determine whether there has been a trial on the merits. At a minimum, the reasons for judgment ought to be transcribed for use on the motion.

A new trial will rarely be granted. If at the trial all the parties had an opportunity to introduce evidence, and the judge has made a decision on the merits, a new trial is generally inappropriate. In those circumstances, the party who was unsuccessful at trial should appeal the decision, rather than move for a new trial.[7]

Upon a motion for a new trial, the Small Claims Court has the power to do the following:

(i) allow the motion and grant a new trial;
(ii) pronounce the judgment that ought to have been given at trial; or
(iii) dismiss the motion.[8]

---

[5] *Ibid.*
[6] *Ibid.*, Rule 15.01.
[7] See *Sears Canada Inc. v. Scott* (1994), 51 A.C.W.S. (3d) 1232 (Ont. Sm. Claims Ct.).
[8] S.C.C.R., Rule 17.04(2).

11.3 WHERE TO APPEAL

The appeal route is generally determined by the amount in issue. In the Small Claims Court, no appeal is available if the action is for the payment of money less than $500, or for the recovery of personal property which has a value of less than $500, excluding costs. It is important to note that it is the amount set out in the claim and not the amount of the judgment which determines the appeal route in the Small Claims Court.[9]

In actions subject to the simplified procedure, it is the amount awarded which determines the appeal court. If the amount awarded is less than $25,000, including pre-judgment interest, but excluding costs, the appeal is to the Divisional Court. If the damages award is $25,000 or less, but the pre-judgment interest brings the total above $25,000, the appeal lies to the Court of Appeal.[10]

An appeal to the Divisional Court must be brought in the region where the trial took place, unless the parties agree otherwise.[11] Appeals of cases in the simplified procedure, where the amount of the judgment is in excess of $25,000, must be brought in the Court of Appeal in Toronto.

11.4 HOW TO APPEAL

The procedure for appeals in the Divisional Court (for Small Claims actions over $500, and simplified procedure awards of less than $25,000, excluding costs) and in the Court of Appeal (for simplified procedure awards greater than $25,000, excluding costs) is governed by the same rule: Rule 61 of the *Rules of Civil Procedure*. The only difference is the court where the various documents are to be filed.

(a) Commencing the Appeal

(i) NOTICE OF APPEAL

The appeal is commenced with the service of a notice of appeal. The notice of appeal shall be served within 30 days of the date of the order appealed from and shall be filed in the office of the registrar within 10 days of service.[12] The notice of appeal must state the relief sought and the grounds for the appeal.[13] The appellant must set out, with some particularity, the errors made by the trial judge in coming to his or her decision. The errors could be errors of fact, such as a failure on the part of the judge to consider, or properly consider, evidence which had

---

[9] *Courts of Justice Act, supra*, note 1, s. 31.
[10] *Ibid.*, ss. 19(1)(a) and 6(1)(b).
[11] *Ibid.*, s. 20(1).
[12] R.C.P., Rule 61.04(1).
[13] *Ibid.*, Rule 61.04(3). See Form 61A Notice of Appeal to an Appellate Court.

been introduced at trial. The appeal could also be based on errors of law, such as allowing or refusing to allow in certain evidence, or in misapplying the law to the evidence.

Within 15 days of receiving the notice of appeal, the responding party may serve a notice of cross-appeal on all parties whose interests may be affected by the cross-appeal. Like the notice of appeal, the notice of cross-appeal must set out the relief sought and the grounds for the cross-appeal. The notice of cross-appeal must be filed with the court office within 10 days of service.[14]

Where the judgment appealed from is for the payment of money, the judgment is automatically stayed when the notice of appeal is delivered.[15]

(ii) Certificate Respecting Evidence

The appellant must serve, with the notice of appeal, the appellant's certificate respecting evidence. The appellant must set out, in the certificate, only the portions of the evidence required for the hearing of the appeal.[16] The appellant may take the position that some of the trial exhibits or evidence are not necessary for the appeal.

Within 15 days of receiving the appellant's certificate of evidence, the responding parties must serve a respondent's certificate of evidence which either confirms the appellant's certificate, or which sets out additions or deletions to the appellant's certificate. If a responding party fails to deliver a respondent's certificate, the responding party is deemed to have confirmed the appellant's certificate.[17]

The parties are not precluded from coming to an agreement with respect to the evidence required on the appeal. Where the parties agree on the evidence for use on the appeal within 30 days after the service of the notice of appeal, it is not necessary to comply with the rules respecting the appellant and respondent's certificates of evidence.[18]

In considering what evidence may be required on the appeal, the parties should ensure that only the evidence relevant to the issues on the appeal are included. In an appeal where the facts are not in dispute, an agreed statement of fact should be used instead of a transcript. A party may be penalized in costs for including irrelevant documents or oral evidence.[19]

---

[14] *Ibid.*, Rule 61.07(1) and (2). See Form 61E Notice of Cross-Appeal.
[15] *Ibid.*, Rule 63.01.
[16] *Ibid.*, Rule 61.05(1) [am. O. Reg. 570/98, s. 5]. See Form 61C Appellant's Certificate Respecting Evidence.
[17] *Ibid.*, Rule 61.05(2) and (3). See Form 61D Respondent's Certificate Respecting Evidence.
[18] *Ibid.*, Rule 61.05(4).
[19] *Ibid.*, Rule 61.05(8).

(iii) ORDERING TRANSCRIPTS

If oral evidence is required for the hearing of the appeal, the appellant must order a copy of the transcript from the court reporter. Proof that the appellant has ordered all oral evidence that the parties have not agreed to omit must be filed with the appeal court office within 30 days after the filing of the notice of appeal. Once the court reporter has finished transcribing the evidence, he or she is required to give notice to all of the parties and the court office that the transcript has been completed.[20]

(b) Perfecting the Appeal

It is the responsibility of the appellant to perfect the appeal.[21] The appellant must forward to the registrar of the court the trial record and the original exhibits from the trial. In addition, the appellant must serve the appeal book and his or her factum. If no transcripts are required for the appeal, the appeal book and factum must be filed within 30 days of filing the notice of appeal. If the transcript is required for the hearing of the appeal, the appellant must serve the appeal book, factum and transcript of the evidence within 30 days of being advised by the court reporter that the transcript has been completed.[22]

(i) APPEAL BOOK

The appeal book must be numbered consecutively and shall contain the following:

(i) table of contents describing each document in the appeal book;
(ii) the notice of appeal and any cross-appeal;
(iii) the issued and entered order appealed from;
(iv) the reasons of the court appealed from and if the reasons are handwritten a transcription of the reasons;
(v) if an earlier order or decision was the subject of the hearing, a copy of that order or decision and any reasons for it, with a typed copy if handwritten;
(vi) the pleadings;
(vii) any affidavit evidence;
(viii) the appellant's and respondent's certificates of evidence;
(ix) any order made regarding the conduct of the appeal;
(x) any other material required for use on the appeal;
(xi) a certificate signed by the appellant's solicitor confirming that the contents of the appeal book are complete and legible.[23]

The appeal book must be bound back and front in buff coloured covers.[24]

---

[20] *Ibid.*, Rule 61.05(5), (6) and (7).
[21] *Ibid.*, Rule 61.09(1).
[22] *Ibid.*, Rule 61.09(2) and (3) [am. O. Reg. 536/96, s. 8].
[23] *Ibid.*, Rule 61.10(1) [am. O. Regs. 441/90, s. 13; 61/96, s. 7; 570/98, s. 7].
[24] *Ibid.*, Rule 4.07(3).

(ii) FACTUMS AND BOOKS OF AUTHORITIES

A factum is to be filed by both the appellant and respondent.[25] The purpose of the factum is to provide a clear summary of the facts and law which will be relied on by each of the parties on the appeal.

The appellant's factum consists of the following five parts and two schedules:

(i) Part I in which the appellant is identified, and sets out the court appealed from and the result in that court;
(ii) Part II, containing a concise overview statement describing the case;
(iii) Part III, containing a summary of the facts relevant to the issues on the appeal;
(iv) Part IV, containing a statement of each issue raised, immediately followed by a statement of the law and authorities relating to that issue;
(v) Part V, containing a statement of the order requested of the appellate court;
(vi) a certificate stating the estimate of time required for his or her oral argument, excluding reply;
(vii) Schedule A, listing the authorities referred to in the appellant's factum; and
(viii) Schedule B, setting out the text of all relevant statutes, regulations and bylaws referred to in the appellant's factum.[26]

The factum must be signed by the appellant's solicitor. The appellant's factum must be bound front and back in white covers.[27]

The responding party must serve a factum within 60 days after receiving the appeal book, transcripts and the appellant's factum.[28] The respondent's factum also consists of five parts and two schedules:

(i) Part I, containing a concise overview statement describing the case;
(ii) Part II, in which the responding party either confirms the facts as set out in the appellant's factum, or sets out where the respondent disagrees with the applicant's facts, and provides a concise statement of any additional facts the respondent will be relying upon;
(iii) Part III, containing the position of the responding party on each issue raised by the appellant in the appellant's factum, immediately followed by a concise statement of the law and authorities relating to that issue;
(iv) Part IV, setting out any additional issues and the statement of law and authorities which relate to those issues;
(v) Part V, containing a statement of the order requested of the appellate court;

---

[25] *Ibid.*, Rules 61.11(1) and 61.12(1).
[26] *Ibid.*, Rule 61.11(1) [am. O. Regs. 534/95, s. 4; O. Reg. 570/98, s. 9; 24/00, s. 9].
[27] *Ibid.*, Rule 4.07(5).
[28] *Ibid.*, Rule 61.12(2) [am. O. Reg. 570/98, s. 10].

(vi) a certificate stating the estimate of time required for his or her oral argument;
(vii) Schedule A, listing the authorities referred to in the respondent's factum; and
(viii) Schedule B, setting out the text of all statutes, regulations or bylaws referred to in the respondent's factum.[29]

The responding party's factum must be signed by the respondent's solicitor. The respondent's factum must be bound front and back in green covers.[30]

If the respondent has brought a cross-appeal, the respondent must deliver a factum as appellant in the cross-appeal, and incorporate it in the respondent's factum. The appellant is required to serve a factum as respondent to the cross-appeal within 10 days of receiving the respondent's factum.[31]

It is important for counsel to note that the factum is to be concise. A lengthy factum may be less persuasive and counsel run the risk of the entire factum not being read. The courts have directed that the factum should not exceed 10 pages in the usual case. Even in exceptional cases, the factum is not to exceed 30 pages.[32]

Although the rules do not require the service and filing of books of authorities, it is good practice to do so. The books of authorities should include all cases to which the solicitor intends to refer in oral argument. The particular passages in the cases should be highlighted.[33]

Where possible, the parties should file a joint book of authorities. If both parties intend to refer to the same case in the joint book, different coloured highlighting can be used to distinguish between the parties. If a joint book of authorities is not being used, the book should clearly indicate on the cover whether it is filed on behalf of the appellant or respondent.

The books of authorities need not be served on the other party to the appeal, but should be filed with the court no later than the Monday of the week preceding the leaving of the appeal.[34]

(iii) COMPENDIUM OF EVIDENCE

In many cases, all of the evidence that has been ordered for the appeal will not be referred to in argument. For this reason the parties are required to file a compendium of evidence that includes only those excerpts of testimony or documents that the party intends to refer to at the appeal. The parties may agree to

---

[29] *Ibid.*, Rule 61.12(3) [am O. Regs. 534/95, s. 5; 570/98, s. 10; 24/00, s. 10].
[30] *Ibid.*, Rule 4.07(5).
[31] *Ibid.*, Rule 61.12(4).
[32] Practice Direction, "Factums in Court of Appeal", May 1, 1993; and "Factums in the Divisional Court", May 24, 1995.
[33] Practice Direction, "Books of Authority — Court of Appeal", May 1, 1993.
[34] *Ibid.*

file a joint compendium that includes the evidence each party will refer to on the appeal.[35]

The compendium must include a table of contents describing each excerpt of transcript and each exhibit. The exhibit must be described by the type of document, date and exhibit number or letter (if for identification). The compendium must also include the actual transcript excerpts and documents, and the documents must be set out in chronological order and not by exhibit number.[36]

The compendium must be served on all parties to the appeal and filed with the court at least 10 days before the hearing of the appeal.[37]

(iv) Certificate of Perfection

After the appeal book, transcripts, factum and compendium have been served, the appellant must file the documents with the registrar of the appropriate appeal court. In appeals pursuant to the Small Claims Court one copy must be filed with the Divisional Court.[38] In appeals of actions subject to the simplified procedure, three copies of the material must be filed with the Divisional Court. If the appeal is to the Court of Appeal and is to be heard by five judges, five copies must be filed with the Court of Appeal.[39]

The appellant must also file a certificate of perfection which states that the trial record, original exhibits, appeal book, transcripts and appellant's factum have been filed. The certificate of perfection must also set out the name, address and telephone number of the solicitor for every party to the appeal, and any other person who may be entitled to intervene in the appeal, or, if a party acts in person, the name, address and telephone number of the person acting on his or her own behalf.[40]

After the certificate of perfection has been filed, the registrar shall place the matter on the list for the hearing of appeals. The notice of listing for hearing shall be served on all persons listed in the certificate of perfection.[41]

If the appellant fails to file proof that the transcript was ordered within 30 days of filing the notice of appeal, or if the certificate of perfection is not filed within the appropriate time limits (30 days after service of the notice of appeal if no transcripts are required, or 30 days after receiving notice from the court reporter that the evidence has been transcribed), the respondent may move before the registrar of the court to dismiss the appeal for reason of delay. The motion must be made on 10 days notice to the appellant.[42]

---

[35] *R.C.P.*, Rule 61.12.1(2).
[36] *Ibid.*, Rule 61.12.1(5).
[37] *Ibid.*, Rule 61.12.1(3).
[38] *Courts of Justice Act*, R.S.O. 1990, c. C.43, s. 21(2)(b).
[39] *R.C.P.*, Rule 61.09(3)(b) [am. O. Reg. 536/96, s. 8].
[40] *Ibid.*, Rule 61.09(3)(c).
[41] *Ibid.*, Rule 61.09(5).
[42] *Ibid.*, Rule 61.13(1).

The registrar may unilaterally dismiss the appeal for delay if the transcript is not filed within 60 days of being advised by the court reporter that the transcript is finished, or if the appellant has not filed a certificate of perfection within one year after filing the notice of appeal. The registrar must give notice to the appellant. The appellant has 10 days to perfect the appeal after receiving the registrar's notice.[43]

11.5 APPEAL HEARING

In Small Claims Court appeals, the appeal will be heard by one judge of the Divisional Court.[44] In simplified procedure actions in the Divisional Court, the appeal will be heard by three members of the Divisional Court.[45] Appeals of simplified procedure actions to the Court of Appeal will be heard by at least three judges, and may be heard by five judges.[46]

Although there are no specific time limits set out in the rules regarding oral argument, the court may have more than one appeal scheduled and will expect the parties to make their arguments as succinctly as possible. The material must be organized in an easily understandable manner, and counsel must be prepared to respond to any questions which may be raised by the judges.

As a general rule, the appeal court judges are reluctant to interfere with the decision of the trial judge on factual issues. The trial judge had the opportunity to assess the credibility of witnesses and determine the facts of the case in a full hearing. An appellate court is not in as good a position to make the same determination and is unlikely to reverse a trial judge on these issues. Parties should consider an appeal only where an error of law, manifest unfairness at trial or a misapprehension of the evidence has led to a plainly unjust decision.

---

[43] *Ibid.*, Rule 61.13(2).
[44] *Courts of Justice Act*, *supra*, note 38, s. 21(2)(b).
[45] *Ibid.*, s. 21(1).
[46] *Ibid.*, s. 7(1).

APPENDIX 1

Conduct of an Action in the Small Claims Court

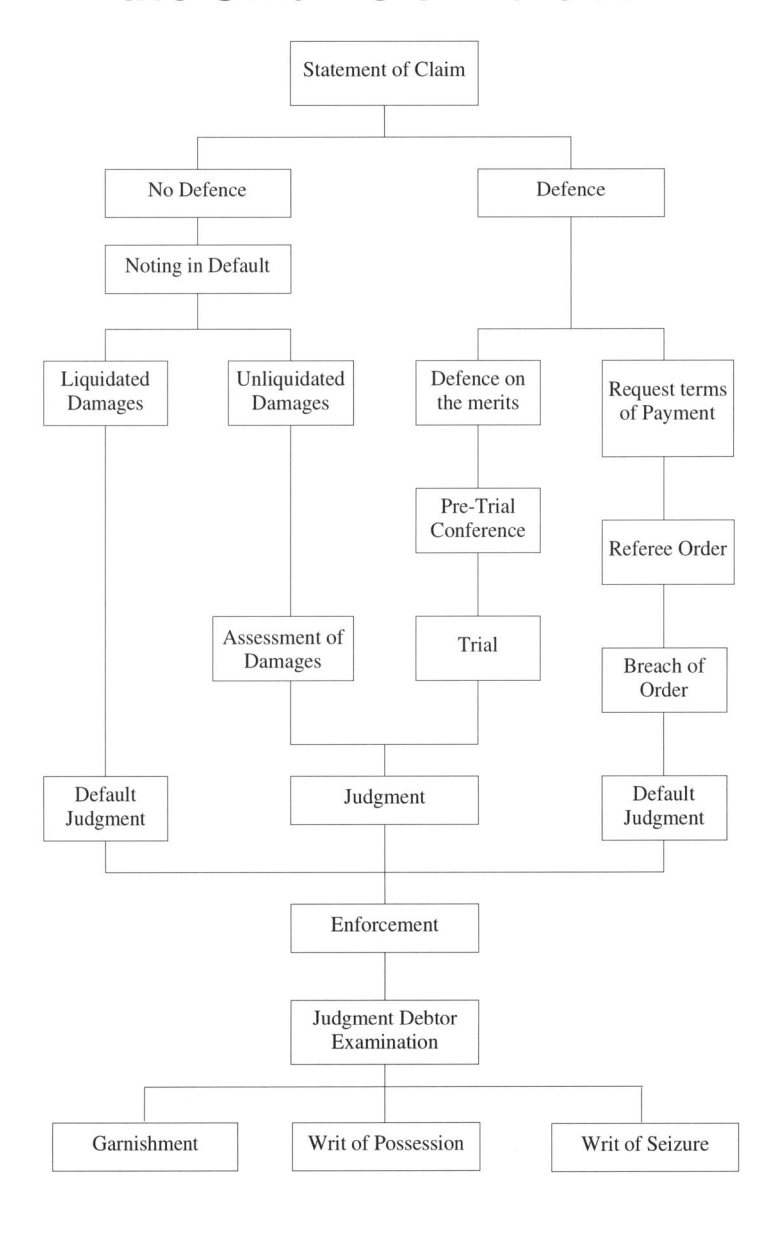

```
                         Statement of Claim
                                │
                ┌───────────────┴───────────────┐
            No Defence                       Defence
                │                               │
         Noting in Default                      │
                │                               │
        ┌───────┴───────┐               ┌───────┴───────┐
    Liquidated      Unliquidated     Defence on      Request terms
     Damages          Damages        the merits       of Payment
        │               │                │               │
        │               │            Pre-Trial        Referee Order
        │               │            Conference          │
        │               │                │               │
        │          Assessment of       Trial         Breach of
        │            Damages                           Order
        │               │                │               │
     Default          Judgment                        Default
     Judgment                                         Judgment
        └───────────────┼───────────────────────────────┘
                        │
                   Enforcement
                        │
                Judgment Debtor
                  Examination
                        │
        ┌───────────────┼───────────────┐
   Garnishment    Writ of Possession   Writ of Seizure
```

APPENDIX 2

Conduct of an Appeal from a Decision of the Small Claims Court

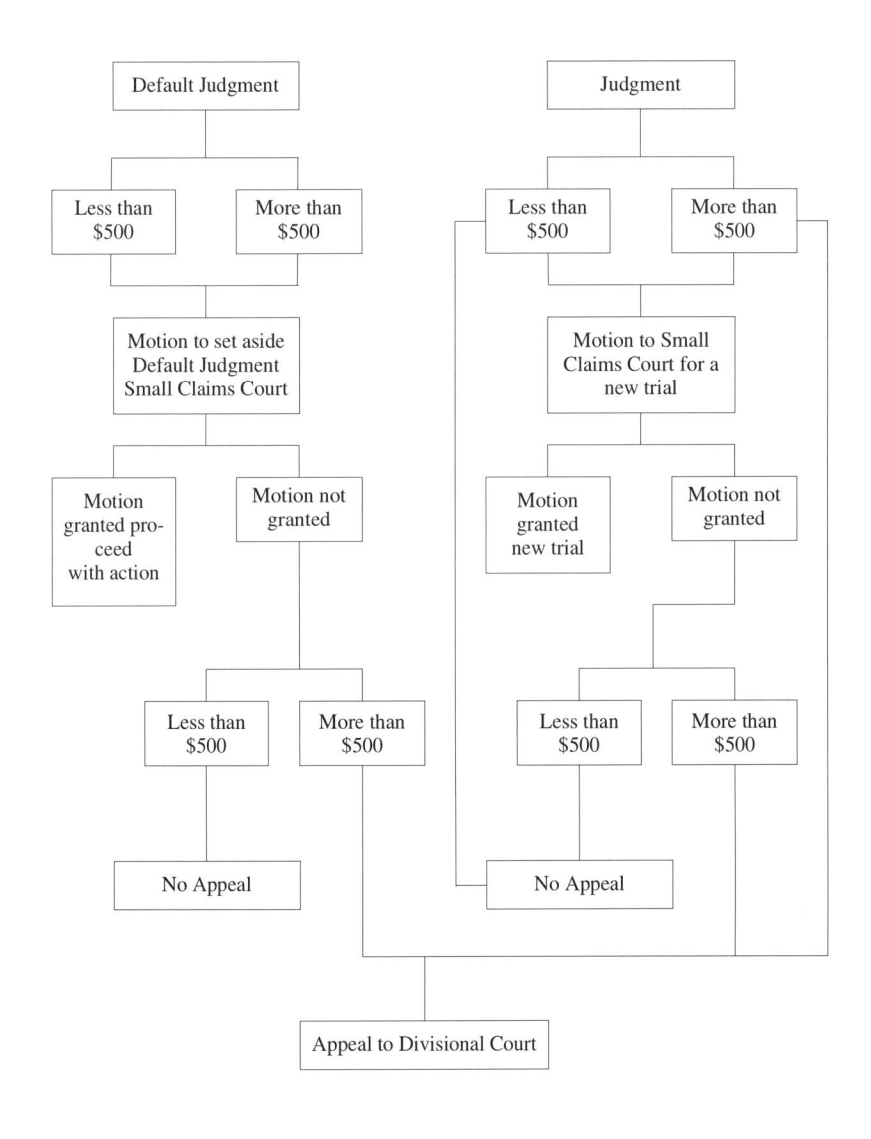

```
Default Judgment
├── Less than $500
└── More than $500
    │
    Motion to set aside
    Default Judgment
    Small Claims Court
    ├── Motion granted proceed with action
    └── Motion not granted
        ├── Less than $500 → No Appeal
        └── More than $500 → Appeal to Divisional Court

Judgment
├── Less than $500
└── More than $500
    │
    Motion to Small Claims Court for a new trial
    ├── Motion granted new trial
    └── Motion not granted
        ├── Less than $500 → No Appeal
        └── More than $500 → Appeal to Divisional Court
```

APPENDIX 3

Conduct of an Action Under the Simplified Procedure

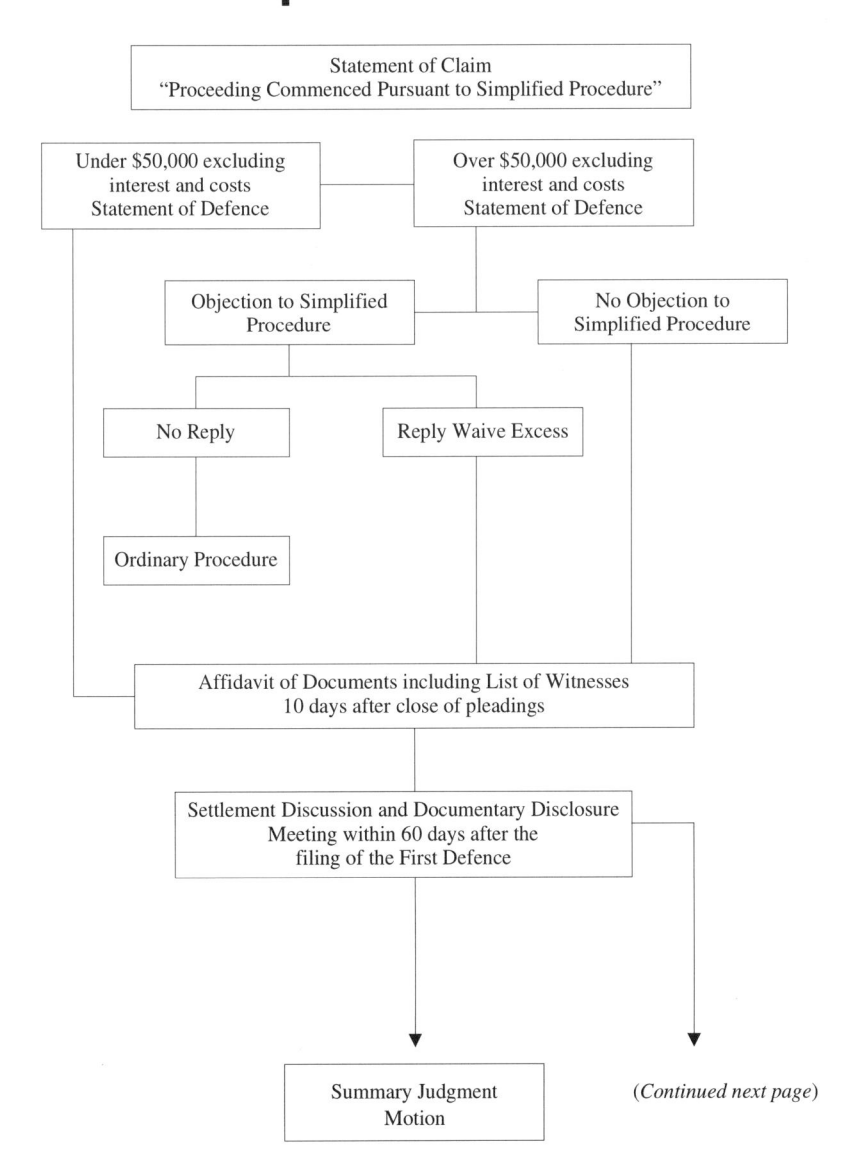

```
Statement of Claim
"Proceeding Commenced Pursuant to Simplified Procedure"
```

- Under $50,000 excluding interest and costs — Statement of Defence
- Over $50,000 excluding interest and costs — Statement of Defence
  - Objection to Simplified Procedure
    - No Reply → Ordinary Procedure
    - Reply Waive Excess
  - No Objection to Simplified Procedure

Affidavit of Documents including List of Witnesses
10 days after close of pleadings

Settlement Discussion and Documentary Disclosure Meeting within 60 days after the filing of the First Defence

Summary Judgment Motion

(Continued next page)

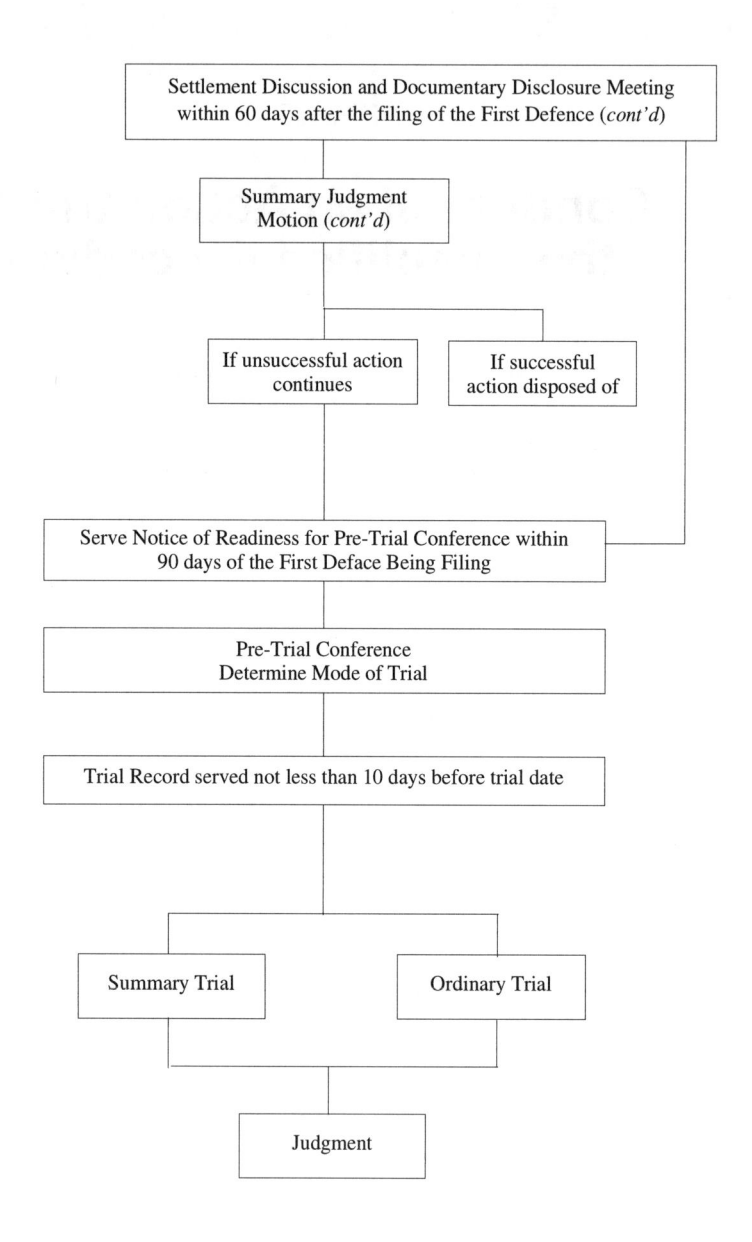

```
┌─────────────────────────────────────────────────────────┐
│ Settlement Discussion and Documentary Disclosure Meeting │
│ within 60 days after the filing of the First Defence (cont'd) │
└─────────────────────────────────────────────────────────┘
                            │
              ┌─────────────────────────┐
              │   Summary Judgment      │
              │   Motion (cont'd)       │
              └─────────────────────────┘
                            │
          ┌─────────────────┴─────────────────┐
┌──────────────────────┐            ┌──────────────────────┐
│ If unsuccessful action│            │    If successful     │
│      continues        │            │  action disposed of  │
└──────────────────────┘            └──────────────────────┘
              │                                 │
┌─────────────────────────────────────────────────────────┐
│ Serve Notice of Readiness for Pre-Trial Conference within │
│   90 days of the First Deface Being Filing               │
└─────────────────────────────────────────────────────────┘
                            │
              ┌─────────────────────────┐
              │   Pre-Trial Conference  │
              │   Determine Mode of Trial│
              └─────────────────────────┘
                            │
┌─────────────────────────────────────────────────────────┐
│ Trial Record served not less than 10 days before trial date │
└─────────────────────────────────────────────────────────┘
                            │
          ┌─────────────────┴─────────────────┐
┌──────────────────────┐            ┌──────────────────────┐
│    Summary Trial     │            │    Ordinary Trial    │
└──────────────────────┘            └──────────────────────┘
                            │
                  ┌─────────────────┐
                  │    Judgment     │
                  └─────────────────┘
```

APPENDIX 4

Conduct of an Appeal from a Decision Under the Simplified Procedure

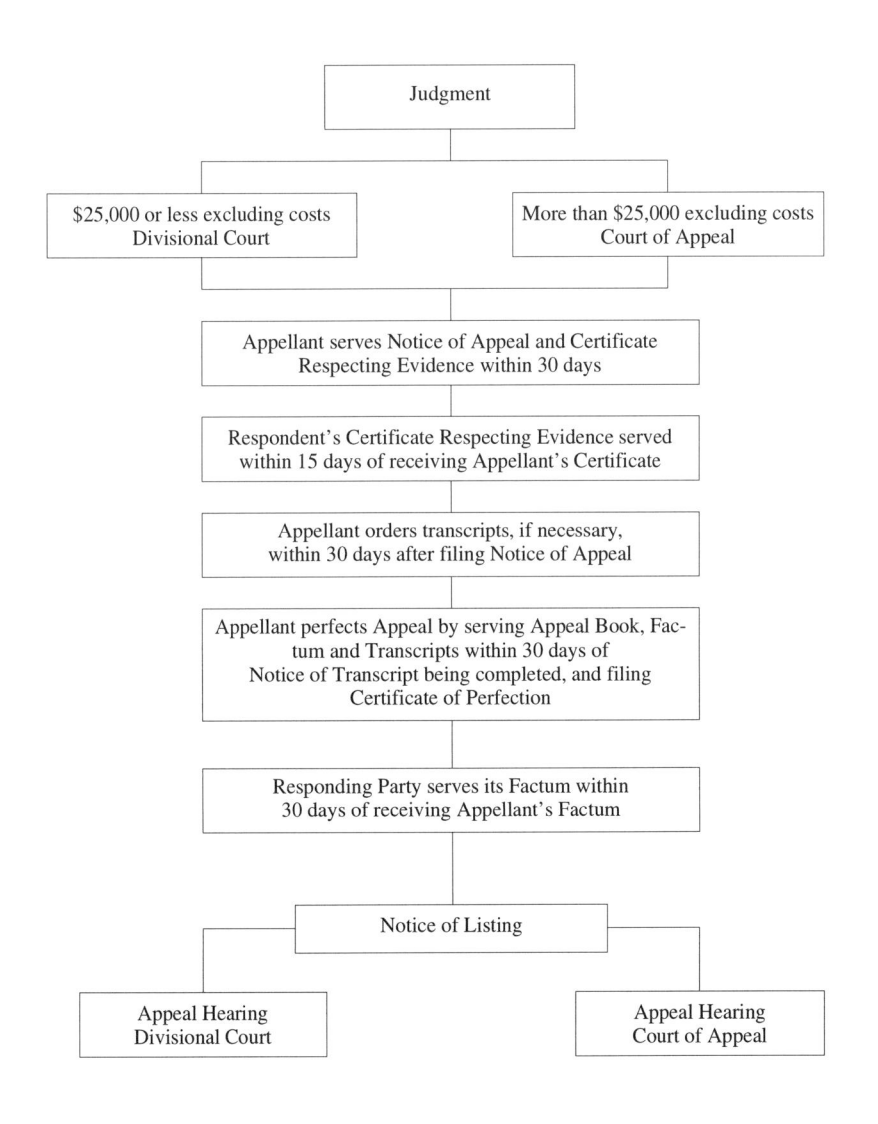

```
                          ┌─────────────┐
                          │  Judgment   │
                          └──────┬──────┘
              ┌──────────────────┴──────────────────┐
┌─────────────────────────────┐      ┌─────────────────────────────────┐
│ $25,000 or less excluding   │      │ More than $25,000 excluding     │
│ costs — Divisional Court    │      │ costs — Court of Appeal         │
└─────────────────────────────┘      └─────────────────────────────────┘
```

- Appellant serves Notice of Appeal and Certificate Respecting Evidence within 30 days
- Respondent's Certificate Respecting Evidence served within 15 days of receiving Appellant's Certificate
- Appellant orders transcripts, if necessary, within 30 days after filing Notice of Appeal
- Appellant perfects Appeal by serving Appeal Book, Factum and Transcripts within 30 days of Notice of Transcript being completed, and filing Certificate of Perfection
- Responding Party serves its Factum within 30 days of receiving Appellant's Factum
- Notice of Listing

┌──────────────────────────┐   ┌──────────────────────────┐
│ Appeal Hearing   │   │ Appeal Hearing   │
│ Divisional Court   │   │ Court of Appeal   │
└──────────────────────────┘   └──────────────────────────┘

APPENDIX 5

Courts of Justice Act

R.S.O. 1990, c. C.43, ss. 22-32, 107 and 127-131
(SMALL CLAIMS COURT)

22.(1) *Small Claims Court* — The Small Claims Court is continued as a branch of the Superior Court of Justice under the name Small Claims Court in English and Cour des petites créances in French.

(2) *Idem* — The Small Claims Court consists of the Chief Justice of the Superior Court of Justice who shall be president of the court and such other judges of the Superior Court of Justice as the Chief Justice designates from time to time.

(3) *Jurisdiction of Judges* — Every judge of the Superior Court of Justice is also a judge of the Small Claims Court.

[S.O. 1996, c. 25, s. 9]

23.(1) *Jurisdiction* — The Small Claims Court,
  (a) has jurisdiction in any action for the payment of money where the amount claimed does not exceed the prescribed amount exclusive of interest and costs; and
  (b) has jurisdiction in any action for the recovery of possession of personal property where the value of the property does not exceed the prescribed amount.

CASE LAW

Von Felix v. Enterprise Rent-A-Car, [2002] O.J. No. 1109 (S.C.J.).

This action for personal injury arising out of a motor vehicle accident, which is subject to s. 267.5 of the *Insurance Act*, R.S.O. 1990, c. I-8, cannot succeed in the Small Claims Court because the most the court can award is $10,000 and the first $15,000 in damages under s. 267.5 are deductible.

Osadca v. Cadillac Fairview Corp., [2000] O.J. No. 3314 (S.C.J.).

Counterclaims, cross-claims and third party claims must also be accounted for in determining the jurisdiction of Small Claims Court. In this action, the sum of monetary damages of main action and those of cross-claim exceeded the Small Claims Court ceiling.

Baslik v. Ontario Teachers Federation, [2000] O.J. No. 1460 (S.C.J.).

This is a motion by the defendant for an order staying the plaintiff's action on the ground that the value of the damages claimed exceeded Small Claims Court jurisdiction. The motion was allowed because of the real possibility that the plaintiff would renew his claim every year in an effort to stay within Small Claims Court jurisdiction.

Associates Financial Services of Canada Ltd. v. Campbell, [1998] O.J. No. 5612 (Gen Div.).

The Small Claims Court has no jurisdiction to lift a stay of proceedings imposed under the *Bankruptcy and Insolvency Act*.[1] Only a Superior Court of Justice sitting in bankruptcy may lift the stay and grant leave to proceed.

Luo v. Canada (Attorney General) (1997), 33 O.R. (3d) 300 (Div. Ct.).

The Small Claims Court is a part of the Ontario Court and has jurisdiction to adjudicate on matters involving the federal crown. (See also *Todd v. Canada (Solicitor General)*, [1993] O.J. No. 3410 (Gen. Div.)).

Beardsley v. Baecker (1993), 20 C.P.C. (3d) 235 (N.S.S.C.).

The Small Claims Court does not have jurisdiction with respect to landlord and tenant matters.

Paul v. Rodgers (1989), 15 W.D.C.P. 158 (Ont. Dist. Ct.).

It is the amount claimed, not the amount awarded, that establishes jurisdiction.

Moore v. Canadian Newspapers Co. (1989), 69 O.R. (2d) 262 (Dist. Ct.).

Although the Provincial Court has jurisdiction to apply equitable principles, it cannot grant equitable relief. Thus, the court did not have jurisdiction to order the libelous defendant to print an apology and retraction.

Ontario (Attorney General) v. Pembina Exploration Can. Ltd., [1989] 1 S.C.R. 206.

The Small Claims Court has jurisdiction to hear an action for damages sustained by a ship in provincial inland waters.

Re Teitel and Theriault (1983), 44 O.R. (2d) 127 (Div. Ct.).

False arrest and false imprisonment are not excluded from the jurisdiction of the Provincial Court.

---

[1] R.S.C. 1985, c. B-3.

(2) Transfer from Superior Court of Justice — An action in the Superior Court of Justice may be transferred to the Small Claims Court by the local registrar of the Superior Court of Justice on requisition with the consent of all parties filed before the trial commences if,

    (a) the only claim is for the payment of money or the recovery of possession of personal property; and

    (b) the claim is within the jurisdiction of the Small Claims Court.

(3) Idem — An action transferred to the Small Claims Court shall be titled and continued as if it had been commenced in that court.

[S.O. 1996, c. 25, s. 9]

CASE LAW

Shoppers Trust Co. v. Mann Taxi Management Ltd. (1993), 16 O.R. (3d) 192 (Gen. Div.).

The plaintiff was permitted to transfer his action from the General Division to the Small Claims Court after the monetary jurisdiction of the Small Claims Court was increased to $6,000.

24.(1) *Composition of court for hearings* — A proceeding in the Small Claims Court shall be heard and determined by one judge of the Superior Court of Justice.

(2) Provincial judge or deputy judge may preside — A proceeding in the Small Claims Court may also be heard and determined by,

    (a) a provincial judge who was assigned to the Provincial Court (Civil Division) immediately before the 1st day of September, 1990; or

    (b) a deputy judge appointed under section 32.

(3) Where deputy judge not to preside — A deputy judge shall not hear and determine an action,

    (a) for the payment of money in excess of the prescribed amount; or

    (b) for the recovery of possession of personal property exceeding the prescribed amount in value.

[S.O. 1996, c. 25, s. 9]

25. *Summary hearings* — The Small Claims Court shall hear and determine in a summary way all questions of law and fact and may make such order as is considered just and agreeable to good conscience.

CASE LAW

Canada (Attorney General) v. Khimani (1985), 50 O.R. (2d) 476 (Div. Ct.).

The Provincial Court (Civil Division) does not have an equitable jurisdiction which would permit a decision contrary to law.

Mandel v. The Permanent (1985), 7 O.A.C. 365 (Div. Ct.).

Where a trial judge intervened to manage a trial in the face of unacceptable conduct by a difficult party, the Divisional Court cautioned against intervention on such a scale (even in a summary hearing) but found nothing improper in the instant case. A trial judge, while obliged to assist a party appearing in person who is unfamiliar with court procedure, is not obliged to become that person's advocate. The judge's role in this respect is limited; he must assist but he must not be unfair to the other party in so doing.

Travel Machine Ltd. v. Madore (1983), 143 D.L.R. (3d) 94 (Ont. H.C.J.).

A trial judge cannot properly, on the basis of "equity and good conscience" ignore statutory law.

Smith v. Galin, [1956] O.W.N. 432 (C.A.).

This section does not provide authority for a judge to ignore general legal principles.

26. *Representation* — **A party may be represented in a proceeding in the Small Claims Court by counsel or an agent but the court may exclude from a hearing anyone, other than a lawyer qualified to practise in Ontario, appearing as an agent on behalf of a party if it finds that such person is not competent properly to represent the party or does not understand and comply at the hearing with the duties and responsibilities of an advocate.**

[S.O. 1994, c. 12, s. 10]

CASE LAW

Re Milligan (1991), 1 C.P.C. (3d) 12 (Ont. Gen. Div.).

The trial judge cannot choose which counsel may appear in his or her court.

27.(1) *Evidence* — **Subject to subsections (3) and (4), the Small Claims Court may admit as evidence at a hearing and act upon any oral testimony and any document or other thing so long as the evidence is relevant to the subject-matter of the proceeding, but the court may exclude anything unduly repetitious.**

(2) *Idem* — **Subsection (1) applies whether or not the evidence is given or proven under oath or affirmation or admissible as evidence in any other court.**

(3) *Idem* — **Nothing is admissible in evidence at a hearing,**

(a) that would be inadmissible by reason of any privilege under the law of evidence; or

(b) that is inadmissible by any Act.

(4) *Conflicts* — Nothing in subsection (1) overrides the provisions of any Act expressly limiting the extent to or purposes for which any oral testimony, documents or things may be admitted or used in evidence in any proceeding.

(5) *Copies* — A copy of a document or any other thing may be admitted as evidence at a hearing if the presiding judge is satisfied as to its authenticity.

CASE LAW

Central Burner Service Ltd. v. Texaco Co. (1989), 36 O.A.C. 239 (Div. Ct.).

The Small Claims Court may decide cases on the basis of hearsay evidence. The trial judge must give the hearsay evidence appropriate weight.

O'Connell v. Custom Kitchen & Vanity (1986), 17 O.A.C. 157 (Div. Ct.).

A judge of the Provincial Court (Civil Division) has a discretion under this section to admit hearsay evidence provided it is relevant.

28. *Installment orders* — The Small Claims Court may order the times and the proportions in which money payable under an order of the court shall be paid.

29. *Limit on costs* — An award of costs in the Small Claims Court, other than disbursements, shall not exceed 15 per cent of the amount claimed or the value of the property sought to be recovered unless the court considers it necessary in the interests of justice to penalize a party, counsel or agent for unreasonable behaviour in the proceeding.

CASE LAW

777812 Ontario Inc. v. Windup Corp., [2002] O.J. No. 1102 (S.C.J.).

The Court has the discretion pursuant to s. 29 of the *Courts of Justice Act* to set a counsel fee for the successful party which includes the cost of the defendant's expert to attend in court. In this case, the defendant was entitled to a counsel fee of $3,000.

30. [Repealed S.O. 1994, c. 12, s. 11].

31. *Appeals* — An appeal lies to the Divisional Court from a final order of the Small Claims Court in an action,

(a) **for the payment of money in excess of $500, excluding costs; or**

(b) for the recovery of possession of personal property exceeding $500 in value.

CASE LAW

Bissoondatt v. Arzadon, [1992] O.J. No. 2312 (Gen. Div.).

The trial judge has an advantage over the appeal court in that he or she has heard and seen the witnesses.

G.B.V.S. Inc. v. DiPaola (1989), 16 A.C.W.S. (3d) 107 (Ont. Div. Ct.).

An appeal was allowed where the trial judge significantly intervenes in the examinations of witnesses and if the right of cross-examination has been denied.

32. (1) *Deputy judges* — **A regional senior judge of the Superior Court of Justice may, with the approval of the Attorney General, appoint a lawyer to act as a deputy judge of the Small Claims Court for a term of three years.**

(2) *Idem* — **A regional senior judge of the Superior Court of Justice may renew the appointment of a deputy judge for one or more three-year terms.**

[S.O. 1994, c. 12, s. 12; 1996, c. 25, s. 9]

CASE LAW

Holovaci v. Zsoldos, [2000] O.J. No. 1633 (S.C.J.).

An appeal of a Small Claims Court judgment that claimed that the deputy judge acted inappropriately was dismissed. The Ontario Divisional Court found that the deputy judge offered the appellant/defendant every opportunity to cross-examine the plaintiff, and said that interventions were made appropriately. The Court found no bias, real or imagined, on the part of the deputy judge.

107.(1) *Consolidation of proceedings in different courts* — **Where two or more proceedings are pending in two or more different courts, and the proceedings,**

(a) **have a question of law or fact in common;**
(b) **claim relief arising out of the same transaction or occurrence or series of transactions or occurrences; or**
(c) **for any other reason ought to be the subject of an order under this section,**

an order may, on motion, be made,

(d) **transferring any of the proceedings to another court and requiring the proceedings to be consolidated, or to be heard at the same time, or one immediately after the other; or**
(e) **requiring any of the proceedings to be,**

(i) stayed until after the determination of any other of them, or

(ii) asserted by way of counterclaim in any other of them.

(2) *Transfer from Small Claims Court* — A proceeding in the Small Claims Court shall not be transferred under clause (1)(d) to the Superior Court of Justice without the consent of the plaintiff in the proceeding in the Small Claims Court.

(3) *Idem* — A proceeding in the Small Claims Court shall not be required under subclause (1)(e)(ii) to be asserted by way of counterclaim in a proceeding in the Superior Court of Justice without the consent of the plaintiff in the proceeding in the Small Claims Court.

(4) *Motions* — The motion shall be made to a judge of the Superior Court of Justice.

(5) *Directions* — An order under subsection (1) may impose such terms and give such directions as are considered just, including dispensing with service of a notice of readiness or listing for trial and abridging the time for placing an action on the trial list.

(6) *Transfer* — A proceeding that is transferred to another court under clause (1)(d) shall be titled in the court to which it is transferred and shall be continued as if it had been commenced in that court.

(7) *Discretion at hearing* — Where an order has been made that proceedings be heard either at the same time or one immediately after the other, the judge presiding at the hearing nevertheless has discretion to order otherwise.

[S.O. 1996, c. 25, ss. 8 and 9]

CASE LAW

Clearnet Inc. v. Blue Line Distribution Ltd., [1999] O.J. No. 1064 (Gen. Div.).

Motion to stay Small Claims Court action was granted given the fact that a similar action involving the same facts was proceeding at the same time in General Division. A stay was appropriate because allowing the Small Claims Court action to continue could give rise to issue estoppel arguments that could have a profound effect on all the parties.

CAD-FM Micro Systems v. Coldmatic Refrigeration of Canada Ltd. (1994), 5 W.D.C.P. (2d) 250 (Gen. Div.).

Where the defendant's counterclaim is in excess of the monetary jurisdiction of the court, and the plaintiff does not consent to the transfer of the action to General Division, the defendant must commence a separate action against the plaintiff in the General Division.

INTEREST AND COSTS

127.(1) *Definitions* — In this section and in sections 128 and 129,

"bank rate" means the bank rate established by the Bank of Canada as the minimum rate at which the Bank of Canada makes short-term advances to banks listed in Schedule I to the *Bank Act* (Canada);

"date of the order" means the date the order is made, even if the order is not entered or enforceable on that date, or the order is varied on appeal, and in the case of an order directing a reference, the date the report on the reference is confirmed;

"postjudgment interest rate" means the bank rate at the end of the first day of the last month of the quarter preceding the quarter in which the date of the order falls, rounded to the next higher whole number where the bank rate includes a fraction, plus 1 per cent;

"prejudgment interest rate" means the bank rate at the end of the first day of the last month of the quarter preceding the quarter in which the proceeding was commenced, rounded to the nearest tenth of a percentage point;

"quarter" means the three-month period ending with the 31st day of March, 30th day of June, 30th day of September or 31st day of December.

(2) *Calculation and publication of interest* — After the first day of the last month of each quarter, a person designated by the Deputy Attorney General shall forthwith,

    (a) determine the prejudgment and postjudgment interest rate for the next quarter; and

    (b) publish in *The Ontario Gazette* a table showing the rate determined under clause (a) for the next quarter and for all the previous quarters during the preceding ten years.

128.(1) *Prejudgment interest* — A person who is entitled to an order for the payment of money is entitled to claim and have included in the order an award of interest thereon at the prejudgment interest rate, calculated from the date the cause of action arose to the date of the order.

(2) *Exception for non-pecuniary loss on personal injury* — Despite subsection (1), the rate of interest on damages for non-pecuniary loss in an action for personal injury shall be the rate determined by the rules of court made under clause 66(2)(w).

(3) *Special damages* — If the order includes an amount for past pecuniary loss, the interest calculated under subsection (1) shall be calculated on

the total past pecuniary loss at the end of each six-month period and at the date of the order.

(4) *Exclusion* — Interest shall not be awarded under subsection (1),
  (a) on exemplary or punitive damages;
  (b) on interest accruing under this section;
  (c) on an award of costs in the proceeding;
  (d) on that part of the order that represents pecuniary loss arising after the date of the order and that is identified by a finding of the court;
  (e) with respect to the amount of any advance payment that has been made towards settlement of the claim, for the period after the advance payment has been made;
  (f) where the order is made on consent, except by consent of the debtor; or
  (g) where interest is payable by a right other than under this section.

[S.O. 1994, c. 12, s. 44]

129.(1) *Postjudgment interest* — Money owing under an order, including costs to be assessed or costs fixed by the court, bears interest at the postjudgment interest rate, calculated from the date of the order.

(2) *Interest on periodic payments* — Where an order provides for periodic payments, each payment in default shall bear interest only from the date of default.

(3) *Interest on orders originating outside Ontario* — Where an order is based on an order given outside Ontario or an order of a court outside Ontario is filed with a court in Ontario for the purpose of enforcement, money owing under the order bears interest at the rate, if any, applicable to the order given outside Ontario by the law of the place where it was given.

(4) *Costs assessed without order* — Where costs are assessed without an order, the costs bear interest at the postjudgment interest rate in the same manner as if an order were made for the payment of costs on the date the person to whom the costs are payable became entitled to the costs.

(5) *Other provision for interest* — Interest shall not be awarded under this section where interest is payable by a right other than under this section.

130.(1) *Discretion of court* — The court may, where it considers it just to do so, in respect of the whole or any part of the amount on which interest is payable under section 128 or 129,
  (a) disallow interest under either section;
  (b) allow interest at a rate higher or lower than that provided in either section;

(c) allow interest for a period other than that provided in either section.

(2) *Idem* — For the purpose of subsection (1), the court shall take into account,

    (a) changes in market interest rates;
    (b) the circumstances of the case;
    (c) the fact that an advance payment was made;
    (d) the circumstances of medical disclosure by the plaintiff;
    (e) the amount claimed and the amount recovered in the proceeding;
    (f) the conduct of any party that tended to shorten or to lengthen unnecessarily the duration of the proceeding; and
    (g) any other relevant consideration.

131.(1) *Costs* — Subject to the provisions of an Act or rules of court, the costs of and incidental to a proceeding or a step in a proceeding are in the discretion of the court, and the court may determine by whom and to what extent the costs shall be paid. R.S.O. 1990, c. C.43, s. 131(1).

(2) *Crown costs* — In a proceeding to which Her Majesty is a party, costs awarded to Her Majesty shall not be disallowed or reduced on assessment merely because they relate to a lawyer who is a salaried officer of the Crown, and costs recovered on behalf of Her Majesty shall be paid into the Consolidated Revenue Fund.

[S.O. 1994, c. 12, s. 45]

APPENDIX 6

Small Claims Court Rules

O. Reg. 258/98

Editorial Note: The Rules reproduced here reflect the Rules as they will read on December 10, 2002, pursuant to O. Reg. 461/01.

ANNOTATED SUMMARY OF CONTENTS

Rule 1. Interpretation
Rule 2. Non-Compliance with the Rules
Rule 3. Time
Rule 4. Parties Under Disability
Rule 5. Partnerships and Sole Proprietorships
Rule 6. Forum and Jurisdiction
Rule 7. Commencement of Proceedings
Rule 8. Service
Rule 9. Defence
Rule 10. Defendant's Claim
Rule 11. Default Proceedings
Rule 12. Amendment
Rule 13. Pre-Trial Conferences
Rule 14. Offer to Settle
Rule 15. Motions
Rule 16. Notice of Trial
Rule 17. Trial
Rule 18. Evidence at Trial
Rule 19. Costs
Rule 20. Enforcement of Orders
Rule 21. Referee

RULE 1 INTERPRETATION

Citation

1.01 These rules may be cited as the Small Claims Court Rules.

Definitions

1.02 In these rules,

"court" means the Small Claims Court;

"disability", where used in respect of a person or party, means that the person or party is,

  (a) a minor,
  (b) mentally incapable within the meaning of section 6 or 45 of the *Substitute Decisions Act,* 1992 in respect of an issue in the proceeding, whether the person or party has a guardian or not, or
  (c) an absentee within the meaning of the *Absentees Act;*

"document" includes data and information in electronic form;

"electronic" includes created, recorded, transmitted or stored in digital form or in other intangible form by electronic, magnetic or optical means or by any other means that has capabilities for creation, recording, transmission or storage similar to those means, and "electronically" has a corresponding meaning;

"holiday" means,

   (a) any Saturday or Sunday,
   (b) New Year's Day,
   (c) Good Friday,
   (d) Easter Monday,
   (e) Victoria Day,
   (f) Canada Day,
   (g) Civic Holiday,
   (h) Labour Day,
   (i) Thanksgiving Day,
   (j) Remembrance Day,
   (k) Christmas Day,
   (l) Boxing Day, and
   (m) any special holiday proclaimed by the Governor General or the Lieutenant Governor,

and if New Year's Day, Canada Day or Remembrance Day falls on a Saturday or Sunday, the following Monday is a holiday, and if Christmas Day falls on a Saturday or Sunday, the following Monday and Tuesday are holidays, and if Christmas Day falls on a Friday, the following Monday is a holiday;

"information technology" [Repealed, O. Reg. 461/01, s. 1]

"order" includes a judgment.

[O. Reg. 461/01, s.1].

General Principle

1.03(1) These rules shall be liberally construed to secure the just, most expeditious and least expensive determination of every proceeding on its merits in accordance with section 25 of the *Courts of Justice Act*.

CASE LAW

Mount Royal Painting & Decorating Inc. v. Central Interiors Inc., [1995] O.J. No. 4031 (Gen. Div.).

The Small Claims Court had a broader discretion to interpret its rules than is granted to other courts in Ontario.

Sahota v. Beauchamp; Firstline Trust Co. (Third party), [1994] O.J. No. 1483 (Sm. Claims Ct.).

The court rejected the suggestion of the moving party to bring a summary judgment motion pursuant to Rule 1.02(1) of the *Small Claims Court Rules*.

Danson v. Ontario (Attorney General) (1987), 60 O.R. (2d) 676 (C.A.), affd (1988) 74 O.R. (2d) 763n (S.C.C.).

The conditional challenge that the *Small Claims Court Rules* may result in judicial abuse was unsuccessful.

Matters Not Provided For

(2) If matters are not provided for in these rules, the practice shall be determined by analogy to them and the court may, at any stage in a proceeding, make any order that is just.

CASE LAW

Suedfeld v. Lancia, [1993] O.J. No. 1693 (Gen. Div.).

The court, keeping in mind the fact that the court rules were to be liberally construed, granted an order to set aside a default judgment.

Weiss v. Prentice Hall Canada Inc. (1995), 66 C.P.R. (3d) 417 (Ont. Sm. Claims Ct.).

The court applied Rule 1.02(2) when awarding damages.

Orders on Terms

1.04 When making an order under these rules, the court may impose such terms and give such directions as are just.

Forms

1.05(1) The forms prescribed by these rules shall be used where applicable and with such variations as the circumstances require.

CASE LAW

Queensway Lincoln Mercury Sales (1980) Ltd. v. 409918 Ont. Ltd. (1981), 34 O.R. (2d) 568 (H.C.J.).

The forms are guides only. Reasonable conformity to them is sufficient.

General Heading

(2) Every document in a proceeding, except a notice of garnishment and certificate of service, shall have a general heading in accordance with Form 1A.

1.06 [Repealed, O. Reg. 461/01, s. 2]

RULE 2 NON-COMPLIANCE WITH THE RULES

Effect of Non-Compliance

2.01 A failure to comply with these rules is an irregularity and does not render a proceeding or a step, document or order in a proceeding a nullity, and the court may grant all necessary amendments or other relief, on such terms as are just, to secure the just determination of the real matters in dispute.

Court May Dispense With Compliance

2.02 If necessary in the interest of justice, the court may dispense with compliance with any rule at any time.

CASE LAW

Smith v. Galin, [1956] O.W.N. 432 (C.A.).

The rule allowing the court to cure a non-compliance does not allow the court to disregard general principles of law, but does allow the court to correct technical defects.

RULE 3   TIME

Computation

3.01 If these rules or an order of the court prescribe a period of time for the taking of a step in a proceeding, the time shall be counted by excluding the first day and including the last day of the period; if the last day of the period of time falls on a holiday, the period ends on the next day that is not a holiday.

Powers of Court

3.02(1) The court may lengthen or shorten any time prescribed by these rules or an order, on such terms as are just.

CASE LAW

Dyce v. Aquarius Management Inc. (1995), 65 B.C.A.C. 316, 106 W.A.C. 316 (C.A.).

The overriding goal of the Small Claims Court procedures is to provide an affordable and quick way to resolve disputes and therefore an extension of time will be permitted by the court rules only where appropriate.

Consent

(2) A time prescribed by these rules for serving or filing a document may be lengthened or shortened by filing the consent of the parties.

[O. Reg. 461/01, s. 3]

RULE 4   PARTIES UNDER DISABILITY

Plaintiff's Litigation Guardian

4.01(1) An action by a person under disability shall be commenced or continued by a litigation guardian, subject to subrule (2).

Exception

(2) A minor may sue for any sum not exceeding $500 as if he or she were of full age.

Consent

(3) A plaintiff's litigation guardian shall, at the time of filing a claim or as soon as possible afterwards, file with the clerk a consent (Form 4A) in which the litigation guardian,
- (a) states the nature of the disability;
- (b) in the case of a minor, states the minor's birth date;
- (c) sets out his or her relationship, if any, to the person under disability;
- (d) states that he or she has no interest in the proceeding contrary to that of the person under disability;
- (e) acknowledges that he or she is aware of his or her liability to pay personally any costs awarded against him or her or against the person under disability, and
- (f) states whether he or she is represented by a lawyer or agent and, if so, gives that person's name and confirms that the person has written authority to act in the proceeding.

Defendant's Litigation Guardian

4.02(1) An action against a person under disability shall be defended by a litigation guardian.

(2) A defendant's litigation guardian shall file with the defence a consent (Form 4B) in which the litigation guardian,
- (a) states the nature of the disability;
- (b) in the case of a minor, states the minor's birth date;
- (c) sets out his or her relationship, if any, to the person under disability;
- (d) states that he or she has no interest in the proceeding contrary to that of the person under disability; and
- (e) states whether he or she is represented by a lawyer or agent and, if so, gives that person's name and confirms that the person has written authority to act in the proceeding.

(3) If it appears to the court that a defendant is a person under disability and the defendant does not have a litigation guardian the court may, after notice to the proposed litigation guardian, appoint as litigation guardian for the defendant any person who has no interest in the action contrary to that of the defendant.

Who May Be Litigation Guardian

4.03(1) Any person who is not under disability may be a plaintiff's or defendant's litigation guardian, subject to subrule (2).

(2) If the plaintiff or defendant,
- (a) is a minor, in a proceeding to which subrule 4.01(2) does not apply,
  - (i) the parent or person with lawful custody or another suitable person shall be the litigation guardian, or
  - (ii) if no such person is available and able to act, the Children's Lawyer shall be the litigation guardian;
- (b) is mentally incapable and has a guardian with authority to act as litigation guardian in the proceeding, the guardian shall be the litigation guardian;
- (c) is mentally incapable and does not have a guardian with authority to act as litigation guardian in the proceeding, but has an attorney under a power of attorney with that authority, the attorney shall be the litigation guardian;
- (d) is mentally incapable and has neither a guardian with authority to act as litigation guardian in the proceeding nor an attorney under a power of attorney with that power,
  - (i) a suitable person who has no interest contrary to that of the incapable person may be the litigation guardian, or
  - (ii) if no such person is available and able to act, the Public Guardian and Trustee shall be the litigation guardian;
- (e) is an absentee,
  - (i) the committee of his or her estate appointed under the *Absentees Act* shall be the litigation guardian,
  - (ii) if there is no such committee, a suitable person who has no interest contrary to that of the absentee may be the litigation guardian, or
  - (iii) if no such person is available and able to act, the Public Guardian and Trustee shall be the litigation guardian;
- (f) is a person in respect of whom an order was made under subsection 72(1) or (2) of the *Mental Health Act* as it read before April 3, 1995, the Public Guardian and Trustee shall be the litigation guardian.

Duties of Litigation Guardian

4.04(1) A litigation guardian shall diligently attend to the interests of the person under disability and take all steps reasonably necessary for the protection of those interests, including the commencement and conduct of a defendant's claim.

Public Guardian and Trustee, Children's Lawyer

(2) The Public Guardian and Trustee or the Children's Lawyer may act as litigation guardian without filing the consent required by subrule 4.01(3) or 4.02(2).

Power of Court

4.05 The court may remove or replace a litigation guardian at any time.

Setting Aside Judgment, etc.

4.06 If an action has been brought against a person under disability and the action has not been defended by a litigation guardian, the court may set aside the noting of default or any judgment against the person under disability on such terms as are just, and may set aside any step that has been taken to enforce the judgment.

Settlement Requires Court's Approval

4.07 No settlement of a claim made by or against a person under disability is binding on the person without the approval of the court.

Money to be Paid into Court

4.08(1) Any money payable to a person under disability under an order or a settlement shall be paid into court, unless the court orders otherwise, and shall afterwards be paid out or otherwise disposed of as ordered by the court.

(2) If money is payable to a person under disability under an order or settlement, the court may order that the money shall be paid directly to the person, and payment made under the order discharges the obligation to the extent of the amount paid.

RULE 5 PARTNERSHIPS AND SOLE PROPRIETORSHIPS

Partnerships

5.01 A proceeding by or against two or more persons as partners may be commenced using the firm name of the partnership.

Defence

5.02 If a proceeding is commenced against a partnership using the firm name, the partnership's defence shall be delivered in the firm name and no person who admits being a partner at any material time may defend the proceeding separately, except with leave of the court.

Notice to Alleged Partner

5.03(1) In a proceeding against a partnership using the firm name, a plaintiff who seeks an order that would be enforceable personally against a person as a partner may serve the person with the claim, together with a notice to alleged partner (Form 5A).

(2) A person served as provided in subrule (1) is deemed to have been a partner at the material time, unless the person defends the proceeding separately denying having been a partner at the material time.

Disclosure of Partners

5.04(1) If a proceeding is commenced by or against a partnership using the firm name, any other party may serve a notice requiring the partnership to disclose immediately in writing the names and addresses of all partners constituting the partnership at a time specified in the notice; if a partner's present address is unknown, the partnership shall disclose the partner's last known address.

(1.1) [Repealed, O. Reg. 461/01, s. 4]

(2) If a partnership fails to comply with a notice under subrule (1), its claim may be dismissed or the proceeding stayed or its defence may be struck out.

[O. Reg. 461/01, s. 4]

Enforcement of Order

5.05(1) An order against a partnership using the firm name may be enforced against the partnership's property.

(2) An order against a partnership using the firm name may also be enforced, if the order or a subsequent order so provides, against any person who was served as provided in rule 5.03 and who,
- (a) under that rule, is deemed to have been a partner at the material time;
- (b) has admitted being a partner at that time; or
- (c) has been adjudged to have been a partner at that time.

Against Person not Served as Alleged Partner

(3) If, after an order has been made against a partnership using the firm name, the party obtaining it claims to be entitled to enforce it against any

person alleged to be a partner other than a person who was served as provided in rule 5.03, the party may move before a judge for leave to do so; the judge may grant leave if the person's liability as a partner is not disputed or, if disputed, after the liability has been determined in such manner as the judge directs.

Sole Proprietorships

5.06(1) If a person carries on business in a business name other than his or her own name, a proceeding may be commenced by or against the person using the business name.

(2) Rules 5.01 to 5.05 apply, with necessary modifications, to a proceeding by or against a sole proprietor using a business name, as though the sole proprietor were a partner and the business name were the firm name of a partnership.

RULE 6   FORUM AND JURISDICTION

6.01(1) An action shall be commenced and tried,
- (a) in the territorial division,
    - (i) in which the cause of action arose, or
    - (ii) in which the defendant or, if there are several defendants, in which any one of them resides or carries on business; or
- (b) at the court's place of sitting that is nearest to the place where the defendant or, if there are several defendants, where any one of them resides or carries on business.

(2) If the court is satisfied that the balance of convenience substantially favours holding the trial of an action at another place than those described in subrule (1), the court may order that the action be tried at that other place.

CASE LAW

Livingstone v. Tomen, [2000] O.J. No. 1462 (S.C.J.).

In determining which court has the appropriate territorial jurisdiction for deciding an action, the balance of convenience is dictated by which court has the closest connection.

Pizza Pizza Ltd. v. Boyack (1995), 38 C.P.C. (3d) 306 (Ont. Gen. Div.).

When deciding the more convenient location for a trial, the onus is on the moving party to prove that the moving parties' location is a more convenient location for the trial.

Dorman Estate v. Korean Air Lines Co., [1995] O.J. No. 1805 (Div. Ct.).

The court granted appeal of a decision where the lower court decided that Ontario courts had jurisdiction based on the fact that the defendant had a business office in Toronto that conducted sales.

Ingersoll Press Automation & Machinery Inc. v. Tom Saab Industries, [1994] O.J. No. 446 (Sm. Claims Ct.).

The court ruled that if the cause of action does not arise in the jurisdiction chosen by the plaintiff, the rule is mandatory and requires the action to be filed in the jurisdiction of the defendant. The jurisdiction of the defendant can be either the defendant's place of residence or place of business.

Shaw v. Auto Caravan Corp. (1989), 15 W.D.C.P. 161 (Ont. Prov. Ct.).

A contract for delivery of a motor vehicle was entered into in Miami and loss or theft of the contents was discovered on delivery in Toronto. The action was dismissed as the whole cause of action did not arise in Toronto. The theft might have occurred at any place and time en route from Florida to Toronto.

Elguindy v. Core Laboratories Can. Ltd. (1987), 8 W.D.C.P. 216 (Ont. Div. Ct.).

A telephone call originating in Alberta induced a breach of contract in Ontario and damages were suffered by the plaintiff in Ontario. Under this rule, the court had jurisdiction where the cause of action arose — in Ontario.

W.B. Knox & Son Ltd. v. St. Amand (1986), 5 W.D.C.P. 333 (Ont. Prov. Ct. (Civ. Div.)).

Although the cause of action did not arise in North York, the plaintiff was entitled, pursuant to this rule, to bring an action in North York because one of the defendants carried on business there.

Interamerican Transport Systems Inc. v. Grand Trunk Western Railroad (1985), 51 O.R. (2d) 568 (Div. Ct.).

The court has jurisdiction to hear a claim against a foreign company which has a sales manager within the jurisdiction, whose duties included solicitation but who had no capacity to contract on behalf of the company.

Xerox Canada Inc. v. Neary (1984), 47 O.R. (2d) 776 (Prov. Ct. (Civ. Div.)).

The court does not have jurisdiction to hear a claim on a contract that was signed outside of the jurisdiction but which provided that payment under the contract would be made within the jurisdiction.

Canada Trust Mastercard v. Nowick (1981), 27 C.P.C. 183 (Ont. Sm. Claims Ct.).

The affidavit filed by the plaintiff (head office in London) failed to establish the jurisdiction of the Middlesex court over a defendant resident in Oshawa.

6.02 A cause of action shall not be divided into two or more actions for the purpose of bringing it within the court's jurisdiction.

CASE LAW

Giroux v. Security National Insurance Co., [2002] O.J. No. 2665 (S.C.J.).

If the plaintiff has split the claim into two separate actions, the most she can recover at the trial of the two actions is the monetary limit of $10,000.

Maple Lodge Farms Ltd. v. Penny Lane Fruit Market Inc., [1997] O.J. No. 4401 (Gen. Div.).

"Splitting" claims to fall within the jurisdiction of the Small Claims Court is strictly prohibited. In this case, the plaintiff was found to have deliberately split a claim into a number of actions. The amount of the claims taken together exceeded the jurisdiction of the Small Claims Court and the plaintiff's action was deemed to be within the jurisdiction of the General Division Court.

Traditional Air Systems Inc. v. Custom Gas Heating Ltd., [1995] O.J. No. 3039, 86 O.A.C. 72 (Div. Ct.).

A cause of action will not be separated into more than one cause of action if the purpose for the separation is to bring the action within the court's jurisdiction. It therefore follows that the trial judge did not have the jurisdiction to commence the trials.

Bernier v. LFD Industries Ltd. (1994), 48 A.C.W.S. (3d) 80 (B.C.S.C.).

Where the matters are distinct and can be tried separately although arising out of the same transaction of occurrence the plaintiff may bring a second action.

Sahota v. Beauchamp; Firstline Trust Co. (Third party), [1994] O.J. No. 1483 (Ont. Sm. Claims Ct.).

A plaintiff cannot bring two actions and avoid Rule 6.02, simply due to the fact that there were two defendants.

Tope v. Stratford (City) (1994), 52 A.C.W.S. (3d) 783 (Ont. Sm. Claims Ct.).

Two personal injury actions arose from the female plaintiff who had been actually injured and by a male plaintiff who brought an action pursuant to the *Family Law Act*.[1] The claims were tried together but remained separate causes of action. There was no splitting of the cause of action to avoid reaching the top monetary level of the Small Claims Court.

---

[1] R.S.O. 1990, c. F.3.

Cox v. Robert Simpson Co. (1973), 1 O.R. (2d) 333 (C.A.).

A cause of action cannot be split. Therefore, when a plaintiff accepts a sum in full satisfaction of the claim made, the plaintiff cannot later commence a new action on the same cause of action.

6.03 If, when an action is called for trial, the trial judge finds that the territorial division where he or she sits is not the proper place of trial, the action shall be tried in a place described in subclause 6.01(1)(a)(i) or clause 6.01(1)(b), unless the judge orders otherwise under subrule 6.01(2).

RULE 7   COMMENCEMENT OF PROCEEDINGS

Plaintiff's Claim

7.01(1) An action shall be commenced by filing a plaintiff's claim (Form 7A) with the clerk, together with a copy of the claim for each defendant.

Contents of Claim, Attachments

(2) The following requirements apply to the claim:
  1. **It shall contain the following information, in concise and non-technical language:**
     - (i) **The full names of the parties to the proceeding and, if relevant, the capacity in which they sue or are sued.**
     - (ii) **The nature of the claim, with reasonable certainty and detail, including the date, place and nature of the occurrences on which the claim is based.**
     - (iii) **The amount of the claim and the relief requested.**
     - (iv) **The name, address and telephone number, and fax number if any, of the lawyer or agent representing the plaintiff or, if the plaintiff is unrepresented, the plaintiff's address and telephone number, and fax number if any.**
     - (v) **The address where the plaintiff believes the defendant may be served.**
  2. **If the plaintiff's claim is based in whole or in part on a document, a copy of the document shall be attached to each copy of the claim, unless it is unavailable, in which case the claim shall state the reason why the document is not attached.**

E-Mail Address

(3) The claim may also contain the e-mail address of the lawyer or agent representing the plaintiff or, if the plaintiff is unrepresented, the e-mail address of the plaintiff.

[O. Reg. 461/01, s. 5]

7.02 [Repealed, O. Reg. 461/01, s. 6]

Issuing Claim

7.03(1) On receiving the plaintiff's claim, the clerk shall immediately issue it by dating, signing and sealing it and assigning it a court file number.

(2) The original of the claim shall remain in the court file and the copies shall be given to the plaintiff for service on the defendant.

CASE LAW

Siemon v. Kuepfer, [1973] 3 O.R. 375 (C.A.).

A claim was filed before the expiry of the limitation period but was issued by the court clerk after the expiry of the limitation period. The time of filing a claim governs for the purposes of the limitation period. (See also *Tummillo v. Prouty* (1990), 42 C.P.C. (2d) 308 (Ont. Dist. Ct.).)

RULE 8   SERVICE

Service of Particular Documents, Plaintiff's or Defendant's Claim

8.01(1) A plaintiff's claim or defendant's claim (Form 7A or 10A) shall be served personally as provided in rule 8.02 or by an alternative to personal service as provided in rule 8.03.

Time for Service of Claim

(2) A claim shall be served within six months after the date it is issued, but the court may extend the time for service, before or after the six months has elapsed.

Defence

(3) A defence shall be served by the clerk, by mail or by fax.

(3.1) [Repealed, O. Reg. 461/01, s. 7]

Notice of Default Judgment

(4) A notice of default judgment (Form 11A) shall be served by the clerk, by mail or fax, on all parties named in the claim.

(4.1) [Repealed, O. Reg. 461/01, s. 7]

Summons to Witness

(5) A summons to witness (Form 18A) shall be served personally by the party who requires the presence of the witness, or by the party's lawyer or agent; at the time of service, attendance money in accordance with the tariff shall be paid or tendered to the witness.

Notice of Garnishment

(6) A notice of garnishment (Form 20E) shall be served by the creditor,
- (a) on the debtor, by mail, personally as provided in rule 8.02 or by an alternative to personal service as provided in rule 8.03; and
- (b) on the garnishee, by mail, personally as provided in rule 8.02 or by an alternative to personal service as provided in rule 8.03.

Notice of Judgment Debtor Examination

(7) A notice of examination of a judgment debtor (Form 20H) may be served by the creditor by mail, personally as provided in rule 8.02 or by an alternative to personal service as provided in rule 8.03.

(8) The notice shall be served at least 30 days before the date fixed for the examination.

A Notice of Contempt Hearing

(9) A notice of a contempt hearing (Form 20I) shall be served by the creditor on the debtor personally as provided in rule 8.02.

CASE LAW

Avco Financial Services Canada Ltd. v. Wall, [2000] O.J. No. 194 (S.C.J.).

Rule 8 does not impose a requirement of personal service that is absolute. Actual notice is sufficient to support a finding of contempt. There must be credible and compelling evidence that proves actual notice to the debtor of the contempt hearing.

Other Documents

(10) A document not referred to in subrules (1) to (9) may be served by mail, by fax, personally as provided in rule 8.02 or by an alternative to personal service as provided in rule 8.03, unless the court orders otherwise.

(11) [Repealed, O. Reg. 461/01, s. 7]

[O. Reg. 461/01, s. 7]

Personal Service

8.02 If a document is to be served personally, the service shall be made,

Individual
(a) on an individual, other than a person under disability, by leaving a copy of the document with him or her;

Municipality
(b) on a municipal corporation, by leaving a copy of the document with the chair, mayor, warden or reeve of the municipality, with the clerk or deputy clerk of the municipality or with a lawyer for the municipality;

Corporation
(c) on any other corporation, by leaving a copy of the document with an officer, director or agent of the corporation, or with a person at any place of business of the corporation who appears to be in control or management of the place of business;

Board or Commission
(d) on a board or commission, by leaving a copy of the document with a member or officer of the board or commission;

Person Outside Ontario Carrying on Business in Ontario
(e) on a person outside Ontario who carries on business in Ontario, by leaving a copy of the document with anyone carrying on business in Ontario for the person;

Crown in Right of Canada
(f) on Her Majesty the Queen in right of Canada, in accordance with subsection 23(2) of the *Crown Liability and Proceedings Act* (Canada);

CASE LAW

Luo v. Canada (Attorney General) (March 7, 1995), Doc. Toronto T5681/1994 (Ont. Sm. Claims Ct.).

Rule 8.03(f), which allows for service upon the Crown in Right of Canada, appears to include within the jurisdiction of the Small Claims Court the capacity to hear cases pursuant to the *Crown Liability and Proceedings Act*[2] and *Proceedings Against the Crown Act*.[3]

Todd v. Canada (Solicitor General), [1993] O.J. No. 3410 (Gen. Div.).

The court considered whether or not an action could be maintained in the Small Claims Court against the Queen in Right of Canada. It was held that Small Claims Court is a branch of the Ontario Court (General Division) which,

---

[2] R.S.C. 1985, c. C-50.
[3] R.S.O. 1990, c. P.27.

according to s. 26(2) of the Federal *Interpretation Act*[4] was a "superior court", and accordingly, the Small Claims branch had the jurisdiction to hear such a matter.

Crown in Right of Ontario
(g) on Her Majesty the Queen in right of Ontario, in accordance with section 10 of the *Proceedings Against the Crown Act*;

Absentee
(h) on an absentee, by leaving a copy of the document with the absentee's committee, if one has been appointed or, if not, with the Public Guardian and Trustee;

Minor
(i) on a minor, by leaving a copy of the document with the minor and, if the minor resides with a parent or other person having his or her care or lawful custody, by leaving another copy of the document with the parent or other person;

Mentally Incapable Person
(j) on a mentally incapable person,
   (i) if there is a guardian or an attorney acting under a validated power of attorney for personal care with authority to act in the proceeding, by leaving a copy of the document with the guardian or attorney,
   (ii) if there is no guardian or attorney acting under a validated power of attorney for personal care with authority to act in the proceeding but there is an attorney under a power of attorney with authority to act in the proceeding, by leaving a copy of the document with the attorney and leaving an additional copy with the person,
   (iii) if there is neither a guardian nor an attorney with authority to act in the proceeding, by leaving a copy of the document bearing the person's name and address with the Public Guardian and Trustee and leaving an additional copy with the person;

Partnership
(k) on a partnership, by leaving a copy of the document with any one or more of the partners or with a person at the principal place of business of the partnership who appears to be in control or management of the place of business; and

Sole Proprietorship
(l) on a sole proprietorship, by leaving a copy of the document with the sole proprietor or with a person at the principal place of busi-

---

[4] R.S.C. 1985, c. I-21.

ness of the sole proprietorship who appears to be in control or management of the place of business.

<u>CASE LAW</u>

Can.-Dom. Leasing Corp. v. Corpex Ltd., [1963] 2 O.R. 497 (M.C.).

For service to be effected, the document must be brought to the notice of the recipient and the recipient must have some knowledge of its contents.

Alternatives to Personal Service

8.03(1) If a document is to be served by an alternative to personal service, service shall be made in accordance with subrule (2), (3) or (5); in the case of a plaintiff's claim or defendant's claim, service may also be made in accordance with subrule (7).

At Place of Residence

(2) If an attempt is made to effect personal service at a person's place of residence and for any reason personal service cannot be effected, the document may be served by,

    (a) leaving a copy in a sealed envelope addressed to the person at the place of residence with anyone who appears to be an adult member of the same household; and

    (b) on the same day or the following day, mailing another copy of the document to the person at the place of residence.

Corporation

(3) If the head office or principal place of business of a corporation or, in the case of an extra-provincial corporation, the attorney for service in Ontario cannot be found at the last address recorded with the Ministry of Consumer and Commercial Relations, service may be made on the corporation by mailing a copy of the document to the corporation or to the attorney for service in Ontario, as the case may be, at that address.

When Effective

(4) Service made under subrule (2) or (3) is effective on the fifth day after the document is mailed.

Acceptance of Service by Lawyer

(5) Service on a party who is represented by a lawyer may be made by leaving a copy of the document with the lawyer or an employee in the law-

yer's office, but service under this subrule is effective only if the lawyer or employee endorses on the document or a copy of it an acceptance of service and the date of the acceptance.

(6) By accepting service the lawyer is deemed to represent to the court that he or she has the client's authority to accept service.

Service of Claim by Mail to Last Known Address

(7) Service of a plaintiff's claim or defendant's claim may be made by sending a copy of it by mail, in an envelope showing the sender's return address, to the last known address of the person to be served.

(8) Service under subrule (7) is deemed to have been effected on the 20th day after the date of mailing if an affidavit of service (Form 8B),
- (a) indicates that the deponent believes the address to which the claim is sent to be the last known address of the person to be served, and states the reasons for the belief;
- (b) indicates that the claim has not been returned to the deponent; and
- (c) indicates that the deponent has no reason to believe that the person to be served did not receive the claim.

(9) The affidavit of service shall not be completed before the day referred to in subrule (8).

Substituted Service

8.04 If it is shown that it is impractical to effect prompt service of a claim personally or by an alternative to personal service, the court may allow substituted service.

CASE LAW

Babineau v. Babineau (1983), 32 C.P.C. 229 (Ont. M.C.).

If denial of substituted service would deny the plaintiff relief, the rule that such service should be allowed only where it is probable that the party being served would receive actual notice may be relaxed and an order made where it is possible that the party will be notified.

Service Outside Ontario

8.05 If the defendant is outside Ontario, the court may allow as costs of the action the costs reasonably incurred in effecting service of the claim on the defendant there.

Proof of Service

8.06(1) The following constitute proof of service of a document:
1. If the document was served by a bailiff or bailiff's officer, a certificate of service (Form 8A) endorsed on a copy of the document.
1.1 [Repealed, O. Reg. 461/01, s. 8]
2. In all other cases, an affidavit of service (Form 8B) made by the person effecting the service.

(2) [Repealed, O. Reg. 461/01, s. 8]

(3) [Repealed, O. Reg. 461/01, s. 8]

[O. Reg. 461/01, s. 8]

Service by Mail

8.07(1) If a document is to be sent by mail under these rules, it shall be sent, by regular lettermail or registered mail, to the last address of the person or of the person's lawyer or agent that is,
(a) on file with the court, if the document is to be served by the clerk;
(b) known to the sender, if the document is to be served by any other person.

When Effective

(2) Service of a document by mail is deemed to be effective on the fifth day following the date of mailing.

Exception

(3) Subrule (2) does not apply when a claim is served by mail under subrule 8.03 (7).

Service by Fax

8.08(1) Service of a document by fax is deemed to be effective,
(a) on the day of transmission, if transmission takes place before 5 p.m. on a day that is not a holiday;
(b) on the next day that is not a holiday, in any other case.

(2) A document containing 16 or more pages, including the cover page and the backsheet, may be served by fax only between 5 p.m. and 8 a.m. the following day, unless the party to be served consents in advance.

8.09 [Repealed, O. Reg. 461/01, s. 9]

Failure to Receive Document

8.10 A person who has been served or who is deemed to have been served with a document in accordance with these rules is nevertheless entitled to show, on a motion to set aside the consequences of default, on a motion for an extension of time or in support of a request for an adjournment, that the document,
- (a) did not come to the person's notice; or
- (b) came to the person's notice only at some time later than when it was served or is deemed to have been served.

[O. Reg. 461/01, s. 9]

CASE LAW

Re Milton and O.M.B. (1978), 20 O.R. (2d) 257 (H.C.J.).

Service by mail is invalid where the sender knows that the letter was not received.

RULE 9 DEFENCE

Defence

9.01(1) A defendant who wishes to dispute a plaintiff's claim shall file a defence (Form 9A), with a copy for every plaintiff (unless subrule 1.06(13) applies because the defence is filed electronically), with the clerk within 20 days of being served with the claim.

(2) On receiving the defence, the clerk shall serve it as described in subrule 8.01(3).

[O. Reg. 461/01, s. 10]

Contents of Defence, Attachments

9.02(1) The following requirements apply to the defence:
1. It shall contain the following information:
    i. The reasons why the defendant disputes the plaintiff's claim, expressed in concise non-technical language with a reasonable amount of detail.
    ii. The defendant's name, address and telephone number, and fax number if any.
    iii. If the defendant is represented by a lawyer or agent, that person's name, address and telephone number, and fax number if any.

2. If the defence is based in whole or in part on a document, a copy of the document shall be attached to each copy of the defence, unless it is unavailable, in which case the defence shall state the reason why the document is not attached.

CASE LAW

American Express Can. Inc. v. Engel (1982), 39 O.R. (2d) 600 (Div. Ct.).

A defence must contain reasons why the claim is disputed. A claim of harassment is not a defence to a claim for debt.

E-mail Address

(2) The defence may also contain the e-mail address of the lawyer or agent representing the defendant or, if the defendant is unrepresented, the e-mail address of the defendant.

[O. Reg. 461/01, s. 11]

Admission of Liability and Proposal of Terms of Payment

9.03(1) A defendant who admits liability for all or part of the plaintiff's claim but wishes to arrange terms of payment may in the defence admit liability and propose terms of payment.

Where No Dispute

(2) If the plaintiff does not dispute the proposal within the 20-day period referred to in subrule (3),
- (a) the defendant shall make payment in accordance with the proposal as if it were a court order;
- (b) in case of failure to make payment in accordance with the proposal, the clerk shall sign judgment for the unpaid balance of the undisputed amount on the filing of an affidavit by the plaintiff swearing to the default and stating the amount paid and the unpaid balance.

Dispute

(3) The plaintiff may dispute the proposal within 20 days after service of the defence by filing with the clerk and serving on the defendant a request for a hearing (Form 9B) before a referee or other person appointed by the court.

(4) The clerk shall fix a time for the hearing, allowing for a reasonable notice period after the date the request is served, and serve a notice of hearing on the parties.

Manner of Service

(4.1) The notice of hearing shall be served by mail or fax.

Order

(5) On the hearing, the referee or other person may make an order (Form 9C) as to terms of payment by the defendant.

Failure to Appear, Default Judgment

(6) If the defendant does not appear at the hearing, the clerk may sign default judgment against the defendant for the part of the claim that has been admitted and shall serve a notice of default judgment (Form 11A) on the defendant in accordance with subrule 8.01(4) immediately.

Failure to Make Payments

(7) Unless the referee or other person specifies otherwise in the order as to terms of payment, if the defendant fails to make payment in accordance with the order, the clerk shall sign judgment for the unpaid balance on the filing of an affidavit by the plaintiff swearing to the default and stating the amount paid and the unpaid balance.

[O. Reg. 461/01, s. 12]

RULE 10   DEFENDANT'S CLAIM

Defendant's Claim

10.01(1) A defendant may make a claim,
- (a) against the plaintiff;
- (b) against any other person,
  - (i) arising out of the transaction or occurrence relied upon by the plaintiff, or
  - (ii) related to the plaintiff's claim; or
- (c) against the plaintiff and against another person in accordance with clause (b).

(2) The defendant's claim shall be in Form 10A and may be issued when a defence is filed or at any time afterwards before trial or default judgment.

Copies

(3) The defendant shall provide a copy of the defendant's claim to the court.

Contents of Defendant's Claim, Attachments

(4) The following requirements apply to the defendant's claim:
   1. It shall contain the following information:
      i. The names of the parties to the plaintiff's claim and to the defendant's claim and, if relevant, the capacity in which they sue or are sued.
      ii. The nature of the claim, expressed in concise non-technical language with a reasonable amount of detail, including the date, place and nature of the occurrences on which the claim is based.
      iii. The amount of the claim and the relief requested.
      iv. The defendant's name, address and telephone number, and fax number if any.
      v. If the defendant is represented by a lawyer or agent, that person's name, address and telephone number, and fax number if any.
      vi. The address where the defendant believes each person against whom the claim is made may be served.
   2. If the defendant's claim is based in whole or in part on a document, a copy of the document shall be attached to each copy of the claim, unless it is unavailable, in which case the claim shall state the reason why the document is not attached.

E-mail Address

(5) The defendant's claim may also contain the e-mail address of the lawyer or agent representing the defendant or, if the defendant is unrepresented, the e-mail address of the defendant.

Issuance

(6) On receiving the defendant's claim, the clerk shall immediately issue it by dating, signing and sealing it, shall assign it the same court file number as the plaintiff's claim and shall place the original in the court file.

(7) [Repealed, O. Reg. 461/01, s. 13]

[O. Reg. 461/01, s. 13]

Service

10.02 A defendant's claim shall be served by the defendant on every person against whom it is made, in accordance with subrules 8.01(1) and (2).

Defence to Defendant's Claim

10.03(1) A party who wishes to dispute the defendant's claim may, within 20 days after service, file a defence (Form 9A) with the clerk, together with a copy for each of the other parties or persons against whom the defendant's or plaintiff's claim is made (unless subrule 1.06(13) applies because the defence is filed electronically).

(2) On receiving the defence to a defendant's claim, the clerk shall retain the original in the court file and shall serve a copy on each party in accordance with subrule 8.01(3).

[O. Reg. 461/01, s. 14]

Defendant's Claim to be Tried with Main Action

10.04(1) A defendant's claim shall be tried and disposed of at the trial of the action, unless the court orders otherwise.

Exception

(2) If it appears that a defendant's claim may unduly complicate or delay the trial of the action or cause undue prejudice to a party, the court may order separate trials or direct that the defendant's claim proceed as a separate action.

Rights of Third Party

(3) If the defendant alleges, in a defendant's claim, that a third party is liable to the defendant for all or part of the plaintiff's claim in the action, the third party may at the trial contest the defendant's liability to the plaintiff.

Application of Rules to Defendant's Claim

10.05(1) These rules apply, with necessary modifications, to a defendant's claim as if it were a plaintiff's claim, and to a defence to a defendant's claim as if it were a defence to a plaintiff's claim.

Exception

(2) However, when a person against whom a defendant's claim is made is noted in default, judgment against that person may be obtained only in accordance with rule 11.03.

RULE 11   DEFAULT PROCEEDINGS

Noting Defendant in Default

11.01(1) If a defendant fails to file a defence with the clerk within the prescribed time, the clerk may, when proof is filed that the claim was served within the territorial division, note the defendant in default.

Service Outside Territorial Division

(2) If all the defendants have been served outside the court's territorial division, the clerk shall not note any defendant in default until it is proved by an affidavit submitted to the clerk, or by evidence presented before the judge, that the action was properly brought in that territorial division.

Default Judgment, Plaintiff's Claim

11.02(1) If a defendant has been noted in default, the clerk may enter judgment in respect of a claim against the defendant for a debt or liquidated demand in money, including interest if claimed.

CASE LAW

Eades v. Kootnikoff (1995), 13 B.C.L.R. (3d) 182 (S.C.).

The court held that whether a claim can be considered a "liquidated demand" is dependent upon whether the amount to which the plaintiff is entitled is specifically named in the contract itself, deduced by further calculation or fixed by a scale of charges agreed upon in or implied by the contract. Some claims on accounts for legal services may be liquidated demands and others may be unliquidated. Unless the pleadings claim that there was an agreement to the specific amount the lawyer was to be paid or a particular method of calculation of the fee, a claim for legal services is not a liquidated demand.

Holden Day Wilson v. Ashton (1993), 14 O.R. (3d) 306 (Div. Ct.).

A solicitor's account was not a "liquidated demand in money" for which default judgment could be signed by a clerk of the Small Claims Court.

American Express Can. Inc. v. Engel (1982), 39 O.R. (2d) 600 (Div. Ct.).

Where a defence discloses no reasons for the dispute, default judgment may issue.

Partial Defence

(2) If a defence is filed in respect of part only of a claim to which subrule (1) applies, the clerk may note the party against whom the claim was made in default and enter default judgment in respect of the part for which no defence was filed.

(3) Entry of judgment under this rule does not affect the plaintiff's right to proceed on the remainder of the claim or against any other defendant for all or part of the claim.

Notice of Default Judgment

(4) A notice of default judgment (Form 11A) shall be served in accordance with subrule 8.01(4).

Default Judgment, Defendant's Claim

11.03 If a party against whom a defendant's claim is made has been noted in default, judgment may be obtained against the party only at trial or on motion.

Trial when Defendant Noted in Default

11.04(1) If a defendant has been noted in default, the plaintiff shall proceed to trial in respect of any claim other than one referred to in subrule 11.02(1), and the clerk shall, after noting the defendant in default, fix a trial date and send a notice of trial (Form 16A) to the plaintiff and any defendant who has filed a defence.

(2) At the trial, the plaintiff is not required to prove liability against a defendant noted in default, but is required to prove the amount of the claim.

Consequences of Noting in Default

11.05(1) A defendant who has been noted in default shall not file a defence or take any other step in the proceeding, except bringing a motion under subrule 11.06(1), without leave of the court or the plaintiff's consent.

(2) Any step in the proceeding may be taken without the consent of a defendant who has been noted in default; the defendant is not entitled to

notice of any step in the proceeding and need not be served with any other document.

(3) Subrule (2) prevails over every other provision of these rules except rule 12.01 (amendment of claim or defence).

Setting Aside Noting of Default or Entry of Default Judgment

11.06(1) On the motion of a party in default, the court may set aside the noting of default or entry of default judgment against the party on such terms as are just.

(2) If the consent of the parties is filed, the clerk may set aside the noting of default or the entry of a default judgment.

[O. Reg. 461/01. s. 15]

CASE LAW

Canadian Shareholders Assn. v. Osiel, [2001] O.J. No. 3662 (S.C.J.).

A motion to set aside noting in default was granted. The plaintiff brought the motion within one month of default judgment being granted.

Adelaide Capital Corp. v. Stinziani, [2001] O.J. No. 1465 (S.C.J.).

A motion to set aside a default judgment order brought approximately five years after judgment was given was dismissed in the absence of evidence, suggesting a breach of the principles of natural justice.

Mount Royal Painting & Decorating Inc. v. Central Interiors Inc., [1995] O.J. No. 4031 (Gen. Div.).

A motion to set aside a judgment characterized as a "default judgment" was granted where the court found that the defendant should not be denied relief because the defendant's request for an adjournment of the trial was denied. Justice and good conscience required that the defendant be given his day in court in the most expeditious and least expensive manner possible.

James Sturino Realty Ltd. v. Andrew Michaels Group Ltd. (1988), 64 O.R. (2d) 410 (Div. Ct.).

On a motion to set aside default judgment, the position of parties should not be jeopardized by the conduct of their solicitors. However, the timing of the motion, the reason for default, and the merits of the defence are all factors to be considered by the court in exercising its discretion.

Watson v. Crystal Mountain Resources Ltd. (1988), 9 A.C.W.S. (3d) 238 (B.C.C.A.).

The setting aside of default judgment and the imposition of terms are matters within the judge's discretion and will not be interfered with by the appeal court so long as there is material capable of supporting the order.

Nagle v. Rosman (1986), 6 W.D.C.P. 58 (Ont. Prov. Ct. (Civ. Div.)).

The defendant's motion to set aside a default judgment was dismissed because the unavailability of a key witness would cause prejudice to the plaintiff.

RULE 12   AMENDMENT

Right to Amend

12.01(1) A plaintiff's or defendant's claim and a defence to a plaintiff's or defendant's claim may be amended by filing with the clerk a copy that is marked "Amended", in which any additions are underlined and any other changes are identified.

CASE LAW

Decoration J.M. Laflamme Inc. v. Arra Chemicals Inc. (1993), 44 A.C.W.S. (3d) 226 (Ont. Div. Ct.).

An amendment to the defence must be granted unless there is prejudice to the plaintiff which cannot be compensated for in costs. Here, the plaintiff was capable of monetary compensation and the amendment ought to have been duly granted.

Turgeon v. Border Supply (EMO) Ltd. (1977), 16 O.R. (2d) 43 (Div. Ct.).

When an action is brought in the name of a partnership and the partnership is dissolved prior to the commencement of the action, the plaintiff has no cause of action and an order cannot be made adding an assignee as a plaintiff at the trial of the action.

W.J. Realty Management Ltd. v. Price (1973), 1 O.R. (2d) 501 (C.A.).

When the original plaintiff does not have a cause of action, the proper person to bring the action cannot be added or substituted for him.

Service

(2) The amended document shall be served by the party making the amendment on all parties, including any parties in default, in accordance with subrule 8.01(10).

Time

(3) Filing and service of the amended document shall take place at least 30 days before the trial, unless the court, on motion, allows a shorter notice period.

Service on Added Party

(4) A person added as a party shall be served with the claim as amended, except that if the person is added as a party at trial, the court may dispense with service of the claim.

Striking Out or Amending Claim or Defence

12.02(1) The court may strike out or amend a claim or defence or anything in a claim or defence on the ground that it,

    (a) discloses no reasonable cause of action or defence, as the case may be;
    (b) is scandalous, frivolous or vexatious;
    (c) may prejudice, embarrass or delay the fair trial of the action; or
    (d) is otherwise an abuse of the court's process.

(2) The court may order the action to be stayed or dismissed or judgment to be entered accordingly, or may impose such terms as are just.

RULE 13 PRE-TRIAL CONFERENCES

Request For Pre-Trial Conference

13.01(1) A party may request a pre-trial conference by filing a request for pre-trial conference (Form 13A) with the clerk.

(2) The court may, before or at the trial, in response to a request for pre-trial conference or on the court's own initiative, direct that a pre-trial conference be held before a judge or another person designated by the court.

(3) The clerk shall fix a time and place for the pre-trial conference and serve a notice of pre-trial conference on the parties.

Failure to Attend

(4) The court may impose appropriate sanctions, by way of costs or otherwise, for the failure of a party who has received a notice of pre-trial conference to attend the pre-trial conference.

Inadequate Preparation

(5) If a person who attends a pre-trial conference is, in the opinion of the judge or designated person conducting the conference, so inadequately prepared as to frustrate the purposes of the conference, the court may award costs against that person.

Limit on Costs

(6) Costs awarded under subrule (4) or (5) shall not exceed $50 unless there are special circumstances.

Notice of Trial

(7) At or after a pre-trial conference, the clerk shall provide the parties with a notice stating that the parties must request a trial date if the action is not disposed of within 30 days after the pre-trial conference, and pay the fee required for setting the action down for trial.

Purposes of Pre-Trial Conference

13.02(1) The purposes of a pre-trial conference are,
- (a) to resolve or narrow the issues in the action;
- (b) to expedite the disposition of the action;
- (c) to facilitate settlement of the action;
- (d) to assist the parties in effective preparation for trial; and
- (e) to provide full disclosure between the parties of the relevant facts and evidence.

(2) At the pre-trial conference, the parties or their representatives shall openly and frankly discuss the issues involved in the action.

Disclosure Restricted

(3) Except as otherwise provided or with the consent of the parties, the matters discussed at the pre-trial conference shall not be disclosed.

Recommendations to Parties

13.03(1) The judge or designated person conducting the pre-trial conference may make recommendations to the parties on any matter relating to the conduct of the action, in order to fulfil the purposes of a pre-trial conference, including recommendations as to,

(a) the formulation and simplification of issues in the action;
(b) the elimination of claims or defences that appear to be unsupported; and
(c) the admission of facts or documents without further proof.

Orders at Pre-Trial Conference

(2) A judge conducting a pre-trial conference may make any order relating to the conduct of the action that the court could make.

(3) Without limiting the generality of subrule (2), the judge may make,
(a) an order for the joinder of parties;
(b) an order amending or striking out a claim or defence under rule 12;
(c) an order referring a matter to a referee under rule 21; and
(d) an order for costs under subrule 13.01(4) or (5).

(4) If the pre-trial conference is conducted by a designated person, a judge may, on that person's recommendation, make any order that could be made under subrule (2).

Memorandum

(5) At the end of the pre-trial conference, the judge or designated person may prepare a memorandum summarizing,
(a) the issues remaining in dispute;
(b) the matters agreed on by the parties;
(c) any evidentiary matters that the judge or designated person considers relevant; and
(d) information relating to the scheduling of the remaining steps in the proceeding.

(6) The memorandum shall be filed with the clerk, and the clerk shall give the trial judge a copy.

Judge Not To Preside At Trial

13.04 A judge who conducts a pre-trial conference in an action shall not preside at the trial of the action unless the parties consent in writing.

CASE LAW

Newlove Estate v. Petrie (June 29, 1995), Doc. Toronto 39122/89 (Ont. Gen. Div.).

The pre-trial judge may schedule or arrange preliminary issues (such as statutory bars or limitation periods) at the outset, so that the litigants know exactly where they stand before they commit themselves to the expense and risk of trial.

Shannon v. Shannon (1995), 6 W.D.C.P. (2d) 534 (Ont. Gen. Div.).

A pre-trial judge is authorized only to resolve or narrow the issues or to settle the procedure at trial. Likewise, a pre-trial judge is restricted to addressing procedural matters in the interest of expediting the trial process. The authority cannot be expanded to include substantive matters which may affect the parties' rights.

Sona Computer Inc. v. Carnegie (March 7, 1995), Doc. Ottawa 596/94 (Ont. Gen. Div.).

Where the defendant did not comply with the payment order of the pre-trial judge, the trial judge made no error in law in awarding judgment on the amount recommended by the pre-trial judge.

Charlebois v. Leadbeater (1993), 4 W.D.C.P. (2d) 195 (Ont. Gen. Div.).

There is nothing to prevent a pre-trial judge from setting out for unrepresented litigants a schedule of time limits within which they must begin or complete certain steps or deliver certain documents.

RULE 14   OFFER TO SETTLE

14.01 A party may serve on any other party an offer to settle a claim on the terms specified in the offer.

Time For Making Offer

14.02 An offer to settle may be made at any time, but if it is made less than seven days before the hearing commences, the costs consequences referred to in rule 14.07 do not apply.

Withdrawal

14.03(1) An offer to settle may be withdrawn at any time before it is accepted, by serving notice of its withdrawal on the party to whom it was made.

Expiry When Court Disposes of Claim

(2) An offer may not be accepted after the court disposes of the claim in respect of which the offer is made.

[O. Reg. 461/01, s. 16]

No Disclosure of Offer to Trial Judge

14.04 If an offer to settle is not accepted, no communication about it shall be made to the trial judge until all questions of liability and the relief to be granted, other than costs, have been determined.

Acceptance

14.05(1) An offer to settle may be accepted by serving an acceptance of the offer on the party who made it, at any time before it is withdrawn or the court disposes of the claim in respect of which it is made.

Payment Into Court As Condition

(2) An offer by a plaintiff to settle a claim in return for the payment of money by a defendant may include a term that the defendant pay the money into court; in that case, the defendant may accept the offer only by paying the money into court and notifying the plaintiff of the payment.

(3) If a defendant offers to pay money to a plaintiff in settlement of a claim, the plaintiff may accept the offer with the condition that the defendant pay the money into court; if the offer is so accepted and the defendant fails to pay the money into court, the plaintiff may proceed as provided in rule 14.06.

Costs

(4) If an accepted offer to settle does not deal with costs, the plaintiff is entitled,

- (a) in the case of an offer made by the defendant, to the plaintiff's disbursements assessed to the date the plaintiff was served with the offer;
- (b) in the case of an offer made by the plaintiff, to the plaintiff's disbursements assessed to the date that the notice of acceptance was served.

Failure to Comply With Accepted Offer

14.06 If a party to an accepted offer to settle fails to comply with the terms of the offer, the other party may,

- (a) make a motion to the court for judgment in the terms of the accepted offer; or
- (b) continue the proceeding as if there had been no offer to settle.

Costs Consequences of Failure to Accept

14.07(1) When a plaintiff makes an offer to settle that is not accepted by the defendant, the court may award the plaintiff an amount not exceeding twice the costs of the action, if the following conditions are met:
 1. The plaintiff obtains a judgment as favourable as or more favourable than the terms of the offer.
 2. The offer was made at least seven days before the trial.
 3. The offer was not withdrawn and did not expire before the trial.

(2) When a defendant makes an offer to settle that is not accepted by the plaintiff, the court may award the defendant an amount not exceeding twice the costs awardable to a successful party, from the date the offer was served, if the following conditions are met:
 1. The plaintiff obtains a judgment as favourable as or less favourable than the terms of the offer.
 2. The offer was made at least seven days before the trial.
 3. The offer was not withdrawn and did not expire before the trial.

(3) If an amount is awarded under subrule (1) or (2) to an unrepresented party, the court may also award the party an amount not exceeding $300 as compensation for inconvenience and expense.

CASE LAW

Baron v. Glowe, [1999] O.J. No. 4192 (S.C.J.).

This is an award of costs made in favour of a successful plaintiff who had made an offer to settle for more than the judgment awarded.

Diefenbacher v. Young (1995), 22 O.R. (3d) 641 (C.A.).

A plaintiff's decreasing offer to settle, and a defendant's increasing offer to settle are considered to be withdrawals of earlier offers when the earlier offers are not mentioned.

Parente v. Van Holland (1988), 24 C.P.C. (2d) 233 (Ont. Dist. Ct.).

Service of an offer to settle by telecopier or facsimile machine was validated as proper service under Rule 16.08 of the *Rules of Practice*. The court recommended that such service be followed by a letter of confirmation.

Roberts v. Dresser Industries Can. Ltd. (1988), 9 A.C.W.S. (3d) 290 (Ont. Dist. Ct.).

A party is entitled to solicitor and client costs under Rule 49.10(1) of the *Rules of Practice* even when the amount by which the order exceeds the offer to settle is nominal.

Niagara Structural Steel (St. Catharines) Ltd. v. W.D. Laflamme Ltd. (1987), 58 O.R. (2d) 773 (C.A.).

Rule 49.10 of the *Rules of Practice*, which is similar to Rule 15.07, does not apply to cases under appeal. Departures from the normal cost consequences should be made only where required by the interests of justice.

King v. Royal Ins. Co. (1987), 10 W.D.C.P. 126 (Ont. Prov. Ct.).

Although the defendant's offer to settle was not accepted and the plaintiff's action was dismissed at trial, the fact that the plaintiff attempted to negotiate at the pre-trial mitigated against the court awarding double costs to the defendant.

Brockman v. Sinclair (1979), 26 O.R. (2d) 276 (Dist. Ct.), affd (1980), 31 O.R. (2d) 436 (Div. Ct.).

The cost provisions of the *Small Claims Court Act*[5] are mandatory and are determined by the amounts awarded at trial.

RULE 15   MOTIONS

Notice of Motion

15.01(1) Unless the court orders otherwise, a motion shall be commenced by the filing of a notice of motion (Form 15A) and an affidavit (Form 15B).

(2) A copy of the notice of motion and the affidavit shall be served at least seven days before the hearing date on every party who has filed a claim or defence.

CASE LAW

Adekunte v. 1211531 Ontario Ltd., [2002] O.J. No. 509 (S.C.J.).

Cross-examination on affidavits filed on motion in the Small Claims Court are not allowed.

Costs

15.02(1) No costs are recoverable in respect of a motion, except that if the court is satisfied that a motion should not have been brought or opposed, or that the motion was necessary because of a party's default, the court may fix the costs of the motion and order that they be paid immediately.

---

[5] R.S.O. 1970, c. 439, s. 83 (then).

(2) The costs of a motion fixed by the court under subrule (1) shall not exceed $50 unless there are special circumstances.

RULE 16   NOTICE OF TRIAL

16.01(1) If a defence has been filed, the clerk shall fix a date for trial and send a notice of trial (Form 16A) on each party who has filed a claim or defence.

Manner of Service

(1.1) The notice of trial shall be served by mail or fax.

(2) If a pre-trial conference is to be conducted under Rule 13, sub-rule 13.01(7) applies instead of subrule (1) of this rule.

[O. Reg. 461/01, s. 17]

RULE 17   TRIAL

Failure to Attend

17.01(1) If an action is called for trial and all the parties fail to attend, the trial judge may strike the action off the trial list.

(2) If an action is called for trial and a party fails to attend, the trial judge may,
- (a) proceed with the trial in the party's absence;
- (b) if the plaintiff attends and the defendant fails to do so, strike out the defence and dismiss the defendant's claim, if any, and allow the plaintiff to prove the plaintiff's claim, subject to subrule (3);
- (c) if the defendant attends and the plaintiff fails to do so, dismiss the action and allow the defendant to prove the defendant's claim, if any; or
- (d) make such other order as is just.

(3) In the case described in clause (2)(b), if an issue as to the proper place of trial under subrule 6.01(1) is raised in the defence, the trial judge shall consider it and make a finding.

Setting Aside or Variation of Judgment

(4) The court may set aside or vary, on such terms as are just, a judgment obtained against a party who failed to attend at the trial.

CASE LAW

Mount Royal Painting & Decorating Inc. v. Central Interiors Inc., [1995] O.J. No. 4031 (Gen. Div.).

Where neither party appears at trial, the defendant should not be denied the relief of an adjournment when it is requested by its representative.

Campbell v. Maritime Engine Specialist Ltd. (October 11, 1995), Doc. AD-0607 (P.E.I.C.A.).

The informality of Small Claims Court proceedings extend to the parties and not to the trial judge. Accordingly, a plaintiff who is surprised at trial should so advise the judge and seek an adjournment.

York v. TV Guide Inc. (1984), 5 O.A.C. 330 (Div. Ct.).

Where the defendant was refused an adjournment and was not prepared to proceed, it was nevertheless an error of law to grant judgment to the plaintiff without calling on the plaintiff to prove his claim.

Re Lachowski and Federated Mutual Ins. Co. (1980), 29 O.R. (2d) 273 (Div. Ct.).

Costs which may be awarded as a condition of adjournment are discussed.

MacInnes v. Leaman (1976), 8 N.R. 297 (S.C.C.).

A request for an adjournment was dismissed because it would be considered to be an abuse of process when the plaintiff had changed solicitors twice after the case had been entered for trial.

Adjournment

17.02 The court may postpone or adjourn a trial on such terms as are just, including the payment by one party to another of an amount as compensation for inconvenience and expense.

Inspection

17.03 The trial judge may, in the presence of the parties or their representatives, inspect any real or personal property concerning which a question arises in the action.

CASE LAW

Swadron v. North York (1985), 8 O.A.C. 204 (Div. Ct.).

A trial judge may use an inspection to better understand the evidence presented in the court, but may not use her own observations as evidence upon which she makes findings of fact.

Motion for New Trial

17.04(1) Within 30 days after the trial, a party may make a motion to the court for a new trial.

CASE LAW

Orion Group R.E. Services Ltd. v. D'Souza, [2002] O.J. No. 1107 (S.C.J.).

A motion for a new trial will not be successful if an appeal has already been brought to the Divisional Court and been dismissed.

Shoppers Mortgage & Loan Corp. v. Health First Wellington Square Ltd. (1995), 38 C.P.C. (3d) 8 (Ont. C.A.).

The trial judge made numerous adversarial interventions during examination-in-chief and cross-examination and refused to hear evidence on a number of issues. The test for bias is whether the image of impartiality is destroyed, and not whether there was prejudice to the defendant's case. The absence of the image of impartiality results in a loss of jurisdiction.

George v. Wagenhoffer (1995), 129 Sask. R. 214 (Q.B.).

A new trial was ordered where the trial judge descended into the arena by becoming counsel to the plaintiff and bringing out facts material to the claim.

Sears Canada Inc. v. Scott (1994), 51 A.C.W.S. (3d) 1232 (Ont. Sm. Claims Ct.).

Jurisdiction to order a new trial exists only where there has not been an adjudication on the merits. Otherwise, an appeal should be sought pursuant to s. 31 of the *Courts of Justice Act*.[6]

DiMenna v. Colborne Auctions (1993), 4 W.D.C.P. (2d) 137 (Ont. Sm. Claims Ct.).

The purpose of Rule 18.04 is to cure mishaps such as the inadvertent non-appearance of a party. It would be inappropriate for a part-time deputy judge to use it to pass judgment on the conduct of another part-time deputy judge or a judge of the General Division sitting in Small Claims Court.

MacDonald v. Porter (1993), 20 C.P.C. (3d) 355 (N.S.S.C.).

---

[6] R.S.O. 1990, c. C.43.

Where a defence is filed, the judge must hear from the defendant before deciding in favour of the plaintiff.

St. Mary's Credit Union Ltd. v. General Doors Inc. (1990), 42 C.P.C. (2d) 115 (Sask. Q.B.).

There was no proper trial of the issues where oral evidence was not given under oath and there was no opportunity for cross-examination.

Bird v. Kehrig (1990), 43 C.P.C. (2d) 97 (Sask. Q.B.).

The court lost jurisdiction and the first summons was rendered a nullity where only the defendant appeared at trial and the court failed to give judgment, grant an adjournment, or dismiss the claim.

Wright v. Bell Canada (1988), 13 W.D.C.P. 228 (Ont. Div. Ct.).

The issue on a second trial was set aside as *res judicata* where the facts alleged were known at the time of the first action and a remedy could have been sought at that time.

Saldanha v. Eastville Hldgs. Ltd. (1985), 2 W.D.C.P. 223 (Ont. Prov. Ct.).

Failure to permit an amendment of a claim at trial is a question of law. Questions of law are the proper subject matter of an appeal, not the granting of a new trial. Grounds for granting new trials are discussed.

Svajlenko v. Appco Paving Ltd. (1985), 3 W.D.C.P. 34 (Ont. Prov. Ct. (Civ. Div.)).

A motion for a new trial under this section is proper where there exists a total failure to have a trial on the merits. Failure of a litigant to correctly anticipate evidence that will be called at the trial is not normally a satisfactory ground for a motion for a new trial.

Field v. Menuck (1985), 2 W.D.C.P. 219 (Ont. Prov. Ct. (Civ. Div.)).

The *Courts of Justice Act, 1984*, reserves discretion to the court to set its own procedures for discontinuance or withdrawal.

394705 Ont. Ltd. v. Moerenhout (1983), 41 O.R. (2d) 637 (Co. Ct.).

An application for a new trial should be made to the original trial judge for a Small Claims Court action of $500 or less.

Order for New Trial or Entry of New Judgment

(2) On the hearing of the motion, the court may,
    (a) if the party demonstrates that a condition referred to in subrule (3) is satisfied,
        (i) grant a new trial, or

(ii) pronounce the judgment that ought to have been given at trial and order judgment to be entered accordingly; or

(b) dismiss the motion.

(3) The conditions referred to in clause (2)(a) are:

1. There was a purely arithmetical error in the determination of the amount of damages.
2. The party was, for a valid reason, unable to attend the first trial.
3. There is relevant evidence that could not reasonably have been expected to be available to the party at the time of the first trial.

RULE 18 EVIDENCE AT TRIAL

Affidavit

18.01 At the trial of an undefended action, the plaintiff's case may be proved by affidavit, unless the trial judge orders otherwise.

Written Statements and Documents

18.02(1) A written statement or document described in subrule (2) that has been served on all parties at least 14 days before the trial date shall be received in evidence, unless the trial judge orders otherwise.

(2) Subrule (1) applies to the following written statements and documents:

1. The signed written statement of any witness, including the written report of an expert, to the extent that the statement relates to facts and opinions to which the witness would be permitted to testify in person.
2. Any other document, including but not limited to a hospital record or medical report made in the course of care and treatment, a financial record, a bill, documentary evidence of loss of income or property damage, and a repair estimate.

Name, Telephone Number and Address of Witness or Author

(3) A party who serves on another party a written statement or document described in subrule (2) shall append to or include in the statement or document the name, telephone number and address for service of the witness or author.

(4) A party who has been served with a written statement or document described in subrule (2) and wishes to cross-examine the witness or author may summon him or her as a witness under subrule 18.03(1).

Where Witness or Author is Summoned

(5) A party who serves a summons to witness on a witness or author referred to in subrule (3) shall, at the time the summons is served, notify all other parties of the summons.

CASE LAW

Trento Motors v. McKinney (1992), 39 M.V.R. (2d) 142, 54 O.A.C. 190 (Div. Ct.).

If a document sought to be admitted under this rule is subject to another statute, that statute must be complied with before the document can be admitted.

Minto Management Ltd. v. Solomonescu (1986), 5 W.D.C.P. 262 (Ont. Prov. Ct. (Civ. Div.)).

The defendant was served with a written statement. He chose not to cross-examine the author of the statement but did question his own witness about the content of the statement. This line of questioning was held to be proper.

O'Connell v. Custom Kitchen & Vanity (1986), 17 O.A.C. 157 (Div. Ct.).

The trial judge has a discretion to admit a document that has not been so served in accordance with Rule 19.02. The judge retains a discretion to allow hearsay under s. 27 of the *Courts of Justice Act*.

Howard v. Canadian National Express (1980), 23 C.P.C. 77 (Ont. Sm. Claims Ct.).

In light of s. 96(a) of the *Small Claims Court Act* (now s. 27 of the *Courts of Justice Act*) and the expense of calling the writers, the court admitted hearsay evidence that had not been produced to opposing counsel.

Summons to Witness

18.03(1) A party who requires the attendance of a person in Ontario as a witness at a trial may serve the person with a summons to witness (Form 18A) requiring him or her to attend the trial at the time and place stated in the summons.

(2) The summons may also require the witness to produce at the trial the documents or other things in his or her possession, control or power relating to the matters in question in the action that are specified in the summons.

(3) A summons to witness shall be served in accordance with subrule 8.01(5) and, at the same time, attendance money shall be paid or tendered to the witness in accordance with the tariff.

(4) Service of a summons to witness and the payment or tender of attendance money may be proved by affidavit.

(5) A summons to witness continues to have effect until the attendance of the witness is no longer required.

Failure to Attend or Remain in Attendance

(6) If a witness whose evidence is material to the conduct of an action fails to attend at the trial or to remain in attendance in accordance with the requirements of a summons to witness served on him or her, the trial judge may, by warrant (Form 18B) directed to all police officers in Ontario, cause the witness to be apprehended anywhere within Ontario and promptly brought before the court.

(7) On being apprehended, the witness may be detained in custody until his or her presence is no longer required or released on such terms as are just, and may be ordered to pay the costs arising out of the failure to attend or remain in attendance.

Abuse of Power to Summon Witness

(8) If satisfied that a party has abused the power to summon a witness under this rule, the court may order that the party pay directly to the witness an amount as compensation for inconvenience and expense.

RULE 19   COSTS

Disbursements

19.01(1) A successful party is entitled to have the party's disbursements, including any costs of effecting service, paid by the unsuccessful party, unless the court orders otherwise.

(2) The clerk shall assess the disbursements in accordance with the regulations made under the *Administration of Justice Act* and in accordance with subrule (3); the assessment is subject to review by the court.

(3) The amount of disbursements assessed for effecting service shall not exceed $20 for each person served.

CASE LAW

Tomarelli v. Co-Operators, [2002] O.J. No. 946 (S.C.J.).

In the appropriate case, a successful party may be entitled to the actual cost of retaining an expert even though the Small Claims Tariff allows for the payment of only $15 for expert fees.

Caringi v. Porco (1989), 17 W.D.C.P. 21 (Ont. Prov. Ct.).

Where there is no tariff to the Provincial Court (Civil Division) Rules, analogy to the tariff under the Provincial Court (Family Division) Rules is allowed. Here, $150 was awarded for preparation of an expert's report and $300 was awarded for the expert's testimony.

Miller v. York Downs Craft & Garden Centre Ltd. (1987), 17 C.P.C. (2d) 142 (Ont. Prov. Ct. (Civ. Div.)).

Reasonable disbursements are discussed.

Limit

19.02 Any power under this Rule to award costs is subject to section 29 of the *Courts of Justice Act*.

Preparation and Filing

19.03 The court may allow a successful party an amount not exceeding $50 for preparation and filing of pleadings.

Counsel Fee

19.04 If the amount claimed by a successful party exceeds $500, exclusive of interest and costs, and the party is represented by a lawyer or student-at-law, the court may allow the party as a counsel fee at trial,
  (a) in the case of a lawyer, an amount not exceeding $300;
  (b) in the case of a student-at-law, an amount not exceeding $150.

CASE LAW

Krackovitch v. Scherer Leasing Inc., [2001] O.J. No. 3349 (S.C.J.).

Costs were denied to the plaintiff who brought action in the Superior Court of Justice but recovered an amount within the monetary jurisdiction of the Small Claims Court.

Catalanotto v. Nina D'Aversa Bakery Ltd., [2001] O.J. No. 4450 (S.C.J.).

A judgment received by the plaintiff in an action brought in the Ontario Superior Court of Justice was within the jurisdiction of the Small Claims Court. The plaintiff ordered to pay the defendant's costs on a party and party basis given the result achieved at trial and the plaintiff's unreasonable failure to make or accept an offer to settle.

Fanaken v. Bell, Temple (1985), 49 C.P.C. 212 (Ont. Assess. Ct.).

Where a law firm defends itself through the use of an employee or partner, no counsel fee should be allowed on assessment of costs.

Shibley v. Harris, [1995] B.C.J. No. 2069 (S.C.).

Where the plaintiff rejected an offer to settle, the plaintiff received his disbursements only up to the date of the offer, after which the defendant was entitled to costs and disbursements.

Weiss v. Prentice Hall Canada Inc. (1995), 7 W.D.C.P. (2d) 99 (Ont. Sm. Claims Ct.).

The $300 maximum costs in s. 20.03 of the *Small Claims Court Rules* is inconsistent with the judicial discretion in s. 29 of the *Courts of Justice Act* to award up to 15% of the amount claimed. Any conflict must be resolved in favour of the Act.

San Francisco Pizza Ltd. v. Granata, [1995] O.J. No. 1408 (Gen. Div.).

The court refused to award costs against a solicitor personally where the conduct complained of was not outrageous and he did not act outside his client's authority.

Yee v. Tight Spot Rentals Ltd. (1995), 11 B.C.L.R. (3d) 291 (S.C.).

Although liability was obvious, it was denied by the defendants, who filed a jury notice. The plaintiff was awarded $1,000 for non-pecuniary damages and the defendants made an application to have costs limited to those available in the Provincial Court. The application was denied as the defendant's jury notice prevented transfer of the matter to the Provincial Court.

Serodio v. White, [1995] O.J. No. 464 (Sm. Claims Ct.).

Section 129 of the *Courts of Justice Act* allows judges sitting in the Small Claims Court to award costs personally against counsel or agents, provided that they have first had the opportunity to make representations on that point.

Garson v. Braithwaite, [1994] O.J. No. 1662 (Gen. Div.).

In accordance with s. 131(1) of the *Courts of Justice Act*, a party is entitled to costs only in connection with the services provided by an agent who is a lawyer, a student-at-law, or a law clerk who is under the supervision of a lawyer.

Purcell v. Taylor (1994), 120 D.L.R. (4th) 161 (Ont. Gen. Div.).

The plaintiff had offered to settle the case for an amount that was within the jurisdiction of the Small Claims Court. The court held that the plaintiff should have transferred the case to the Small Claims Court when it became obvious that the damages were "very modest".

Lamont v. Nieuwenhuis, [1988] O.J. No. 2625 (Prov. Ct.).

An action, which had been unduly complicated and lengthened by the plaintiff, was dismissed with costs to the defendant. The court ordered the plaintiff to pay to the defendant $200 and the cost of the subpoenas for inconvenience and expense.

Fossil Fuel Dev. Ltd. v. Tudex Petroleums Ltd. (1987), 6 A.C.W.S. (3d) 65 (Sask. C.A.).

Costs are discretionary and follow the event except in unusual situations. The trial court ought to have granted costs in the dismissed counterclaim, despite the fact that it was a secondary matter at trial.

DeCorte v. Methot (1981), 11 A.C.W.S. (2d) 101 (Ont. Sm. Claims Ct.).

The *Small Claims Court Act* does not provide for an award of costs on a motion for a contempt of court order.

Re Lachowski and Federated Mutual Ins. Co. (1980), 29 O.R. (2d) 273 (Div. Ct.).

Awards of costs are limited to the provisions of the *Small Claims Court Act* and the tariff of that court. Examples of the type of costs that may be awarded as a condition of adjournment are transportation, babysitters and reimbursement for loss of pay.

Compensation for Inconvenience and Expense

19.05 The court may order an unsuccessful party to pay to a successful party an amount not exceeding $300 as compensation for inconvenience and expense, if,
- **(a) the successful party is unrepresented;**
- **(b) the amount claimed exceeds $500, exclusive of interest and costs; and**
- **(c) the court is satisfied that the proceeding has been unduly complicated or prolonged by the unsuccessful party.**

CASE LAW

Fuss v. Fidelity Electronics of Canada Ltd. (1996), 7 W.D.C.P. (2d) 66 (Ont. Gen. Div.).

Costs are not available to a solicitor who acts in his own cause, as personal preparation costs are denied to all other non-solicitor litigants.

Khokhar v. Blackburn (1993), 20 C.P.C. (3d) 313 (Alta. Q.B.).

The court may make an order for costs to be paid to an unrepresented appellant for the cost of preparing and arguing the appeal. Costs cannot be awarded for the appellant's lost wages.

RULE 20   ENFORCEMENT OF ORDERS

Definitions

20.01 In rules 20.02 to 20.10,

"creditor" means a person who is entitled to enforce an order for the payment or recovery of money;

"debtor" means a person against whom an order for the payment or recovery of money may be enforced.

Power of Court

20.02(1) The court may,
  (a) stay the enforcement of an order of the court, for such time and on such terms as are just; and
  (b) vary the times and proportions in which money payable under an order of the court shall be paid, if it is satisfied that the debtor's circumstances have changed.

Enforcement Limited While Periodic Payment Order in Force

(2) While an order for periodic payment is in force, no step to enforce the judgment may be taken or continued against the debtor by a creditor named in the order, except issuing a writ of seizure and sale of land and filing it with the sheriff.

Termination on Default

(3) An order for periodic payment terminates immediately if the debtor is in default under it for 21 days.

General

20.03 In addition to any other method of enforcement provided by law,
  (a) an order for the payment or recovery of money may be enforced by,
     (i) a writ of seizure and sale of personal property (Form 20C) under rule 20.06,
     (ii) a writ of seizure and sale of land (Form 20D) under rule 20.07, and
     (iii) garnishment under rule 20.08; and
  (b) a further order as to payment may be made under subrule 20.10(7).

Certificate of Judgment

20.04(1) If there is default under an order for the payment or recovery of money, the clerk shall, at the creditor's request, supported by an affidavit stating the amount still owing, issue a certificate of judgment (Form 20A) to the clerk of the territorial division specified by the creditor.

(2) The certificate of judgment shall state,
- **(a) the date of the order and the amount awarded;**
- **(b) the rate of postjudgment interest payable; and**
- **(c) the amount owing, including postjudgment interest.**

CASE LAW

Miller v. York Downs Craft & Garden Centre Ltd. (1987), 17 C.P.C. (2d) 142 (Ont. Prov. Ct.).

The court has the discretion to specifically award disbursements which were reasonable and necessary to the proceedings.

Delivery of Personal Property

20.05(1) An order for the delivery of personal property may be enforced by a writ of delivery (Form 20B) issued by the clerk to a bailiff, on the request of the person in whose favour the order was made, supported by an affidavit of that person or the person's agent stating that the property has not been delivered.

Seizure of Other Personal Property

(2) If the property referred to in a writ of delivery cannot be found or taken by the bailiff, the person in whose favour the order was made may make a motion to the court for an order directing the bailiff to seize any other personal property of the person against whom the order was made.

(3) The bailiff shall keep personal property seized under subrule (2) until the court makes a further order for its disposition.

Storage Costs

(4) The person in whose favour the order is made shall pay the bailiff's storage costs, in advance and from time to time; if the person fails to do so, the seizure shall be deemed to be abandoned.

Writ of Seizure and Sale of Personal Property

20.06(1) If there is default under an order for the payment or recovery of money, the clerk shall, at the creditor's request, supported by an affidavit stating the amount still owing, issue to a bailiff a writ of seizure and sale of personal property (Form 20C), and the bailiff shall enforce the writ for the amount owing, postjudgment interest and the bailiff's fees and expenses.

Duration and Renewal

(2) A writ of seizure and sale of personal property remains in force for six months after the date of its issue and for a further six months after each renewal.

(3) A writ of seizure and sale of personal property may be renewed before its expiration by filing with the clerk a request to renew it.

(4) A writ of seizure and sale of personal property shall show the creditor's name, address and telephone number and the name, address and telephone number of the creditor's lawyer or agent, if any.

Inventory of Property Seized

(5) Within a reasonable time after a request is made by the debtor or the debtor's agent, the bailiff shall deliver an inventory of personal property seized under a writ of seizure and sale of personal property.

Sale of Personal Property

(6) Personal property seized under a writ of seizure and sale of personal property shall not be sold by the bailiff unless notice of the time and place of sale has been,
- (a) mailed to the creditor at the address shown on the writ or the creditor's lawyer or agent and to the debtor at the debtor's last known address, at least 14 days before the sale; and
- (b) advertised in a manner that is likely to bring it to the attention of the public.

Writ of Seizure and Sale of Land

20.07(1) If an order for the payment or recovery of money is unsatisfied, the clerk shall at the creditor's request, supported by an affidavit stating the amount still owing, issue to the sheriff specified by the creditor a writ of seizure and sale of land (Form 20D).

(2) A writ of seizure and sale of land issued under subrule (1) has the same force and effect and may be renewed or withdrawn in the same

manner as a writ of seizure and sale issued under Rule 60 of the *Rules of Civil Procedure.*

Garnishment

20.08(1) A creditor may enforce an order for the payment or recovery of money by garnishment of debts payable to the debtor by other persons.

Joint Debts Garnishable

(2) If a debt is payable to the debtor and to one or more co-owners, one-half of the indebtedness or a greater or lesser amount specified in an order made under subrule (15) may be garnished.

Obtaining Notice of Garnishment

(3) A creditor who seeks to enforce an order by garnishment shall file with the clerk in the territorial division in which the debtor resides or carries on business,
  (a) an affidavit stating,
      (i) the date of the order and the amount awarded,
      (ii) the territorial division in which the order was made,
      (iii) the rate of postjudgment interest payable,
      (iv) the total amount of any payments received since the order was granted,
      (v) the amount owing, including postjudgment interest,
      (vi) the name and address of each person to whom a notice of garnishment is to be directed,
      (vii) the creditor's belief that those persons are or will become indebted to the debtor, and the grounds for the belief, and
      (viii) any particulars of the debts that are known to the creditor; and
  (b) a certificate of judgment (Form 20A), if the order was made in another territorial division.

(4) On the filing of the material required by subrule (3), the clerk shall issue notices of garnishment (Form 20E) naming as garnishees the persons named in the affidavit.

(5) A notice of garnishment issued under subrule (4) shall name only one debtor and only one garnishee.

Service of Notice of Garnishment

(6) The notice of garnishment shall be served by the creditor in accordance with subrule 8.01(6).

Garnishee Liable From Time of Service

(7) The garnishee is liable to pay to the clerk any debt of the garnishee to the debtor, up to the amount shown in the notice of garnishment, within 10 days after service of the notice on the garnishee or 10 days after the debt becomes payable, whichever is later.

(8) For the purpose of subrule (7), a debt of the garnishee to the debtor includes,
- (a) a debt payable at the time the notice of garnishment is served; and
- (b) a debt payable (whether absolutely or on the fulfilment of a condition) within 24 months after the notice is served.

Payment by Garnishee to Clerk

(9) A garnishee who admits owing a debt to the debtor shall pay it to the clerk in the manner prescribed by the notice of garnishment, subject to section 7 of the *Wages Act*.

Equal Distribution Among Creditors

(10) If the clerk has issued notices of garnishment in respect of a debtor at the request of more than one creditor and receives payment under any of the notices of garnishment, he or she shall distribute the payment equally among the creditors who have filed a request for garnishment and have not been paid in full.

Disputing Garnishment

(11) A garnishee referred to in subrule (12) shall, within 10 days after service of the notice of garnishment, file with the court a statement (Form 20F) setting out the particulars.

(12) Subrule (11) applies to a garnishee who,
- (a) wishes to dispute the garnishment for any reason; or
- (b) pays to the clerk less than the amount set out in the notice of garnishment as owing by the garnishee to the debtor, because the debt is owed to the debtor and to one or more co-owners or for any other reason.

Service on Creditor and Debtor

(13) If the garnishee's statement indicates that the debt is owed to the debtor and to one or more co-owners, the garnishee shall also serve copies of the statement on the creditor and the debtor.

Notice to Co-Owner of Debt

(14) A creditor who is served with a garnishee's statement under subrule (13) shall forthwith send to the co-owners of the debt, in accordance with subrule 8.01(10), a notice to co-owner of debt (Form 20G) and a copy of the garnishee's statement.

Garnishment Hearing

(15) At the request of a creditor, debtor, garnishee, co-owner of the debt or any other interested person, the court may,
- (a) if it is alleged that the garnishee's debt to the debtor has been assigned or encumbered, order the assignee or encumbrancer to appear and state the nature and particulars of the claim;
- (b) determine the rights and liabilities of the garnishee, any co-owner of the debt, the debtor and any assignee or encumbrancer;
- (c) vary or suspend periodic payments under a notice of garnishment; or
- (d) determine any other matter in relation to a notice of garnishment.

Time to Request Hearing

(16) A person who has been served with a notice to co-owner of debt is not entitled to dispute the enforcement of the creditor's order for the payment or recovery of money or a payment made by the clerk unless the person requests a garnishment hearing within 30 days after the notice is sent.

Enforcement Against Garnishee

(17) If the garnishee does not pay to the clerk the amount set out in the notice of garnishment and does not send a garnishee's statement, the creditor is entitled to an order against the garnishee for payment of the amount set out in the notice, unless the court orders otherwise.

Payment to Person other than Clerk

(18) If, after service of a notice of garnishment, the garnishee pays a debt attached by the notice to a person other than the clerk, the garnishee remains liable to pay the debt in accordance with notice.

Effect of Payment to Clerk

(19) Payment of a debt by a garnishee in accordance with a notice of garnishment is a valid discharge of the debt as between the garnishee and the debtor and any co-owner of the debt, to the extent of the payment.

(20) Unless a hearing has been requested under subrule (15), the clerk shall, when proof is filed that the notice of garnishment was served on the debtor, distribute to a creditor payments received under a notice of garnishment as they are received.

Payment if Debt Jointly Owned

(21) If a payment of a debt owed to the debtor and one or more co-owners has been made to the clerk, no request for a garnishment hearing is made and the time for doing so under subrule (16) has expired, the creditor may file with the clerk, within 30 days after that expiry,
   (a) proof of service of the notice to co-owner; and
   (b) an affidavit stating that the creditor believes that no co-owner of the debt is a person under disability, and the grounds for the belief.

(22) The affidavit required by subrule (21) may contain statements of the deponent's information and belief, if the source of the information and the fact of the belief are specified in the affidavit.

(23) If the creditor does not file the material referred to in subrule (21) the sheriff shall return the money to the garnishee.

[O. Reg. 461/01, s. 18]

CASE LAW

720659 Ontario Inc. v. Wells, [2001] O.J. No. 3666 (S.C.J.).

If a debtor against whom judgment is granted becomes bankrupt before garnishment proceedings commence, the garnishment will be set aside.

Canada Mortgage and Housing Corp. v. Apostolou (1995), 22 O.R. (3d) 190 (Gen. Div.).

The issue of the motion was the priority of a garnishment issued and served by a judgment creditor and another creditor to whom the debtor had assigned wages under a registered financing statement. The court ruled that the garnishment had priority over the earlier wage assignment because garnishment places direct influence and restrictions upon the garnishee.

Dacon Corp. v. Treats Ontario Inc. (1995), 6 W.D.C.P. (2d) 174 (Ont. Gen. Div.).

Rents payable under a sublease agreement are a proper object of garnishment and the sublessee is obliged to pay garnished rent to the sheriff.

Chrich Holdings & Buildings Ltd. and David Hall v. Eugene Madore o/a Absolute Office Furniture Services, Garnishee (December 20, 1994), Doc. 633/94, Searle Dep. J. (Ont. Sm. Claims Ct.).

There is no valid garnishment of wages and no liability to remit payment if the debtor is not an employee at the time that the notice of garnishment is served.

Director of Support and Custody Enforcement v. Jones (1991), 3 C.P.C. (3d) 206 (Ont. Div. Ct.).

At common law, a judgment creditor may not garnish payments made into a debtor's joint bank account, as this would require the court to apportion ownership of the funds in the account and, in effect, rewrite the joint account agreement.

667801 Ontario Ltd. v. Moir (1990), 1 W.D.C.P. (2d) 266 (Ont. Prov. Ct.).

The judgment debtor owed the garnishee money pursuant to loans. The notice of garnishment took priority over the loans.

Bank of N.S. v. Cameron; Inco Ltd., Garnishee (1985), 1 W.D.C.P. 483 (Ont. Prov. Ct. (Civ. Div.)).

If a garnishee receives notices of garnishment from different courts, payments should be made on the basis of priority of receipt of the notices and not on a pro rata basis. The first garnishment notice must be paid in full before the subsequent garnishments can be paid.

Bain v. Rosen and Erie Meat Markets Ltd., Garnishee (1984), 45 O.R. (2d) 672 (H.C.J.).

Where a judgment debtor's employer received an income tax demand and a garnishee order, the income tax demand was applied after determination of the exception based on the employee's net income.

Avco Financial Services Can. Ltd. v. Bowe; Steenbakkers Lumber Ltd., Garnishee (1979), 23 O.R. (2d) 264 (Div. Ct.).

When an employee is paid regularly in advance, money owing to him at the beginning of each period can properly be made the subject of garnishment proceedings.

Nunez-de-Cela v. May Co. (1973), 1 O.R. (2d) 217 (C.A.).

A judgment in a Small Claims Court action given against a defendant in a trade name may be enforced against the defendant himself without any additional order.

Bonus Finance Ltd. v. Smith; Crown Trust Co., Garnishee, [1971] 3 O.R. 732 (H.C.J.).

Money payable under a pension is immune from attachment by the *Pension Benefits Act.*[7]

Consolidation Order

20.09(1) A debtor against whom there are two or more unsatisfied orders for the payment of money may make a motion to the court for a consolidation order.

(2) The debtor shall file with the motion an affidavit stating,
- **(a) the names and addresses of the creditors who have obtained an order for the payment of money against the debtor;**
- **(b) the amount owed to each creditor;**
- **(c) the amount of the debtor's income from all sources, identifying them; and**
- **(d) the debtor's current financial obligations and any other relevant facts.**

Notice of Motion

(3) Notice of the motion and a copy of the affidavit shall be served on each of the creditors mentioned in the affidavit, at least seven days before the hearing date.

Contents of Consolidation Order

(4) At the hearing of the motion, the court may make a consolidation order setting out,
- **(a) a list of unsatisfied orders for the payment of money against the debtor, indicating in each case the date, court and amount and the amount unpaid;**
- **(b) the amounts to be paid into court by the debtor under the consolidation order; and**
- **(c) the times of the payments.**

(5) The total of the amounts to be paid into court by the debtor under a consolidation order shall not exceed the portion of the debtor's income that is subject to seizure or garnishment under section 7 of the *Wages Act.*

Creditor May Make Submissions

(6) At the hearing of the motion, a creditor may make submissions as to the amount and times of payment.

---

[7] R.S.O. 1990, c. P.8 (now).

Further Orders Obtained After Consolidation Order

(7) If an order for the payment of money is obtained against the debtor after the date of the consolidation order for a debt incurred before the date of the consolidation order, the creditor may file with the clerk a certified copy of the new order; the creditor shall be added to the consolidation order and shall share in the distribution under it from that time.

(8) A consolidation order terminates immediately if an order for the payment of money is obtained against the debtor for a debt incurred after the date of the consolidation order.

Enforcement Limited While Consolidation Order in Force

(9) While the consolidation order is in force, no step to enforce the judgment may be taken or continued against the debtor by a creditor named in the order, except issuing a writ of seizure and sale of land and filing it with the sheriff.

Termination on Default

(10) A consolidation order terminates immediately if the debtor is in default under it for 21 days.

Effect of Termination

(11) If a consolidation order terminates under subrule (8) or (10), the clerk shall notify the creditors named in the consolidation order, and no further consolidation order shall be made in respect of the debtor for one year after the date of termination.

Manner of Sending Notice

(11.1) The notice that the consolidation order is terminated shall be sent by mail or fax.

Equal Distribution Among Creditors

(12) All payments into a consolidation account belong to the creditors named in the consolidation order, who shall share equally in the distribution of the money.

(13) The clerk shall distribute the money paid into the consolidation account at least once every six months.

[O. Reg. 461/01, s. 19]

CASE LAW

Dainard v. Dainard (1981), 22 C.P.C. 283 (Ont. Prov. Ct.).

A support order made pursuant to the *Family Law Act*[8] cannot be included in a Small Claims Court consolidation order.

Re Young (1973), 4 O.R. (2d) 390 (Sm. Claims Ct.).

Consolidation was refused where one of the creditors was a wife who had filed a maintenance order in the Small Claims Court.

Re Landry (1973), 1 O.R. (2d) 107 (Sm. Claims Ct.).

A judgment of a Superior or District Court that is filed in a Small Claims Court is not a judgment within the consolidation order section.

Examination of Debtor or Other Person

20.10(1) If there is default under an order for the payment or recovery of money, the clerk of the territorial division where the debtor or other person to be examined resides or carries on business shall, at the creditor's request, issue a notice of examination (Form 20H) directed to the debtor or other person.

(2) The creditor's request shall be accompanied by,
- **(a) an affidavit setting out,**
  - **(i) the date of the order and the amount awarded,**
  - **(ii) the territorial division in which the order was made,**
  - **(iii) the rate of postjudgment interest payable,**
  - **(iv) the total amount of any payments received since the order was granted, and**
  - **(v) the amount owing, including postjudgment interest; and**
- **(b) a certificate of judgment (Form 20A), if the order was made in another territorial jurisdiction.**

Service of Notice of Examination

(3) The notice of examination shall be served in accordance with subrules 8.01(7) and (8).

(4) The debtor, any other persons to be examined and any witnesses whose evidence the court considers necessary may be examined in relation to,

---

[8] *Supra*, note 1.

(a) the reason for nonpayment;
(b) the debtor's income and property;
(c) the debts owed to and by the debtor;
(d) the disposal the debtor has made of any property either before or after the order was made;
(e) the debtor's present, past and future means to satisfy the order;
(f) whether the debtor intends to obey the order or has any reason for not doing so; and
(g) any other matter pertinent to the enforcement of the order.

Who May Be Examined

(5) An officer or director of a corporate debtor, or, in the case of a debtor that is a partnership or sole proprietorship, the sole proprietor or any partner, may be examined on the debtor's behalf in relation to the matters set out in subrule (4).

Examinations Private

(6) The examination shall be held in the absence of the public, unless the court orders otherwise.

Order As To Payment

(7) After the examination or if the debtor's consent is filed, the court may make an order as to payment.

Enforcement Limited while Order as to Payment in Force

(8) While an order as to payment is in force, no step to enforce the judgment may be taken or continued against the debtor by a creditor named in the order, except issuing a writ of seizure and sale of land and filing it with the sheriff.

Contempt Hearing

(9) The court may find a person on whom a notice of examination has been served to be in contempt of court, and may order that he or she attend before the court for a contempt hearing, if the person,
(a) fails to attend as required by the notice of examination, and the court is satisfied that the failure to attend is wilful; or
(b) attends and refuses to answer questions.

Notice of Contempt Hearing

(10) When an order for a contempt hearing is made under subrule (9), a notice (Form 20I) setting out the time, date and place of the hearing shall be,
- (a) sent to the creditor by mail or fax; and
- (b) served on the person by the creditor in accordance with subrule 8.01(9).

Powers of Court at Contempt Hearing

(11) At the contempt hearing, the court may,
- (a) order that the person attend at an examination under this rule;
- (b) make an order as to payment; or
- (c) order that the person be jailed for a period not exceeding 40 days.

Warrant of Committal

(12) If an order is made under clause (11)(c), the clerk shall issue a warrant of committal (Form 20J) directed to all police officers in Ontario.

(13) The warrant authorizes any police officer in Ontario to take the debtor or other person named in the warrant and deliver him or her to the nearest correctional institution.

(14) The warrant remains in force for 12 months after its date of issue and may be renewed by order of the court made on the creditor's motion, for 12 months at each renewal.

Discharge

(15) The person shall be discharged from custody on the order of the court or when the time prescribed in the warrant expires, whichever is earlier.

[O. Reg. 461/01, s. 20]

CASE LAW

Consumers Gas Co. v. Ferreira (1990), 1 W.D.C.P. (2d) 257 (Ont. Prov. Ct.).

A renewal of a warrant of committal should not be granted when the court is not satisfied that the debtor had notice of the claim, the default judgment and the warrant. Where substituted service was the method of service in every step of the action, this was insufficient to so satisfy the court.

RULE 21   REFEREE

21.01(1) A referee shall assist the court by performing the advisory duties and functions that it directs.

(2) Without limiting the generality of subrule (1), if the court so directs, a referee shall conduct pre-trial conferences under Rule 13 and examinations under rule 20.10 (examination of debtor).

(3) Except under subrule 9.03(5) (order as to terms of payment), a referee shall not make a final decision in any matter referred to him or her but shall report his or her findings and recommendations to the court.

CASE LAW

Lagadin v. King (1985), 2 W.D.C.P. 259 (Ont. Prov. Ct.).

At a resolution hearing, with the plaintiffs appearing, the defendant absent and no defence entered, the referee exceeded jurisdiction by recommending judgment in respect of an unliquidated claim. This cannot be done without the written consent to same by all parties.

Bussineau v. Roberts (1982), 15 A.C.W.S. (2d) 367 (Ont. Sm. Claims Ct.).

The duties of a pre-trial hearing referee in Small Claims Court do not include conducting a trial by hearing evidence from the parties and their witnesses. The referee cannot dismiss the claim for failure of the plaintiff to attend or give judgment for the plaintiff for failure of the defendant to attend a hearing.

APPENDIX 7

Rule 76 Simplified Procedure*

Editorial Note: The Rules reproduced here reflect the Rules as they will read on December 31, 2002, pursuant to O. Reg. 206/02.

APPLICATION OF RULE

76.01(1) The simplified procedure set out in this Rule does not apply to actions under,

    (a) the *Class Proceedings Act*, 1992;
    (b) the *Construction Lien Act*;
    (c) Rule 69, 70 or 77.

CASE LAW

McEvenue v. Robin Hood Multifoods Inc. (1997), 33 O.R. (3d) 315 (Gen. Div.).

The simplified procedure is available for actions which are commenced before March 11, 1996, only with the consent of the defendants. In an action commenced before March 11, 1996, a plaintiff cannot unilaterally transfer the action to the simplified procedure, even if the plaintiff amends the claim to reduce the amount sought to less than $25,000.

Application of Other Rules

(2) The rules that apply to an action apply to an action that is proceeding under this Rule, unless this Rule provides otherwise.

[O. Reg. 533/95, s. 6; O. Reg. 60/96, s. 1; O. Reg. 284/01, s. 25]

AVAILABILITY OF SIMPLIFIED PROCEDURE

When Mandatory

76.02(1) The procedure set out in this Rule shall be used in an action if the following conditions are satisfied:

---

* *Rules of Civil Procedure*, R.R.O. 1990, Reg. 194, Rule 76 [am. O. Reg. 533/95, s. 6; O. Reg. 60/96, s. 1; O. Reg. 118/97, s. 4; O. Reg. 627/98, s. 8; O. Reg. 284/01, s. 25; O. Reg. 457/01, s. 9; O. Reg. 206/02, ss. 19 and 20].

1. The plaintiff's claim is exclusively for one or more of the following:
    i. Money.
    ii. Real property.
    iii. Personal property.
2. The total of the following amounts is $50,000 or less, exclusive of interest and costs:
    i. The amount of money claimed, if any.
    ii. The fair market value of any real property and of any personal property, as at the date the action is commenced.

CASE LAW

Moffatt & Powell Ltd. v. Armour Steel Supply Ltd., [2002] O.J. No. 1475 (S.C.J.).

If the plaintiff's claim exceeds the monetary jurisdiction of the simplified procedure, and the defendant does not object to the Statement of Defence, the plaintiff is entitled to any judgment that is awarded following trial, even if the judgment exceeds the monetary jurisdiction of simplified procedure.

Dusto v. Hooper-Holmes Canada Ltd., [2002] O.J. No. 1289 (S.C.J.).

The January 1, 2002 amendments have a retroactive effect and apply to actions commenced before the amendments came into force. The rules are mandatory and therefore a claim for less than $50,000 is to be automatically converted to simplified procedure.

McIntosh v. C.T.F. Supply Ltd., [2001] O.J. No. 5062 (S.C.J.).

Although the defendant's conduct in the action justified a punitive damage award, such an award could not be made because to do so would exceed the $25,000 cap on damage awards under simplified procedure.

Lillie v. Bisson, [1999] O.J. No. 1008 (C.A.).

The court should encourage a liberal interpretation of Rule 76 to carry out the policy of reducing the cost of litigation claims of modest sums. As such, deductions pursuant to automobile insurance litigation cannot be taken into account when determining whether a claim falls within simplified procedure.

Rizzi v. Great Atlantic and Pacific Co. of Canada (1999), 46 O.R. (3d) 509 (S.C.J.).

The plaintiff who opts for simplified procedure is precluded from seeking an amendment to increase prayer for relief in order to be consistent with a possible higher jury award. Allowing the plaintiff to amend would result in prejudice to the defendant, who could not be compensated for in costs or adjournment.

Bonneville v. IITC Holdings Ltd., [1999] O.J. No. 428 (Gen. Div.).

Deductions cannot be made on an original claim of assessed damages in order to bring the plaintiff's claim within simplified procedure. (See *Lillie v. Bisson*, [1999] O.J. No. 1008 (C.A.)).

(2) If there are two or more plaintiffs, the procedure set out in this Rule shall be used if each plaintiff's claim, considered separately, meets the requirements of subrule (1).

When Optional

(3) The procedure set out in this Rule may be used in any other action at the option of the plaintiff, subject to subrules (4) to (9).

CASE LAW

Stapley v. Intermap Technologies Ltd., [1999] O.J. No. 1411 (Gen. Div.).

The Rule relating to converting actions to simplified procedure does not limit the court's jurisdiction to consider a plaintiff's re-election to proceed under simplified procedure. The court ought to allow an amendment to the plaintiff's Statement of Claim, reconverting the action to a simplified action, unless there is prejudice to the defendant.

Lechier-Kimel v. Friedlander, [1999] O.J. No. 1614 (Gen. Div.).

The trial judge does not have the right to refuse the parties' mutual agreement to proceed under the simplified rules procedure.

Alcox v. Woolley, [1997] O.J. No. 2821 (Gen. Div.).

A plaintiff who wishes to amend the Statement of Claim to reduce the amount sought to $25,000 to bring the action within the simplified procedure need not provide a justification for the amendment. The plaintiff may even be able to amend the claim to bring it within the simplified procedure without notice to the other parties.

McEvenue v. Robin Hood Multifoods Inc. (1997), 33 O.R. (3d) 315 (Gen. Div.).

The simplified procedure is available for actions which are commenced before March 11, 1996, only with the consent of the defendants. In an action commenced before March 11, 1996, a plaintiff cannot unilaterally transfer the action to the simplified procedure, even if the plaintiff amends the claim to reduce the amount sought to less than $25,000.

Originating Process

(4) The statement of claim (Form 14A, 14B or 14D) or notice of action (Form 14C) shall indicate that the action is being brought under this Rule.

Action Continues to Proceed Under Rule

(5) An action commenced under this Rule continues to proceed under this Rule unless,
- (a) the defendant objects in the statement of defence to the action proceeding under this Rule because the plaintiff's claim does not comply with subrule (1), and the plaintiff does not abandon in the reply the claims or parts of claims that do not comply; or
- (b) a defendant by counterclaim, crossclaim or third party claim objects in the statement of defence to the counterclaim, crossclaim or third party claim proceeding under this Rule because the counterclaim, crossclaim or third party claim does not comply with subrule (1), and the defendant does not abandon in the reply to the counterclaim, crossclaim or third party claim the claims or parts of claims that do not comply.

CASE LAW

Applewood Holdings Inc. v. Maximum Sales Corp., [1999] O.J. No. 5387 (Gen. Div.).

The defendant was allowed to amend the Statement of Defence to object to the action being brought under simplified procedure, despite delay in bringing the application to amend. The application was allowed in light of the fact that the plaintiff would not be prejudiced by the defendant's amendment. (Contra: *Munro v. Thompson, Tooze, McLean, Rollo & Elkin*, [1998] O.J. No. 3839 (Gen. Div.).

Continuance Under Ordinary Procedure – Where Notice Required

(6) If an action commenced under this Rule may no longer proceed under this Rule because of an amendment to the pleadings or as a result of the operation of subrule (5),
- (a) the action is continued under the ordinary procedure or under Rule 77, as the case may be; and
- (b) the plaintiff shall deliver, after all the pleadings have been delivered or at the time of amending the pleadings, as the case may be, a notice (Form 76A) stating that the action and any related proceedings are continued as an ordinary action or under Rule 77, as the case may be.

Continuance Under Simplified Procedure – Where Notice Required

(7) An action that was not commenced under this Rule is continued under this Rule if,

(a) a party's pleading is amended;
(b) the amended pleading complies with subrule (1);
(c) all other claims, counterclaims, crossclaims or third party claims comply with this Rule; and
(d) the consent of all the parties is filed.

(8) The plaintiff shall deliver a notice (Form 76A) stating that the action and any related proceedings are continued under this Rule.

Effect of Abandonment

(9) A party who abandons a claim or part of a claim or amends a pleading so that the claim, counterclaim, crossclaim or third party claim complies with subrule (1) may not bring the claim or part in any other proceeding.

[O. Reg. 533/95, s. 6; O. Reg. 118/97, s. 4; O. Reg. 284/01, s. 25]

AFFIDAVIT OF DOCUMENTS

Copies of Documents

76.03(1) A party to an action under this Rule shall, within 10 days after the close of pleadings and at the party's own expense, serve on every other party,
(a) an affidavit of documents (Form 30A or 30B) disclosing to the full extent of the party's knowledge, information and belief all documents relating to any matter in issue in the action that are or have been in the party's possession, control or power; and
(b) copies of the documents referred to in Schedule A of the affidavit of documents.

CASE LAW

Willis v. Ontario, [1999] O.J. No. 3656 (S.C.J.).

Parties to a simplified procedure action are entitled to discovery of all relevant documents.

List of Potential Witnesses

(2) The affidavit of documents shall include a list of the names and addresses of persons who might reasonably be expected to have knowledge of matters in issue in the action, unless the court orders otherwise.

Effect of Failure to Disclose

(3) At the trial of the action, a party may not call as a witness a person whose name has not been disclosed in the party's affidavit of documents or any supplementary affidavit of documents, unless the court orders otherwise.

Lawyer's Certificate

(4) The lawyer's certificate under subrule 30.03(4) (full disclosure in affidavit) shall include a statement that the lawyer has explained to the deponent the necessity of complying with subrules (1) and (2).

[O. Reg. 533/95, s. 6; O. Reg. 284/01, s. 25; O. Reg. 206/02, s. 19]

NO DISCOVERY, CROSS-EXAMINATION ON AN AFFIDAVIT OR EXAMINATION OF A WITNESS

76.04 The following are not permitted in an action under this Rule:
1. Examination for discovery under rule 31.03 or 31.10.
2. Examination for discovery by written questions and answers under Rule 35.
3. Cross-examination of a deponent on an affidavit under rule 39.02.
4. Examination of a witness on a motion under rule 39.03.

CASE LAW

Mills v. MacFarlane, [2000] O.J. No. 2874 (S.C.J.).

The master erred in ordering written examination for discovery. Neither written nor oral examination is available under the simplified procedure.

Canadian Imperial Bank of Commerce v. Glackin, [1999] O.J. No. 842 (Gen. Div.).

The court found that cross-examination was available in enforcement proceedings despite the fact that judgment was obtained under simplified procedure. Once judgment is obtained under Rule 76, simplified procedure is spent and enforcement proceedings for the action are governed by Rule 60.

Gasparini v. Waterfront Tennis and Squash Club Ltd., [1997] O.J. No. 785 (Gen. Div.).

As there are no discoveries in the simplified procedure, parties should set out as much particularity in the pleadings as possible.

Alcox v. Woolley, [1997] O.J. No. 2821 (Gen. Div.).

Where discoveries have been partially completed, and the plaintiff wishes to amend the claim to bring it within the simplified procedure, the earlier discovery is rescinded and all copies are to be sealed in the court file.

MOTIONS

Motion Form

76.05(1) The moving party shall serve a motion form (Form 76B) in accordance with rule 37.07 and shall submit it to the court before the motion is heard.

Place of Hearing

(2) Unless the parties agree otherwise or the court orders otherwise, the motion shall be heard in the county where the action was commenced.

Procedure

(3) Depending on the practical requirements of the situation, the motion may be made,
- **(a) with or without supporting material or a motion record;**
- **(b) by attendance, in writing, by fax or under rule 1.08 (telephone and video conferences).**

Motions Dealt With by Registrar

(4) When a motion described in subrule (5) meets one of the following conditions, the registrar shall make an order granting the relief sought:
1. **The motion is for an order on consent, the consent of all parties is filed and the consent states that no party affected by the order is under disability.**
2. **No responding material is filed and the notice of motion or the motion form states that no party affected by the order is under disability.**

(5) Subrule (4) applies to a motion for,
- **(a) amendment of a pleading or notice of motion;**
- **(b) addition, deletion or substitution of a party whose consent is filed;**
- **(c) removal of a solicitor as solicitor of record;**
- **(d) setting aside the noting of a party in default;**
- **(e) setting aside a default judgment;**
- **(f) discharge of a certificate of pending litigation;**
- **(g) security for costs in a specified amount; or**
- **(h) dismissal of a proceeding with or without costs.**

Disposition

(6) The court or registrar shall record the disposition of the motion on the motion form.

(7) No formal order is required unless,
- (a) the court or registrar orders otherwise;
- (b) an appeal is made to a judge; or
- (c) an appeal or motion for leave to appeal is made to an appellate court.

[O. Reg. 533/95, s. 6; O. Reg. 284/01, s. 25]

DISMISSAL BY REGISTRAR

If No Defence Filed

76.06(1) The registrar shall make an order dismissing an action as abandoned if the following conditions are satisfied, unless the court orders otherwise:
1. More than 180 days have passed since the date the originating process was issued.
2. No statement of defence has been filed.
3. The action has not been disposed of by final order or judgment.
4. The action has not been set down for trial or summary trial.
5. The registrar has given 45 days notice that the action will be dismissed as abandoned.

If Defence Filed

(2) The registrar shall make an order dismissing an action as abandoned if the following conditions are satisfied, unless the court orders otherwise:
1. More than 150 days have passed since the filing of the first statement of defence or notice of intent to defend.
2. The action has not been disposed of by final order or judgment.
3. The action has not been set down for trial or summary trial.
4. The registrar has given 45 days notice that the action will be dismissed as abandoned.

CASE LAW

Hudon v. Colliers Macaulay Nicolls Inc. (c.o.b. Colliers International), [2001] O.J. No. 1588 (Div. Ct.).

In a motion to set aside a dismissal of an action for delay, the master must consider whether the delay was intentional, inordinate or gave rise to serious prejudice to the opposing party. Plaintiffs are not precluded by simplified rules from commencing a new action after having the first action dismissed as abandoned.

Grieco v. Marquis (1998), 38 O.R. (3d) 314 (Gen. Div.).

In a motion to set aside default judgment signed by the registrar, the defendant must show that there is a genuine issue for trial such that the issues cannot be decided without cross-examinations or it would be otherwise unjust to decide the issues on a motion.

Service on Parties

(3) The registrar shall serve a copy of the order made under subrule (1) or (2) on the parties.

Effect on Subsequent Action

(4) The dismissal of an action as abandoned has the same effect as a dismissal for delay under rule 24.05.

[O. Reg. 533/95, s. 6; O. Reg. 627/98, s. 8; O. Reg. 284/01, s. 25]

SUMMARY JUDGMENT

Where Available

76.07(1) After the close of pleadings, a party may move before a judge with supporting affidavit material for summary judgment.

Place of Hearing

(2) Unless the parties agree otherwise or the court orders otherwise, the motion shall be heard in the county where the action was commenced.

Application of Summary Judgment Procedure

(3) Rules 20.05, 20.07, 20.08 and 20.09 (summary judgment procedure) apply to the motion, but rules 20.01 to 20.04 (availability, affidavits, factums, disposition of motion) and rule 20.06 (costs) do not apply.

Responding Party's Material

(4) In response to affidavit material supporting the motion, the responding party may not rest on the mere allegations or denials of the party's pleadings, but is required to set out, in affidavit material, specific facts to show that judgment ought not to be granted.

Contents of Affidavit

(5) An affidavit for use on the motion may be made on information and belief as permitted by subrule 39.01(4), but on the hearing of the motion an adverse inference may be drawn, if appropriate, from a party's failure to provide the evidence of persons having personal knowledge of contested facts.

Motion Record Required

(6) The moving party shall serve a motion record on every other party to the motion and file it, with proof of service, in the court office where the motion is to be heard, at least two days before the hearing of the motion.

Contents of Motion Record

(7) The motion record shall contain, in consecutively numbered pages arranged in the following order,
- (a) a table of contents describing each document, including each exhibit, by its nature and date and, in the case of an exhibit, by exhibit number or letter;
- (b) a copy of the notice of motion;
- (c) a copy of all affidavits served by any party for use on the motion; and
- (d) a copy of the pleadings, including those relating to any counterclaim, crossclaim or third party claim.

Factums Required

(8) Every party to the motion shall serve on every other party a factum consisting of a concise statement of the facts and law relied upon by the party and file it, with proof of service, in the court office where the motion is to be heard, at least two days before the hearing of the motion.

Test for Summary Judgment

(9) The presiding judge shall grant judgment on the motion unless,
- (a) he or she is unable to decide the issues in the action without cross-examination; or
- (b) it would be otherwise unjust to decide the issues on the motion. O. Reg. 284/01, s. 25.

CASE LAW

Itravel2000.com Inc. v. Contestix.com Corp., [2002] O.J. No. 2462 (S.C.J.).

The focus of a summary judgment motion brought pursuant to the simplified procedure rules is whether the judge can decide the issue without cross-examination and whether there is injustice in granting judgment. The focus is not on whether there is a genuine issue for trial.

Torstar Electronic Publishing Ltd. v. Asian Television Network Inc., [2000] O.J. No. 2748 (S.C.J.).

The test for summary judgment includes a consideration of whether there is a genuine issue for trial; however, the test is less onerous than under the ordinary procedure rules.

32262 BC Ltd. v. Mark's Work Wearhouse Ltd., [1999] O.J. No. 1471 (Gen. Div.).

Under Rule 76.04, the judge *shall* grant summary judgment unless the judge is unable to decide the issues in the action in the absence of cross-examination.

Royal Bank of Canada v. Mancuso, [1999] O.J. No. 5055 (S.C.J.).

The unrepresented defendant was unaware that he could object to the plaintiff's choice to proceed under simplified procedure, and this effectively deprived him of an opportunity to cross-examine on affidavits. The plaintiff's motion for summary judgment was dismissed because there were genuine issues of complexity.

Guarantee Co. of North America v. Witts, [1997] O.J. No. 1657 (Gen. Div.).

It is mandatory that summary judgment be granted unless the judge is unable to decide the issue in the action, or it would be otherwise unjust to decide the issues on such a motion.

Bank of Nova Scotia v. Pelletier (January 9, 1997), Doc. 98844/96 (Ont. Gen. Div.).

Where it does not appear that any additional evidence would be available to the trial judge, summary judgment should be granted.

Trans Canada Credit Corp. v. Wheeler (May 22, 1997), Doc. 96-CU-112524 (Ont. Gen. Div.).

An action within the simplified procedure may be tried together with an action in the ordinary procedure. If so, it would not be appropriate to proceed upon a summary judgment motion pursuant to Rule 76.06.

Conestoga Tire & Rim Inc. v. Sisson, [1997] O.J. No. 1993 (Gen. Div.).

Summary judgment under simplified procedure is appropriate in cases where little additional information can be brought forward at trial.

Craig Gilchrist Equipment Rental Ltd. v. Robertson (1997), 10 C.P.C. (4th) 372 (Ont. Gen. Div.).

The parties must put forward their complete and best evidence in support of their position on a summary judgment motion.

Terra Cotta Cookie Co. v. Dek Packaging Ltd., [1997] O.J. No. 995 (Gen. Div.).

The emphasis in Rule 76 is purely upon the resolution of the litigation. Consideration suggests that fairness is the governing criteria rather than a determination of a genuine issue at trial.

K. & R. Painting v. Abraham J. Green Ltd. (12 November 1996), Doc. SR/96/CU/104604 (Ont. Gen. Div.).

The test under Rule 76.06 is less demanding than Rule 20. Where there is conflicting testimony and there is an issue of creditability which cannot be determined without cross-examination, summary judgment will not be granted and the matter must proceed to trial.

Bradley-Kelly Construction Ltd. v. Ottawa-Carleton Regional Transit Commission (1996), 30 O.R. (3d) 301 (Gen. Div.).

Where there are really no facts in dispute, and the determination of the action is based on the interpretation of the contract, it is appropriate to decide the case on a summary judgment motion.

Robertson v. Ball (1996), 31 O.R. (3d) 30 (Gen. Div.).

Rule 76.06 is a different test from Rule 20. Under simplified procedure the consideration of justice and fairness govern the criteria on a motion for summary judgment rather than a determination for the genuine issue for trial. Rule 76.06 should apply only where a brief and summary review of the affidavit evidence would demonstrate a clear case which would warrant immediate judgment. If it is not a clear case, the matter should proceed to trial.

If Trial Necessary

(10) If summary judgment is refused or is granted only in part, the presiding judge shall determine the mode of trial that is appropriate in all the circumstances.

[O. Reg. 355/95, s. 6; O. Reg. 284/01, s. 25]

SETTLEMENT DISCUSSION AND DOCUMENTARY DISCLOSURE

76.08 Within 60 days after the filing of the first statement of defence or notice of intent to defend, the parties shall, in a meeting or telephone call, consider whether,

    (a) all documents relating to any matter at issue have been disclosed; and

    (b) settlement of any or all issues is possible.

[O. Reg. 533/95, s. 6; O. Reg. 284/01, s. 25]

HOW DEFENDED ACTION IS SET DOWN FOR TRIAL OR SUMMARY TRIAL

Notice of Readiness for Pre-Trial Conference

76.09(1) Despite rule 48.02 (how action set down for trial), the plaintiff shall, within 90 days after the first statement of defence or notice of intent to defend is filed, set the action down for trial by serving a notice of readiness for pre-trial conference (Form 76C) on every party to the action and any counterclaim, crossclaim or third party claim and forthwith filing the notice with proof of service.

(2) If the plaintiff does not act under subrule (1), any other party may do so.

Certificate

(3) The party who sets the action down for trial shall certify in the notice of readiness for pre-trial conference that there was a settlement discussion.

[O. Reg. 533/95, s. 6; O. Reg. 284/01, s. 25]

PRE-TRIAL CONFERENCE

Notice

76.10(1) The registrar shall serve notice of a pre-trial conference at least 45 days before the scheduled date.

Attendance

(2) A party and his or her lawyer shall, unless the court orders otherwise, participate in the pre-trial conference,
- (a) by personal attendance; or
- (b) under rule 1.08 (telephone and video conferences) if personal attendance would require undue amounts of travel time or expense.

Authority to Settle

(3) A party who requires another person's approval before agreeing to a settlement shall, before the pre-trial conference, arrange to have ready telephone access to the other person throughout the conference, whether it takes place during or after regular business hours.

Documents

(4) At least five days before the pre-trial conference, each party shall,

(a) file,
- (i) a copy of the party's affidavit of documents and copies of the documents relied on for the party's claim or defence,
- (ii) a copy of any expert report, and
- (iii) any other material necessary for the conference; and

(b) deliver,
- (i) a two-page statement setting out the issues and the party's position with respect to them, and
- (ii) a trial management checklist (Form 76D).

Trial Date

(5) The pre-trial conference judge or master shall fix a date for trial, subject to the direction of the regional senior judge.

Mode of Trial

(6) The parties may agree that the trial shall be an ordinary trial or a summary trial under rule 76.12; if they do not agree, the pre-trial conference judge or master shall determine the mode of trial that is appropriate in all the circumstances.

(7) If the trial is to be a summary trial under rule 76.12, the pre-trial conference judge or master,

(a) shall set a timetable for the delivery of all the parties' affidavits; and

(b) may vary the order and time of presentation.

[O. Reg. 533/95, s. 6; O. Reg. 284/01, s. 25; O. Reg. 457/01, s. 9]

PLACING DEFENDED ACTION ON TRIAL LIST

Registrar

76.11(1) The registrar shall place a defended action on the appropriate trial list immediately after the pre-trial conference.

Trial Record

(2) At least 10 days before the date fixed for trial, the party who set the action down for trial shall serve a trial record on every party to the action and any counterclaim, crossclaim or third party claim, and file the record with proof of service.

(3) In the case of an ordinary trial, the trial record shall be prepared in accordance with rule 48.03.

(4) In the case of a summary trial under rule 76.12, the trial record shall contain, in consecutively numbered pages arranged in the following order,

(a) a table of contents describing each document, including each exhibit, by its nature and date and, in the case of an exhibit, by exhibit number or letter;
(b) a copy of the pleadings, including those relating to any counterclaim, crossclaim or third party claim;
(c) a copy of any demand or order for particulars of a pleading and the particulars delivered in response;
(d) a copy of any order respecting the trial;
(e) a copy of all the affidavits served by all the parties for use on the summary trial; and
(f) a certificate signed by the solicitor of the party filing the trial record, stating that it contains the documents described in clauses (a) to (e).

[O. Reg. 284/01, s. 25]

SUMMARY TRIAL

Procedure

76.12(1) At a summary trial, the evidence and argument shall be presented as follows, subject to any direction under subrule 76.10(7):
1. The plaintiff shall adduce evidence by affidavit.
2. A party who is adverse in interest may cross-examine the deponent of any affidavit served by the plaintiff.
3. The plaintiff may re-examine any deponent who is cross-examined under this subrule for not more than 10 minutes.
4. When any cross-examinations and re-examinations of the plaintiff's deponents are concluded, the defendant shall adduce evidence by affidavit.
5. A party who is adverse in interest may cross-examine the deponent of any affidavit served by a defendant.
6. A party shall complete all of the party's cross-examinations within 50 minutes.
7. A defendant may re-examine any deponent who is cross-examined under this subrule for not more than 10 minutes.
8. When any cross-examinations and re-examinations of the defendant's deponents are concluded, the plaintiff may, with leave of the trial judge, adduce any proper reply evidence.
9. After the presentation of evidence, each party may make oral argument for not more than 45 minutes.

CASE LAW

Chakie v. Elton, [1996] O.J. No. 4447 (Gen. Div.).

The time limit of 50 minutes for cross-examination applies to the total cross-examinations of all witnesses, and a party is not entitled to cross-examine each deponent for 50 minutes. The time limits set out in Rule 76.06(16) will be strictly enforced.

(2) The trial judge may extend a time provided in subrule (1).

(3) A party who intends to cross-examine the deponent of an affidavit at the summary trial shall, at least 10 days before the date fixed for trial, give notice of that intention to the party who filed the affidavit, who shall arrange for the deponent's attendance at the trial.

Judgment after Summary Trial

(4) The judge shall grant judgment after the conclusion of the summary trial.

[O. Reg. 284/01, s. 25]

CASE LAW

Moshiri v. 1142682 Ontario Ltd., [1997] O.J. No. 2592 (Gen. Div.).

A judge hearing a summary trial has no authority to put the matter over for a full trial under the ordinary procedure. If the trial judge cannot decide the case based on the evidence on the summary trial, the party with the onus of proof has failed.

Realffe v. Abou-Assaf, [1996] O.J. No. 3066 (Gen. Div.).

If the parties proceed to a regular trial when a summary trial would have been appropriate because the plaintiff objected to the use of the summary trial, the plaintiff may be denied costs.

COSTS CONSEQUENCES

Opting In

76.13(1) Regardless of the outcome of the action, if this Rule applies as the result of amendment of the pleadings under subrule 76.02(7), the party whose pleadings are amended shall pay, on a substantial indemnity basis, the costs incurred by the opposing party up to the date of the amendment that would not have been incurred had the claim originally complied with subrule 76.02(1), unless the court orders otherwise.

CASE LAW

Leo (Litigation guardian of) v. Hamilton-Wentworth Roman Catholic Separate School Board, [2000] O.J. No. 1803 (S.C.J.).

The defendant was awarded its costs for examination for discovery on solicitor and client scale based on the plaintiff's request to continue the action under simplified procedure after examinations for discovery. No reasons were given by the plaintiff for amending the claim.

Plaintiff Denied Costs

(2) Subrules (3) to (10) apply to a plaintiff who obtains a judgment that satisfies the following conditions:

1. **The judgment awards exclusively one or more of the following:**
   i. **Money.**
   ii. **Real property.**
   iii. **Personal property.**
2. **The total of the following amounts is $50,000 or less, exclusive of interest and costs:**
   i. **The amount of money awarded, if any.**
   ii. **The fair market value of any real property and of any personal property awarded, as at the date the action is commenced.**

CASE LAW

Snider v. Salerno, [2002] O.J. No. 1004 (S.C.J.).

In an action arising out of a motor vehicle accident (Bill 59), the statutory deductible of $15,000 is not to be taken into account when determining entitlement and assessment of costs.

Grossinger v. Olympia Business Machines Canada Ltd., [2001] O.J. No. 1108 (S.C.J.).

In view of the plaintiff's offers to settle in an effort to avoid a trial, the plaintiff was entitled to costs on a solicitor-client scale for action brought under simplified procedure.

Bois v. Majestech Corp. Canada, [2001] O.J. No. 3762 (S.C.J.).

In ordering costs fixed at $5500 in favour of the plaintiff, the court took into account the principles of law submitted by the plaintiff's counsel, the time expended on the file, the result and not having heard submissions from the defendant on the issue of costs. (Note: The court does not discuss the legal principles it considered in making its costs award.)

Seltzer-Soberano v. Kogut (c.o.b. Majestic Home Inspection), [2001] O.J. No. 9 (S.C.J.).

The monetary limit on damages claimed does not limit the amount that can be recovered on an assessment of solicitor-client costs.

Osan Financial Corp. v. Bhatti, [2000] O.J. No. 4104 (S.C.J.).

Security for costs allowed for simplified action. The security was to cover the period up to the point of setting down the action for trial. (*Contra: Azulev, S.A. v. Tilerama Ltd.*, [1999] O.J. No. 2765 (Gen. Div.).)

Azulev, S.A. v. Tilerama Ltd., [1999] O.J. No. 2765 (Gen. Div.)

The motion by the defendant for security for costs was dismissed because it was inappropriate to order security for costs under simplified procedure, especially when the amount in issue was $9,000. This does not mean that security for costs should never be ordered in a simplified procedure case, but the fact that the action is under simplified procedure is a factor that should be considered.

(3) The plaintiff shall not recover any costs unless,
  (a) the action was proceeding under this Rule at the commencement of the trial; or
  (b) the court is satisfied that it was reasonable for the plaintiff,
    (i) to have commenced and continued the action under the ordinary procedure or under Rule 77, as the case may be, or
    (ii) to have allowed the action to be continued under the ordinary procedure or under Rule 77, as the case may be, by not abandoning claims or parts of claims that do not comply with subrule 76.02(1).

(4) Subrule (3) applies despite subrule 49.10(1) (plaintiff's offer to settle).

(5) Subrule (3) does not apply if this Rule was unavailable because of the counterclaim, crossclaim or third party claim of another party.

CASE LAW

Polish National Union of Canada Inc. v. Dopke (No. 2) (2001), 55 O.R. (3d) 728 (S.C.J.).

If the award at trial is less than the monetary limit of the simplified procedure, but the action was subject to ordinary procedure at the commencement of trial, the court does not have discretion to award costs to the plaintiff.

Dowe-Salter v. Pickering (Town), [2000] O.J. No. 3818 (S.C.J.).

Costs were not available to the plaintiff because she improperly commenced and continued her action under ordinary procedure when she should have brought it under simplified procedure. Costs are intended to be a major sanction for those who do not use the simplified procedure when the action meets the criteria.

Dronshek v. Martchenkov, [2000] O.J. No. 5193 (S.C.J.).

Even though judgment obtained was significantly less than $25,000 in an action brought under ordinary procedure, the court awarded costs to the plaintiff.

The plaintiff could not be expected to use simplified procedure as credibility was a key issue in the action.

Helsberg v. Allison, [2000] O.J. No. 3618 (S.C.J.), affd [2002] O.J. No. 1529 (C.A.).

Costs were not awarded to either party. Even though it was not reasonable in all the circumstances for the plaintiff to commence and continue his action under the ordinary procedure, the actions of the defendants militated against an award of costs in their favour.

Marion Community Homes Corp. v. Kinston (City), [2000] O.J. No. 1329 (S.C.J.).

The plaintiff was awarded its costs on party and party scale despite the fact that judgment awarded in the plaintiff's favour was only $6,900. It was proper for the plaintiff to commence action under ordinary procedure because the issues in dispute were complex and the monetary result was not apparent to the parties prior to the issuance of the claim. Monetary result is only one factor to be considered in awarding costs.

Plaintiff may be Ordered to Pay Defendant's Costs

(6) The plaintiff may, in the trial judge's discretion, be ordered to pay all or part of the defendant's costs, including substantial indemnity costs, in addition to any costs the plaintiff is required to pay under subrule 49.10(2) (defendant's offer to settle).

Defendant Objecting to Simplified Procedure

(7) In an action that includes a claim for real or personal property, if the defendant objected to proceeding under this Rule on the ground that the property's fair market value exceeded $50,000 at the date the action was commenced and the court finds the value did not exceed that amount at that date, the defendant shall pay, on a substantial indemnity basis, the costs incurred by the plaintiff that would not have been incurred had the claim originally complied with subrule 76.02(1), unless the court orders otherwise.

Burden of Proof

(8) The burden of proving that the fair market value of the real or personal property at the date of commencement of the action was $50,000 or less is on the plaintiff.

Counterclaims, Crossclaims and Third Party Claims

(9) Subrules (1) to (8) apply, with necessary modifications, to counterclaims, crossclaims and third party claims.

Transition

(10) In the case of an action that was commenced before January 1, 2002, subrules (2), (7) and (8) apply as if "$50,000" read "$25,000".

[O. Reg. 284/01, s. 25; O. Reg. 206/02, s. 20]

APPENDIX 8

Small Claims Court Forms*

Form	1A	General Heading
Form	1B	[Repealed, O. Reg. 461/01, s. 22 (in force December 10, 2002)]
Form	1C	[Repealed, O. Reg. 461/01, s. 22 (in force December 10, 2002)]
Form	4A	Consent to Act as Plaintiff's Litigation Guardian
Form	4B	Consent to Act as Defendant's Litigation Guardian
Form	5A	Notice to Alleged Partner
Form	7A	Plaintiff's Claim
Form	8A	Certificate of Service — Bailiff or Bailiff's Officer
Form	8B	Affidavit of Service
Form	8C	[Repealed, O. Reg. 461/01, s. 23 (in force December 10, 2002)]
Form	9A	Defence
Form	9B	Request for a Hearing (Dispute of Proposal of Terms of Payment)
Form	9C	Order as to Terms of Payment
Form	10A	Defendant's Claim
Form	11A	Notice of Default Judgment
Form	13A	Request for Pre-Trial Conference
Form	15A	Notice of Motion
Form	15B	Affidavit
Form	16A	Notice of Trial
Form	18A	Summons to Witness
Form	18B	Warrant for Arrest of Defaulting Witness
Form	20A	Certificate of Judgment
Form	20B	Writ of Delivery
Form	20C	Writ of Seizure and Sale of Personal Property
Form	20D	Writ of Seizure and Sale of Land
Form	20E	Notice of Garnishment
Form	20F	Garnishee's Statement
Form	20G	Notice to Co-Owner of Debt
Form	20H	Notice of Examination
Form	20I	Notice of Contempt Hearing
Form	20J	Warrant of Committal

---

* *Small Claims Court Rules*, O. Reg. 258/98, as am.

FORM 1A

GENERAL HEADING

Superior Court of Justice

.....................Small Claims Court

| Claim No. | / |

Plaintiff #1

Full name
Address for Service *(street and number, city, postal code)*
Phone No. Fax No. (If any) E-Mail Address (Optional)
Plaintiff's Lawyer/Agent (Full Name)
Lawyer/Agent's Address for Service
Lawyer/Agent's Phone No. Fax No. (If any) E-Mail Address (Optional)

Plaintiff #2 (if applicable)

Full Name
Address for Service *(street and number, city, postal code)*
Phone No. Fax No. (If any) E-Mail Address (Optional)
Plaintiff's Lawyer/Agent (Full Name)
Lawyer/Agent's Address for Service
Lawyer/Agent's Phone No. Fax No. (If any) E-Mail Address (Optional)

Defendant #1

Full name
Address for Service *(street and number, city, postal code)*
Phone No. Fax No. (If any) E-Mail Address (Optional)
Defendant's Lawyer/Agent (Full Name)

Defendant #2 (if applicable)

Full Name
Address for Service *(street and number, city, postal code)*
Phone No. Fax No. (If any) E-Mail Address (Optional)
Defendant's Lawyer/Agent (Full Name)

Lawyer/Agent's Address for Service	Lawyer/Agent's Address for Service
Lawyer/Agent's Phone No. Fax No. (If any) E-Mail Address (Optional)	Lawyer/Agent's Phone No. Fax No. (If any) E-Mail Address (Optional)

Defendant #3	**Defendant #4 (if applicable)**
Full name	Full Name
Address for Service *(street and number, city, postal code)*	Address for Service *(street and number, city, postal code)*
Phone No. Fax No. (If any) E-Mail Address (Optional)	Phone No. Fax No. (If any) E-Mail Address (Optional)
Defendant's Lawyer/Agent (Full Name)	**Defendant's Lawyer/Agent** (Full Name)
Lawyer/Agent's Address for Service	Lawyer/Agent's Address for Service
Lawyer/Agent's Phone No. Fax No. (If any) E-Mail Address (Optional)	Lawyer/Agent's Phone No. Fax No. (If any) E-Mail Address (Optional)

[O. Reg. 295/99, s. 1; O. Reg. 461/01, s. 21]

[Note: For greater certainty, the amendments made by Ontario Regulation 295/99 do not affect the application of section 10 of the *Courts Improvement Act, 1996*. See: O. Reg. 295/99, s. 2.]

Form 4A

CONSENT TO ACT AS PLAINTIFF'S LITIGATION GUARDIAN

I, ...
(name of litigation guardian)

living at ....
(street and number)

....
(city, province, postal code)

....
(telephone number and fax number, if any)

Consent to act as litigation guardian for the plaintiff in this action.

I have given written authority

to ....
(name of lawyer/agent with authority to act in this proceeding)

of ....
(street and number)

....
(city, province, postal code)

....
(telephone number and fax number, if any)

to act in this proceeding.

The Plaintiff is under the following disability:

    ☐   a minor whose birth date is ....
                                       (state date of birth of minor)

    ☐   mentally incapable within the meaning of section 6 or section 45 of the *Substitute Decisions Act, 1992* in respect of an issue in a proceeding.

    ☐   an absentee within the meaning of the *Absentees Act*.

My relationship to the plaintiff is...
(state relationship, if any)

I have no interest in this action adverse to that of the plaintiff and I acknowledge that I know that I may be personally liable for any costs awarded against me or against the plaintiff.

....
         (Date)   (Signature of litigation guardian)

Form 4B

CONSENT TO ACT AS DEFENDANT'S LITIGATION GUARDIAN

I, ...
                           (name of litigation guardian)

living at ....
               (street and number)

              ....
               (city, province, postal code)

              ....
               (telephone number and fax number, if any)

Consent to act as litigation guardian for the defendant in this action.

I have given written authority

to ....
      (name of lawyer/agent with authority to act in this proceeding)

of ....
      (street and number)

     ....
     (city, province, postal code)

     ....
     (telephone number and fax number, if any)

to act in this proceeding.

The Defendant is under the following disability:

- ☐   a minor whose birth date is ....
                                            (state date of birth of minor)

- ☐   mentally incapable within the meaning of section 6 or section 45 of the *Substitute Decisions Act, 1992* in respect of an issue in a proceeding.

- ☐   an absentee within the meaning of the *Absentees Act*.

My relationship to the defendant is ....
(state relationship, if any)

I have no interest in this action adverse to that of the defendant and I acknowledge that I know that I may be personally liable for any costs awarded against me or against the defendant.

....
(Date)   (Signature of litigation guardian)

Form 5A

NOTICE TO ALLEGED PARTNER

To ....
    (name of alleged partner)

....
    (street and number)

....
    (city, province, postal code)

....
    (phone number and fax number, if any of alleged partner)

YOU ARE ALLEGED TO HAVE BEEN A PARTNER on ....

(or during the period) .... in the partnership of...........................
                      (Date)

.... a party named in this proceeding.
  (Firm Name)

IF YOU WISH TO DENY THAT YOU WERE A PARTNER at any material time, you must defend this proceeding separately from the partnership, denying that you were a partner at the material time. If you fail to do so you will be deemed to have been a partner on the date (or during the period) set out above.

AN ORDER AGAINST THE PARTNERSHIP MAY BE ENFORCED AGAINST YOU PERSONALLY if you are deemed to have been a partner, if you admit that you were a partner, or if the court finds that you were a partner at the material time.

....
    (Date)   (Name of Plaintiff or Plaintiff's lawyer/agent)

Form 7A

PLAINTIFF'S CLAIM

TO THE DEFENDANT:

....
(Name of Defendant)

The Plaintiff claims from you $ ...., and costs for the reason(s) set out below.

IF YOU DO NOT FILE A DEFENCE WITH THE COURT WITHIN TWENTY (20) DAYS AFTER YOU HAVE RECEIVED THIS CLAIM, JUDGMENT MAY BE ENTERED AGAINST YOU.

TYPE OF CLAIM

❏ Unpaid Account	❏ Contract	❏ Motor Vehicle Accident
❏ Promissory Note	❏ Services Rendered	❏ N.S.F. cheque
❏ Damage to Property	❏ Lease	❏ Other/ ....

REASONS FOR CLAIM AND DETAILS

(Explain what happened, where and when *and* the amounts of money involved.)

....

....

If the claim is based in whole or in part on a document, attach a copy of the document to the claim, or if the document is lost or unavailable, explain why it is not attached.

....
(Date)   (Clerk's signature)

Form 8A

CERTIFICATE OF SERVICE
BAILIFF OR BAILIFF'S OFFICER

I, ... ,

bailiff (or bailiff's officer) of the ....

Small Claims Court, certify that I have served the ....

....
(name of document)

❑ Personally on .... ,
                  (Name of Person Served)

    on ....
               (Date)

OR

❑ by leaving a copy of document in a sealed envelope addressed to the defendant with:

   .... at ....
   (Name of Person document was   (Address)
   left with)

and by mailing another copy of the document addressed to the defendant at:

....
(Address where mailed to)

    on ....
           (Date)

....
      (Date)   (Signature of bailiff/deputy bailiff)

Form 8B

AFFIDAVIT OF SERVICE

I, ..., of the ....
   (full name)   (City, Town, etc.)

of .... in the .... of
   (Name of City/Town)   (County/Regional Municipality, etc.)
                                (Name of County/Regional Municipality)

MAKE OATH AND SAY (or AFFIRM):

I have served the .... on ....
                  (Name of document)   (Name of person)

❑ personally on .... by leaving a copy with him/her
                        (Date)

at ....
                        (Address where document was served)

....

I was able to identify the person by means of (state the means by which the person's identity was ascertained.) ....
....

OR

❑ by leaving a copy of the ....
                              (Name of document)

in a sealed envelope addressed to ....
                                    (Name of party to be served)

with .... who appeared to be an adult
        (Identify person served, if known)

member of the same household in which

....
                        (Name of person to be served)

resides at ....
(Address where service was made)

.... and by sending another copy of the
(Name of Document)

.... by regular lettermail addressed to

.... at the same address on
(Name of party to be served)

....;
(Date)

OR

❏ by sending a copy of the ....
(Name of document)

in an envelope showing my return address to ....
(Name of party to be served)

by regular lettermail/registered mail at ....
(Cross out method of mail not used)   (Address to which the document
 was mailed)

on ....
(Date)

I believe that this is the address of ....
(Name of party to be served)

because..
(State reason for belief here)

....

The document has not been returned to me and I have no reason to believe that it

was not received by ....
(Name of party to be served)

NOTE: A claim served by mail is not considered to have been served until twenty days have elapsed from the date of mailing. Accordingly, the affidavit of service cannot be completed until twenty days from mailing have elapsed.

OR

☐ Specify other method of service, e.g. service on a corporation *(identify person served and position in the corporation)*, service on a party's solicitor, etc.

....

....

SWORN (OR AFFIRMED) BEFORE ME AT

this .... day of .... 20 .....

....
Signature

....
A COMMISSIONER FOR TAKING AFFIDAVITS
(or as may be)

WARNING	IT IS A CRIMINAL OFFENCE TO KNOWINGLY SWEAR A FALSE AFFIDAVIT

Form 9A

DEFENCE

- ☐ I/We dispute the full claim made by the plaintiff.
- ☐ I/We admit the plaintiff's full claim and propose the following terms of payment.

    $ ....per ....…..……….commencing

    ……………………………………….

- ☐ I/We admit part of the plaintiff's claim amounting to $ ………………..
  and propose the following terms of payment: $ ……………………….
  per …………………....commencing………………………………………....

- ☐ I/we dispute the balance of the claim.

REASONS FOR DISPUTING THE CLAIM AND DETAILS:

…………………………………………………………………………………

…………………………………………………………………………………

If the defence is based in whole or in part on a document, attach a copy of the document to the defence, or if the document is lost or unavailable, explain why it is not attached.

NOTE:

If the defence contains a proposal for terms of payment, the plaintiff is deemed to have accepted the terms unless the plaintiff, in writing to the clerk, disputes the proposal and requests a hearing within 20 days of service of a copy of the DEFENCE.

IF THE DEFENDANT FAILS TO MAKE PAYMENT IN ACCORDANCE WITH THE TERMS OF PAYMENT PROPOSED, THE CLERK MAY SIGN JUDGMENT FOR THE UNPAID BALANCE WITHOUT A HEARING.

………………………………   …………………………………………………
(Date)   (Defendant's Signature or
                                                   Solicitor/Agent's Name)

Form 9B

REQUEST FOR A HEARING
(DISPUTE OF PROPOSAL OF TERMS OF PAYMENT)

TO THE COURT:

I, ………...………………………………………………, dispute the defendant's proposal to terms of payments to the claim filed, and request that a hearing be held in this proceeding for the following reasons: *(Give reasons for request).*

....

....

....
(Signature of party, solicitor or agent)

Form 9C

ORDER AS TO TERMS OF PAYMENT

At a hearing held on ....the
                         (Date)   (Year)

following terms of payment for a total of $ .... and
                                                          (Claim)

$ ....were ordered.
      (Costs)

....

....

....
(Date order made)   (Signature of referee/designated person)

NOTE:
If the defendant fails to make payment in accordance with this order, the clerk shall sign judgment for the balance without a hearing.

Form 10A

DEFENDANT'S CLAIM

TO THE DEFENDANT IN THE DEFENDANT'S CLAIM: ……………….

……………………………………………..

The Plaintiff in the defendant's claim in this action claims from you $ …………, and costs for the reason(s) set out below.

IF YOU DO NOT FILE A DEFENCE WITH THE COURT WITHIN TWENTY (20) DAYS AFTER YOU HAVE RECEIVED THIS DEFENDANT'S CLAIM, JUDGMENT MAY BE ENTERED AGAINST YOU.

TYPE OF CLAIM

❏ Unpaid Account	❏ Contract	❏ Motor Vehicle Accident
❏ Promissory Note	❏ Services Rendered	❏ N.S.F. cheque
❏ Damage to Property	❏ Lease	❏ Other

REASONS FOR CLAIM AND DETAILS

(Explain what happened, where and when *and* the amounts of money involved.)
Reasons for claim and details
……………………………………………………………………………………

……………………………………………………………………………………

If the claim is based in whole or in part on a document, attach a copy of the document to the defendant's claim, or if the document is lost or unavailable, explain why it is not attached.

………………………   ……………………………………………………
    (Date)   (Signature of Clerk)

Form 11A

NOTICE OF DEFAULT JUDGMENT

NOTE: Take notice that default judgment has been entered in this action as against...for the following sums:

Debt	$ ....
Pre-judgment Interest	$ ....
Costs	$ ....
Sub-Total	$ ....

Post-judgment Interest at .... per cent per annum commencing this date.

....
(Date)   (Clerk)

Form 13A

REQUEST FOR PRE-TRIAL CONFERENCE

TO THE COURT:

1, ………………………………………………….. request that a pre-trial conference be held in this proceeding.

………..……………………………………
(Signature of party, solicitor or agent)

Form 15A

NOTICE OF MOTION

TAKE NOTICE:

A motion will be made to the court by .... at
                                                    (Name of party)

.... on
                     (Name and location of court)

.... at .... (or so soon thereafter
   (Date)   (Time)

as the motion can be heard) for the following order: *(Specify)*

....

....

The following material will be relied on at the hearing of the motion: *(Specify, and where an affidavit is to be relied on, attach a copy.)*

....

....

TAKE NOTICE: If you fail to appear at the hearing of this motion, an order may be made in your absence.

....
   (Date)   (Signature of party or party's lawyer/agent)

Form 15B

AFFIDAVIT

I, (full name) ...., of the (City, Town, etc.)

.... of .... in the (County,

Regional Municipality, etc.) of ....

MAKE OATH AND SAY (or AFFIRM):

(Give facts in support of the motion. If the facts are not within your own personal knowledge, give the source of your information or the grounds for your belief.)

....

....

SWORN (or AFFIRMED) BEFORE ME AT

this .... day of ...., 20........

....
(Signature)

....
A COMMISSIONER FOR TAKING
AFFIDAVITS (or as may be)

WARNING	IT IS A CRIMINAL OFFENCE TO KNOWINGLY SWEAR A FALSE AFFIDAVIT

Form 16A

NOTICE OF TRIAL

TAKE NOTICE: The trial of this action will be held in the ....

.... at ....……...
(Name of court)   (Location of Court)

on ………………. at ……………..or so soon thereafter as the trial may be held.
    (Date)   (Time)

TAKE NOTICE: IF YOU FAIL TO APPEAR, THIS ACTION MAY BE DISPOSED OF WITHOUT FURTHER NOTICE TO YOU.

Dated at ………………..this ………..day of ……………20…..

....
(Clerk)

Form 18A

SUMMONS TO WITNESS

TO: ……………………………………………………………………………..
(Name of witness)

YOU ARE REQUIRED TO ATTEND TO GIVE EVIDENCE IN COURT

at the trial of this action on ……………., at ……..……. at ……………………..
(date)   (time)

……………………………………………………………………………………
(address of court)

and to remain until your attendance is no longer required.

YOU ARE REQUIRED TO BRING WITH YOU and produce at the trial the following documents and things:

……………………………………………………………………………………

……………………………………………………………………………………
(State particular documents and things required)

and all other documents relating to the action in your custody, possession or control.

IF YOU FAIL TO ATTEND OR TO REMAIN IN ATTENDANCE AS REQUIRED BY THIS SUMMONS, A WARRANT MAY BE ISSUED FOR YOUR ARREST.

………………………..   …………………………………..
(Date)   (Signature of Clerk)

Form 18B

WARRANT FOR ARREST OF DEFAULTING WITNESS

TO ALL police officers in Ontario AND TO the officers of all correctional institutions in Ontario.

1. The witness ....
   (name)

   of ....
   (address)

was served with a summons to witness to give evidence at the trial of this action, and the prescribed attendance money was paid or tendered.

2. The witness failed to (attend)/(remain in attendance) at the trial, and I am satisfied that the evidence of the witness is material to this proceeding.

YOU ARE ORDERED to arrest and bring the witness ....
(name of witness)

before the court to give evidence in this action, and if the court is not then sitting or if the witness cannot be brought before the court immediately, to deliver the witness to a provincial correctional institution or other secure facility, to be admitted and detained there until the witness can be brought before the court.

....
(Date)   (Signature of judge)

Form 20A

CERTIFICATE OF JUDGMENT

TO THE CLERK OF THE …………………..**SMALL CLAIMS COURT**

Person requesting Certificate is ……………………………………………
(Name of person requesting Certificate)

of ……………………………………………………………………………
(Address)

A Judgment was recovered in this action against ………………………………

………………………………………………………………………………
(Name of person against whom judgment was recovered)

on ………………..**in the** ……………..**Small Claims Court** …………………
   (Date)

for the following:

Debt	$ ……………………………..
Pre-Judgment Interest	$ ……………………………..
Costs	$ ……………………………..
Subtotal	$ ……………………………..
Amount paid	$ ……………………………..
Balance Due	$ ……………………………..
Additional Cost	$ ……………………………..
Total	$ ……………………………..

The amount unpaid on the judgment is $…………………………….. **as stated**
(Total)
in this certificate and the rate of postjudgment interest is ………..**per cent.**

……………………….   ……………………………………………
   (Date)   (Signature of Clerk)

Form 20B

WRIT OF DELIVERY

TO THE BAILIFF OF THE........................ **SMALL CLAIMS COURT**

Under an order of this court made on ....
(Date)

YOU ARE DIRECTED to seize from ....…............................
(Name of person against whom
the order was made)

and to deliver without delay to ....…..
(Name of person in whose
favour the order was made)

the following personal property: *(set out a description of the property to be delivered together with any identifying marks or serial numbers)*

....

....

....
(Date)   (Signature of Clerk)

Form 20C

WRIT OF SEIZURE AND SALE OF PERSONAL PROPERTY

TO: BAILIFF OF ……………………………...**SMALL CLAIMS COURT**

Under an order of this court made on …………………………….in favour of
(date)

……………………………………. **YOU ARE DIRECTED** to seize and sell
(name of creditor)

the personal property of …………………………..situate within your jurisdiction
(name of debtor)

and to realize from the seizure and sale the following sums:

(A) Debt $ …………………

   Pre-Judgment Interest at ……….
   per cent per annum commencing ……….. $ …………………

(B) Costs $ …………………

   Post-Judgment Interest at ……….
   per cent per annum commencing ………. $ …………………

   Subsequent costs incurred after judgment $ …………………..

        This Execution $ …………………..

                                                  $ …………………..

(C) Your fees and expenses in enforcing this
    writ $ …………………

YOU ARE DIRECTED to pay the proceeds over to the clerk of this court for the creditor

………………………………….   …………………………………………..
(Date)   (Signature of Clerk)

THIS WRIT REMAINS IN FORCE FOR SIX (6) MONTHS FROM THE DATE OF ITS ISSUE.

Form 20D

WRIT OF SEIZURE AND SALE OF LAND

TO: THE SHERIFF OF ....
                                             (name of area)

Under an order of this court made on ....in favour of
                                                          (date)

.... **YOU ARE DIRECTED** to seize and
          (name of creditor)

sell the real property of ....situate within your jurisdiction
                                       (name of debtor)

and to realize from the seizure and sale the following sums:

(A) Debt $ ....

   Pre-Judgment Interest at ....
   per cent per annum commencing .... $ ....

(B) Costs $ ....

   Post-Judgment Interest at ....
   per cent per annum commencing .... $ ....

   Subsequent costs incurred after judgment $...................

   This Execution $ ....

                                                                         $ ....

(C) Your fees and expenses in enforcing this writ $ ....

YOU ARE DIRECTED to pay out the proceeds according to law and to report on the execution of this writ if required by the party or solicitor who filed it.

....   Issued by ....
         (Date)   (Clerk)

                              Court office ....

Form 20E

NOTICE OF GARNISHMENT

Superior Court of Justice

............................Small Claims Court

Refer to No. /
Amount Unsatisfied $ ....

Creditor

Full name
Address for Service *(street and number, city, postal code)*
Phone No. Fax No. (If any)
Creditor's Lawyer/Agent (Full Name)
Lawyer/Agent's Address for Service
Lawyer/Agent's Phone No. Fax No. (If any)

Debtor

Full name
Address for Service *(street and number, city, postal code)*
Phone No. Fax No. (If any)
Debtor's Lawyer/Agent (Full Name)
Lawyer/Agent's Address for Service
Lawyer/Agent's Phone No. Fax No. (If any)

Garnishee
Full name
Address for Service *(street and number, city, postal code)*
Phone No. Fax No. (If any)

TO: GARNISHEE

A LEGAL PROCEEDING in this court between the creditor and the debtor has resulted in an order that the debtor pay a sum of money to the creditor. The creditor claims that you owe a debt to the debtor. A debt to the debtor includes both a debt payable to the debtor and a debt payable to the debtor and one or more co-owners. The creditor has had this notice of garnishment directed to you as garnishee in order to seize any debt that you owe or will owe to the debtor. Where the debt is payable to the debtor and to one or more co-owners, you must pay one-half of the indebtedness or a greater or lesser amount specified in an order made under subrule 20.08 (15).

Subject to the exemptions provided by section 7 of the *Wages Act.*

YOU ARE REQUIRED TO PAY to the clerk of the ....

.... Small Claims Court
   (Issuing Court)

(a) within ten days after this notice is served on you, all debts now payable by you to the debtor; and

(b) within ten days after they become payable, all debts that become payable by you to the debtor within twenty-four (24) months after this notice is served on you.

The total amount of all your payments to the clerk is not to exceed $ ....

IF YOU DO NOT PAY THE TOTAL AMOUNT OR SUCH LESSER AMOUNT AS YOU ARE LIABLE TO PAY UNDER THIS NOTICE WITHIN TEN DAYS after this notice is served on you, you must file with the clerk a statement signed by you setting out the particulars of why you have not done so. **EACH PAYMENT MUST BE SENT** to the clerk at the address shown below.

IF YOU FAIL TO OBEY THIS NOTICE, AN ORDER MAY BE OBTAINED AGAINST YOU BY THE CREDITOR for payment of the amount set out above and the costs of the creditor as may be ordered by the court.

IF YOU MAKE PAYMENT TO ANYONE OTHER THAN THE CLERK, YOU MAY BE LIABLE TO PAY AGAIN.

TO THE CREDITOR, THE DEBTOR AND THE GARNISHEE:

Any party may make a motion to determine any matter in relation to this notice of garnishment.

....
(Date)

....
(Signature of Clerk)

....
(Address of court office)

THIS NOTICE SHALL BE SERVED TOGETHER WITH THE NOTICE TO GARNISHEE.

[Note: For greater certainty, the amendments made by Ontario Regulation 295/99 do not affect the application of section 10 of the *Courts Improvement Act, 1996*. See: O. Reg. 295/99, s. 2.]

Form 20F

GARNISHEE'S STATEMENT

Superior Court of Justice

| Claim No. | / |

.... **Small Claims Court**

Creditor

Full name
Address for Service *(street and number, city, postal code)*
Phone No. Fax No. (If any)
Creditor's Lawyer/Agent (Full Name)
Lawyer/Agent's Address for Service
Lawyer/Agent's Phone No. Fax No. (If any)

Debtor

Full name
Address for Service *(street and number, city, postal code)*
Phone No. Fax No. (If any)
Debtor's Lawyer/Agent (Full Name)
Lawyer/Agent's Address for Service
Lawyer/Agent's Phone No. Fax No. (If any)

Garnishee
Full name
Address for Service *(street and number, city, postal code)*
Phone No. Fax No. (If any)

1. I/We acknowledge that I/we owe or will owe the debtor or the debtor and one or more co-owners the sum of $ ……………………………, payable on

   …………………………….. because:
   (date)

(Give reasons why you owe the debtor or the debtor and one or more co-owners money. If you are making payment of less than the amount stated in line 2 of this paragraph because the debt is owed to the debtor and to one or more co-owners or for any other reason, give a full explanation of the reason. If you owe the debtor wages, state how often the debtor is paid. State the gross amount of the debtor's wages before any deductions and the net amount after all deductions and attach a copy of a pay slip.)

………………………………………………………………………………

………………………………………………………………………………

1.1 (If debt owed to debtor and one or more co-owners, check here ❑ and complete the following:)

Co-owner(s) of the Debt …………………………………………………
(name, address)

2. (If you do not owe the debtor money, explain why. Give any other information that will explain your financial relationship with the debtor.)

………………………………………………………………………………

………………………………………………………………………………

3. (If you have been served with any other notice of garnishment or a writ of execution against the debtor, give particulars.)

| Name of Creditor | Location of Sheriff | Date of Notice or writ | Date of Service on you |

4. (If you have been served outside Ontario and you wish to object on the ground that service outside Ontario was improper, give particulars of your objection.)

....
(Date)   (Signature of or for garnishee)

....
(Name of garnishee)

....
(Address)

....
(Telephone Number)

[Note: For greater certainty, the amendments made by Ontario Regulation 295/99 do not affect the application of section 10 of the *Courts Improvement Act, 1996*. See: O. Reg. 295/99, s. 2.]

Form 20G

NOTICE TO CO-OWNER OF DEBT

Superior Court of Justice

Claim No.	/

...................**Small Claims Court**

Creditor

Full name
Address for Service *(street and number, city, postal code)*
Phone No. Fax No. (If any)
Creditor's Lawyer/Agent (Full Name)
Lawyer/Agent's Address for Service
Lawyer/Agent's Phone No. Fax No. (If any)

Debtor

Full name
Address for Service *(street and number, city, postal code)*
Phone No. Fax No. (If any)
Debtor's Lawyer/Agent (Full Name)
Lawyer/Agent's Address for Service
Lawyer/Agent's Phone No. Fax No. (If any)

Garnishee

Full name
Address for Service *(street and number, city, postal code)*
Phone No. Fax No. (If any)

To   ……………………………..
           (Name of co-owner of Debt)

           ……………………………..
           (Street and number)

           ……………………………..
           (City, province, postal code)

           ……………………………..
           (Phone number and fax number, if any of co-owner of Debt)

A LEGAL PROCEEDING in this court between the creditor and the debtor has resulted in an order that the debtor pay a sum of money to the creditor. The creditor has given a notice of garnishment to……………………………………….. (Name of Garnishee) claiming that the garnishee owes a debt to the debtor. A debt to the debtor includes both a debt payable to the debtor and a debt payable to the debtor and one or more other co-owners. The garnishee has indicated in the attached garnishee's statement that you are a co-owner. Under the notice of garnishment the garnishee has paid one-half of the indebtedness or a greater or lesser amount specified in an order made under subrule 20. 08 (15) to the clerk of the Small Claims Court.

IF YOU HAVE A CLAIM to the money being paid to the clerk of the Small Claims Court by the garnishee, you have 30 days from service of this notice to make a motion to the court for a garnishment hearing. If you fail to do so, you may not hereafter dispute the enforcement of the creditor's order for the payment or recovery of money under the Rules of the Small Claims Court and the funds may be paid out to the creditor unless the court orders otherwise.

………………………………….
     (Date)

[Note: For greater certainty, the amendments made by Ontario Regulation 295/99 do not affect the application of section 10 of the *Courts Improvement Act, 1996*. See: O. Reg. 295/99, s. 2.]

Form 20H

NOTICE OF EXAMINATION

Superior Court of Justice

| Claim No. | / |

……………………..Small Claims Court

Creditor

Full name
Address for Service *(street and number, city, postal code)*
Phone No. Fax No. (If any)
Creditor's Lawyer/Agent (Full Name)
Lawyer/Agent's Address for Service
Lawyer/Agent's Phone No. Fax No. (If any)

Debtor

Full name
Address for Service *(street and number, city, postal code)*
Phone No. Fax No. (If any)
Debtor's Lawyer/Agent (Full Name)
Lawyer/Agent's Address for Service
Lawyer/Agent's Phone No. Fax No. (If any)

TO: ....
           (name of person to be summoned)

On ...., the plaintiff recovered judgment against
           (Date)

....in the
           (name of person/party against whom judgment was made)

.... for $ ....and $ ....costs.
           (name of court)

The judgment remains outstanding.

YOU ARE REQUIRED TO ATTEND AN EXAMINATION to determine

the means .... has to satisfy this
                                    (name of defendant)

judgment and whether ....intends to satisfy it or *has* any
                                    (name of defendant)

reason for not doing so.

THE EXAMINATION WILL BE HELD at the next sitting of this court at

.... on ....
           (location of court)   (Date)

at ....
           (Time)

TAKE NOTICE THAT IF YOU DO NOT ATTEND AS REQUIRED BY THIS NOTICE OR YOU REFUSE TO ANSWER QUESTIONS, THE COURT MAY FIND YOU IN CONTEMPT OF COURT AND ORDER YOU TO ATTEND FOR A CONTEMPT HEARING.

....
           (Date)   (Signature of Clerk)

[Note: For greater certainty, the amendments made by Ontario Regulation 295/99 do not affect the application of section 10 of the *Courts Improvement Act, 1996*. See: O. Reg. 295/99, s. 2.]

Appendix 8

Form 20I

NOTICE OF CONTEMPT HEARING

TAKE NOTICE:

That an order for a contempt hearing has been made against you for:

(a) failure to attend as required by the notice of examination; or
(b) refusal to answer questions at the examination

The contempt hearing is to be held at ....on
                                    (Address)

.... on .... beginning at ....
        (Date)   (Date)   (Time)

If you fail to attend this contempt hearing, the court may:

(a) order that you attend at an examination;
(b) make an order as to payment; or
(c) order that you be jailed for a period not exceeding 40 days.

....
      (Date)   (Signature of Clerk)

Form 20J

WARRANT OF COMMITTAL

TO ALL POLICE OFFICERS IN ONTARIO

AND TO THE OFFICERS OF ALL CORRECTIONAL INSTITUTIONS IN ONTARIO:

A NOTICE OF CONTEMPT HEARING was issued from this court by which

.... was required to attend the
(Name of person required to attend Contempt Hearing)

sittings of this court at .... on ....
                                  (time)   (date)

WHEREAS it has been duly proved that the notice of contempt hearing has been properly served on ....
                                               (name)

WHEREAS *(state facts relating to failure to attend or refusal to answer questions)*

....

....

WHEREAS a judge of this court thereupon ordered ....
                                                             (name)

to be committed.

YOU ARE ORDERED to take the person named above to the nearest correctional institution and admit and detain him or her there for ....days.

This Warrant expires twelve (12) months from the date of issue, unless renewed by court order.

....
     (Date)   (Signature of Clerk)

APPENDIX 9

Simplified Procedure Court Forms[*]

Form	14D	Statement of Claim (Action Commenced by Notice of Action)
Form	18A	Statement of Defence
Form	18B	Notice of Intent to Defend
Form	24.1A	Notice of Name of Mediator and Date of Session
Form	24.1B	Notice by Assigned Mediator
Form	24.1C	Statement of Issues
Form	24.1D	Certificate of Non-Compliance
Form	25A	Reply
Form	27A	Counterclaim (Against Parties to Main Action Only)
Form	27C	Defence to Counterclaim
Form	27D	Reply to Defence to Counterclaim
Form	28A	Crossclaim
Form	28B	Defence to Crossclaim
Form	28C	Reply to Defence to Crossclaim
Form	29A	Third Party Claim
Form	29B	Third Party Defence
Form	29C	Reply to Third Party Defence
Form	30A	Affidavit of Documents (Individual)
Form	76A	Notice Whether Action Under Rule 76
Form	76B	Simplified Procedure Motion Form
Form	76C	Notice of Readiness for Pre-Trial Conference
Form	76D	Trial Management Checklist

---

[*] *Rules of Civil Procedure*, R.R.O. 1990, Reg. 194, as am.

Form 14D

STATEMENT OF CLAIM
(ACTION COMMENCED BY NOTICE OF ACTION)

(Court file no.)

ONTARIO
SUPERIOR COURT OF JUSTICE

BETWEEN:

(name)

Plaintiff

and

(name)

Defendant

STATEMENT OF CLAIM
Notice of action issued on *date*

(In an action under the simplified procedure provided in Rule 76, add:)

THIS ACTION IS BROUGHT AGAINST YOU UNDER THE SIMPLIFIED PROCEDURE PROVIDED IN RULE 76 OF THE RULES OF CIVIL PROCEDURE.

1. The plaintiff claims: *State here the precise relief claimed.*

(Then set out in separate, consecutively numbered paragraphs each allegation of material fact relied on to substantiate the claim.)

(Where the statement of claim is to be served outside Ontario without a court order, set out the facts and the specific provisions of Rule 17 relied on in support of such service.)

The plaintiff proposes that this action be tried at *(place)*.

(Date)   *(Name, address and telephone number
                                       of solicitor or plaintiff)*

[O. Reg. 533/95, s. 8; O. Reg. 652/00, s. 4]

Form 18A

STATEMENT OF DEFENCE

(Court file no.)

ONTARIO
SUPERIOR COURT OF JUSTICE

BETWEEN:

(name)

Plaintiff

and

(name)

Defendant

STATEMENT OF DEFENCE

1. The defendant admits the allegations contained in paragraphs .... of the statement of claim.

2. The defendant denies the allegations contained in paragraphs ....of the statement of claim.

3. The defendant has no knowledge in respect of the allegations contained in paragraphs .... of the statement of claim.

4. *Set out in separate, consecutively numbered paragraphs each allegation of material fact relied on by way of defence.*

(Date)   *(Name, address and telephone number of defendant's solicitor or defendant)*

TO   *(Name and address of plaintiff's solicitor or plaintiff)*

Form 18B

NOTICE OF INTENT TO DEFEND

(Court file no.)

ONTARIO
SUPERIOR COURT OF JUSTICE

BETWEEN:

(name)

Plaintiff

and

(name)

Defendant

NOTICE OF INTENT TO DEFEND

The defendant (or defendant added by counterclaim or third party) intends to defend this action.

(Date)   *(Name, address and telephone number of solicitor or party serving notice)*

TO   *(Name and address of solicitor or party on whom notice is served)*

Form 24.1A

Courts of Justice Act

(Court file no.)

ONTARIO
SUPERIOR COURT OF JUSTICE

BETWEEN:

(name)

Plaintiff

and

(name)

Defendant

NOTICE OF NAME OF MEDIATOR AND DATE OF SESSION

TO: MEDIATION CO-ORDINATOR

1. I certify that I have consulted with the parties and that the parties have chosen the following mediator for the mediation session required by Rule 24.1: *(name)*

2. The mediator is named in the list of mediators for *(name county)*.

(or)

2. The mediator is not named in a list of mediators, but has been chosen by the parties under clause 24.1.08(2)(a) or (c).

3. The mediation session will take place on *(date)*.

(Date)   *(Name, address, telephone number and fax number of plaintiff's lawyer or of plaintiff)*

[O. Reg. 453/98, s. 2; O. Reg. 627/98, s. 10; O. Reg. 244/01, s. 7]

Form 24.1B

Courts of Justice Act

(*Court file no.*)

ONTARIO
SUPERIOR COURT OF JUSTICE

BETWEEN:

(*name*)

Plaintiff

and

(*name*)

Defendant

NOTICE BY ASSIGNED MEDIATOR

TO:
AND TO:

The notice of name of mediator and date of session (Form 24.1A) required by rule 24.1.09 of the *Rules of Civil Procedure* has not been filed in this action. Accordingly, the mediation co-ordinator has assigned me to conduct the mediation session under Rule 24.1. I am a mediator named in the list of mediators for (*name county*).

The mediation session will take place on (*date*), from (*time*) to (*time*), at (*place*).

Unless the court orders otherwise, you are required to attend this mediation session. If you have a lawyer representing you in this action, he or she is also required to attend.

You are required to file a statement of issues (Form 24.1C) by (*date*) (seven days before the mediation session). A blank copy of the form is attached.

When you attend the mediation session, you should bring with you any documents that you consider of central importance in the action. You should plan to remain throughout the scheduled time. If you need another person's approval before agreeing to a settlement, you should make arrangements before the mediation session to ensure that you have ready telephone access to that person throughout the session, even outside regular business hours.

YOU MAY BE PENALIZED UNDER RULE 24.1.13 IF YOU FAIL TO FILE A STATEMENT OF ISSUES OR FAIL TO ATTEND THE MEDIATION SESSION.

(Date) *(Name, address, telephone number and fax number of mediator)*

cc. Mediation co-ordinator

[O. Reg. 453/98, s. 2; O. Reg. 244/01, s. 7]

Form 24.1C

Courts of Justice Act

(Court file no.)

**ONTARIO
SUPERIOR COURT OF JUSTICE**

BETWEEN:

(name)

Plaintiff

and

(name)

Defendant

STATEMENT OF ISSUES

(To be provided to mediator and parties at least seven days before the mediation session)

1. Factual and legal issues in dispute

The plaintiff *(or* defendant*)* states that the following factual and legal issues are in dispute and remain to be resolved.

(Issues should be stated briefly and numbered consecutively.)

2. Party's position and interests (what the party hopes to achieve)

(Brief summary.)

3. Attached documents

Attached to this form are the following documents that the plaintiff *(or* defendant*)* considers of central importance in the action: *(list)*

(date)   *(party's signature)*

(Name, address, telephone number and fax number of lawyer of party filing statement of issues, or of party)

NOTE: When the plaintiff provides a copy of this form to the mediator, a copy of the pleadings shall also be included.

Appendix 9

NOTE: Rule 24.1.14 provides as follows:

All communications at a mediation session and the mediator's notes and records shall be deemed to be without prejudice settlement discussions.

[O. Reg. 453/98, s. 2; O. Reg. 244/01, s. 7]

Form 24.1D

Courts of Justice Act

(Court file no.)

ONTARIO
SUPERIOR COURT OF JUSTICE

BETWEEN:

(name)

Plaintiff

and

(name)

Defendant

CERTIFICATE OF NON-COMPLIANCE

TO: MEDIATION CO-ORDINATOR

I, *(name)*, mediator, certify that this certificate of non-compliance is filed because:

( )   *(Identify party(ies))* failed to provide a copy of a statement of issues to the mediator and the other parties *(or* to the mediator *or* to *party(ies))*.

( )   *(Identify plaintiff)* failed to provide a copy of the pleadings to the mediator.

( )   *(Identify party(ies))* failed to attend within the first 30 minutes of a scheduled mediation session.

(Date)

(Name, address, telephone number and fax number, if any, of mediator)

[O. Reg. 453/98, s. 2; O. Reg. 244/01, s. 7]

Form 25A

REPLY

(Court file no.)

ONTARIO
SUPERIOR COURT OF JUSTICE

BETWEEN:

(name)

Plaintiff

and

(name)

Defendant

REPLY

1. The plaintiff admits the allegations contained in paragraphs ……. of the statement of defence.

2. The plaintiff denies the allegations contained in paragraphs …….. of the statement of defence.

3. The plaintiff has no knowledge in respect of the allegations contained in paragraphs ……… of the statement of defence.

4. *(Set out in separate, consecutively numbered paragraphs each allegation of material fact relied on by way of reply to the statement of defence.)*

(Date) *(Name, address and telephone number of plaintiff's solicitor or plaintiff)*

TO *(Name and address of defendant's solicitor or defendant)*

Form 27A

COUNTERCLAIM
(AGAINST PARTIES TO MAIN ACTION ONLY)

(Where the counterclaim includes as a defendant to the counterclaim a person who is not already a party to the main action, use Form 27B.)

(Include the counterclaim in the same document as the statement of defence, and entitle the document STATEMENT OF DEFENCE AND COUNTERCLAIM. *The counterclaim is to follow the last paragraph of the statement of defence. Number the paragraphs in sequence commencing with the number following the number of the last paragraph of the statement of defence.)*

COUNTERCLAIM

The defendant *(name if more than one defendant)* claims: *(State here the precise relief claimed.)*

(Then set out in separate, consecutively numbered paragraphs each allegation of material fact relied on to substantiate the counterclaim.)

(Where the defendant to the counterclaim is sued in a capacity other than that in which the defendant is a party to the main action, set out the capacity.)

(Date)   *(Name, address and telephone number of plaintiff by counterclaim's solicitor or plaintiff by counterclaim)*

TO   *(Name and address of solicitor for defendant to the counterclaim or of defendant to the counterclaim)*

Appendix 9

Form 27C

DEFENCE TO COUNTERCLAIM

(Court file no.)

ONTARIO
SUPERIOR COURT OF JUSTICE

BETWEEN:

(name)

Plaintiff
(Defendant by Counterclaim)

and

(name)

Defendant
(Plaintiff by Counterclaim)

(A plaintiff who delivers a reply in the main action must include the defence to counterclaim in the same document as the reply, and the document is to be entitled REPLY AND DEFENCE TO COUNTERCLAIM. *The defence to counterclaim is to follow immediately after the last paragraph of the reply and the paragraphs are to be numbered in sequence commencing with the number following the number of the last paragraph of the reply.)*

DEFENCE TO COUNTERCLAIM

1. The defendant to the counterclaim admits the allegations contained in paragraphs .... of the counterclaim.

2. The defendant to the counterclaim denies the allegations contained in paragraphs .... of the counterclaim.

3. The defendant to the counterclaim has no knowledge in respect of the allegations contained in paragraphs .... of the counterclaim.

4. *(Set out in separate, consecutively numbered paragraphs each allegation of material fact relied on by way of defence to the counterclaim.)*

(Date)

(Name, address and telephone number of solicitor for defendant to the counterclaim or defendant to the counterclaim)

TO   *(Name and address of plaintiff by counterclaim's solicitor or of plaintiff by counterclaim)*

Form 27D

REPLY TO DEFENCE TO COUNTERCLAIM

(Court file no.)

ONTARIO
SUPERIOR COURT OF JUSTICE

BETWEEN:

(name)

Plaintiff
(Defendant by Counterclaim)

and

(name)

Defendant
(Plaintiff by Counterclaim)

REPLY TO DEFENCE TO COUNTERCLAIM

1. The plaintiff by counterclaim admits the allegations contained in paragraphs ……. of the defence to counterclaim.

2. The plaintiff by counterclaim denies the allegations contained in paragraphs …….. of the defence to counterclaim.

3. The plaintiff by counterclaim has no knowledge in respect of the allegations contained in paragraphs …….. of the defence to counterclaim.

4. *(Set out in separate, consecutively numbered paragraphs each allegation of material fact relied on by way of reply to the defence to counterclaim.)*

(Date)   *(Name, address and telephone number of plaintiff by counterclaim's solicitor or plaintiff by counterclaim)*

TO   *(Name and address of solicitor for the defendant to the counterclaim or defendant to the counterclaim)*

Form 28A

CROSSCLAIIM

(Include the crossclaim in the same document as the statement of defence, and entitle the document STATEMENT OF DEFENCE AND CROSSCLAIM. *The crossclaim is to follow the last paragraph of the statement of defence. Number the paragraphs in sequence commencing with the number following the number of the last paragraph of the statement of defence.)*

CROSSCLAIM

The defendant *(name)* claims against the defendant *(name)*: *(State here the precise relief claimed).*

(Then set out in separate, consecutively numbered paragraphs each allegation of material fact relied on to substantiate the crossclaim.)

(Where a defendant to the crossclaim is sued in a capacity other than that in which the defendant is a party to the main action, set out the capacity. Where the statement of defence and crossclaim is to be served outside Ontario without a court order, include the facts and the specific provisions of Rule 17 relied on in support of such service.)

(Date) *(Name, address and telephone number of crossclaiming defendant's solicitor or crossclaiming defendant)*

TO *(Name and address of defendant to crossclaim's solicitor or defendant to crossclaim)*

Form 28B

DEFENCE TO CROSSCLAIM

(Court file no.)

ONTARIO
SUPERIOR COURT OF JUSTICE

BETWEEN:

(name)

Plaintiff

and

(name)

Defendant

DEFENCE TO CROSSCLAIM

1. The defendant *(name)* admits the allegations contained in paragraphs .... of the crossclaim.

2. The defendant *(name)* denies the allegations contained in paragraphs .... of the crossclaim.

3. The defendant *(name)* has no knowledge in respect of the allegations contained in paragraphs .... of the crossclaim.

4. *(Set out in separate, consecutively numbered paragraphs each allegation of material fact relied on by way of defence to the crossclaim.)*

(Date)   *(Name, address and telephone number of defendant to crossclaim's solicitor or defendant to crossclaim)*

TO   *(Name and address of crossclaiming defendant's solicitor or crossclaiming defendant)*

Appendix 9

Form 28C

REPLY TO DEFENCE TO CROSSCLAIM

(Court file no.)

ONTARIO
SUPERIOR COURT OF JUSTICE

BETWEEN:

(name)

Plaintiff

and

(name)

Defendant

REPLY TO DEFENCE TO CROSSCLAIM

1. The defendant *(name)* admits the allegations contained in paragraphs......... of the defence to crossclaim.

2. The defendant *(name)* denies the allegations contained in paragraphs .... of the defence to crossclaim.

3. The defendant *(name)* has no knowledge in respect of the allegations contained in paragraphs .... of the defence to crossclaim.

4. *(Set out in separate, consecutively numbered paragraphs each allegation of material fact relied on by way of reply to the defence to crossclaim.)*

(Date) *(Name, address and telephone number of crossclaiming defendant's solicitor or crossclaiming defendant)*

TO *(Name and address of defendant to crossclaim's solicitor or defendant to crossclaim)*

Form 29A

THIRD PARTY CLAIM

(Court file no.)

ONTARIO
SUPERIOR COURT OF JUSTICE

BETWEEN:

(name)

Plaintiff

(Court Seal) and

(name)

Defendant

and

(name)

Third Party

THIRD PARTY CLAIM

TO THE THIRD PARTY

A LEGAL PROCEEDING HAS BEEN COMMENCED AGAINST YOU by way of a third party claim in an action in this court.

The action was commenced by the plaintiff against the defendant for the relief claimed in the statement of claim served with this third party claim. The defendant has defended the action on the grounds set out in the statement of defence served with this third party claim. The defendant's claim against you is set out in the following pages.

IF YOU WISH TO DEFEND THIS THIRD PARTY CLAIM, you or an Ontario lawyer acting for you must prepare a third party defence in Form 29B prescribed by the Rules of Civil Procedure, serve it on the lawyers for the other parties or, where a party does not have a lawyer, serve it on the party, and file it, with proof of service, WITHIN TWENTY DAYS after this third party claim is served on you, if you are served in Ontario.

If you are served in another province or territory of Canada or in the United States of America, the period for serving and filing your third party defence is forty days. If you are served outside Canada and the United States of America, the period is sixty days.

Instead of serving and filing a third party defence, you may serve and file a notice of intent to defend in Form 18B prescribed by the Rules of Civil Procedure. This will entitle you to ten more days within which to serve and file your third party defence.

YOU MAY ALSO DEFEND the action by the plaintiff against the defendant by serving and filing a statement of defence within the time for serving and filing your third party defence.

IF YOU FAIL TO DEFEND THIS THIRD PARTY CLAIM, JUDGMENT MAY BE GIVEN AGAINST YOU IN YOUR ABSENCE AND WITHOUT FURTHER NOTICE TO YOU. IF YOU WISH TO DEFEND THIS PROCEEDING BUT ARE UNABLE TO PAY LEGAL FEES, LEGAL AID MAY BE AVAILABLE TO YOU BY CONTACTING A LOCAL LEGAL AID OFFICE.

(Where the third party claim is for money only, include the following:)

IF YOU PAY THE AMOUNT OF THE THIRD PARTY CLAIM AGAINST YOU, and $ …….. for costs, within the time for serving and filing your third party defence, you may move to have the third party claim dismissed by the court. If you believe the amount claimed for costs is excessive, you may pay the amount of the third party claim and $400.00 for costs and have the costs assessed by the court.

Date _____ Issued by _____
                                                                Local registrar

                                        Address of
                                        court office _____
                                                            _____

TO   *(Name and address of third party)*

CLAIM

1. The defendant claims against the third party: *(State here the precise relief claimed.)*

(Then set out in separate, consecutively numbered paragraphs each allegation of material fact relied on to substantiate the third party claim.)

(Where the third party claim is to be served outside Ontario without a court order, set out the facts and the specific provisions of Rule 17 relied on in support of such service.)

(Date of issue)   *(Name, address and telephone number of defendant's solicitor or defendant)*

[O. Reg. 292/99, s. 1; O. Reg. 653/00, s. 16]

Appendix 9

Form 29B

THIRD PARTY DEFENCE

(Court file no.)

ONTARIO
SUPERIOR COURT OF JUSTICE

BETWEEN:

(name)

Plaintiff

(Court seal) and

(name)

Defendant

and

(name)

Third Party

THIRD PARTY DEFENCE

1. The third party admits the allegations contained in paragraphs .... of the third party claim.

2. The third party denies the allegations contained in paragraphs .... of the third party claim.

3. The third party has no knowledge in respect of the allegations contained in paragraphs .... of the third party claim.

4. *(Set out in separate, consecutively numbered paragraphs each allegation of material fact relied on by way of defence to the third party claim.)*

(Date)   *(Name, address and telephone number of third party's solicitor or third party)*

TO   *(Name and address of defendant's solicitor or defendant)*

Form 29C

REPLY TO THIRD PARTY DEFENCE

(Court file no.)

ONTARIO
SUPERIOR COURT OF JUSTICE

BETWEEN:

(name)

Plaintiff

(Court seal) and

(name)

Defendant

and

(name)

Third Party

REPLY TO THIRD PARTY DEFENCE

1. The defendant admits the allegations contained in paragraphs .... of the third party defence.

2. The defendant denies the allegations contained in paragraphs .... of the third party defence.

3. The defendant has no knowledge in respect of the allegations contained in paragraphs .... of the third party defence.

4. *(Set out in separate, consecutively numbered paragraphs each allegation of material fact relied on by way of reply to the third party defence.)*

(Date) *(Name, address and telephone number of defendant's solicitor or defendant)*

TO *(Name and address of third party's solicitor or third party)*

Appendix 9

Form 30A

AFFIDAVIT OF DOCUMENTS
(INDIVIDUAL)

(Court file no.)

ONTARIO
SUPERIOR COURT OF JUSTICE

BETWEEN:

(name)

Plaintiff

and

(name)

Defendant

AFFIDAVIT OF DOCUMENTS

I, *(full name of deponent)*, of the *(*City, Town*, etc.)* of ...., in the (County, Regional Municipality, *etc.*) of......., the plaintiff *(or as may be)* in this action, MAKE OATH AND SAY *(or* AFFIRM*)*:

1. I have conducted a diligent search of my records and have made appropriate enquiries of others to inform myself in order to make this affidavit. This affidavit discloses, to the full extent of my knowledge, information and belief, all documents relating to any matter in issue in this action that are or have been in my possession, control or power.

2. I have listed in Schedule A those documents that are in my possession, control or power and that I do not object to producing for inspection.

3. I have listed in Schedule B those documents that are or were in my possession, control or power and that I object to producing because I claim they are privileged, and I have stated in Schedule B the grounds for each such claim.

4. I have listed in Schedule C those documents that were formerly in my possession, control or power but are no longer in my possession, control or power, and I have stated in Schedule C when and how I lost possession or control of or power over them and their present location.

5. I have never had in my possession, control or power any document relating to any matter in issue in this action other than those listed in Schedules A, B and C.

6. I have listed in Schedule D the names and addresses of persons who might reasonably be expected to have knowledge of transactions or occurrences in issue. (*Strike out this paragraph if the action is not being brought under the simplified procedure.*)

SWORN (*etc.*)

_____

(*Signature of deponent*)

LAWYER'S CERTIFICATE

I CERTIFY that I have explained to the deponent,
- (a) the necessity of making full disclosure of all documents relating to any matter in issue in the action;
- (b) what kinds of documents are likely to be relevant to the allegations made in the pleadings; and
- (c) if the action is brought under the simplified procedure, the necessity of providing the list required under rule 76.03.

SCHEDULE A

Documents in my possession, control or power that I do not object to producing for inspection.

(Number each document consecutively. Set out the nature and date of the document and other particulars sufficient to identify it.)

SCHEDULE B

Documents that are or were in my possession, control or power that I object to producing on the grounds of privilege.

(Number each document consecutively. Set out the nature and date of the document and other particulars sufficient to identify it. State the grounds for claiming privilege for each document.)

SCHEDULE C

Documents that were formerly in my possession, control or power but are no longer in my possession, control or power.

(Number each document consecutively. Set out the nature and date of the document and other particulars sufficient to identify it. State when and how possession or control of or power over each document was lost, and give the present location of each document.)

SCHEDULE D

(To be filled in only if the action is being brought under the simplified procedure.)

Names and addresses of persons who might reasonably be expected to have knowledge of transactions or occurrences in issue.

[O. Reg. 533/95, s. 9; O. Reg. 652/00, s. 5; O. Reg. 206/02, s. 26 (in force December 31, 2002)]

Form 76A

Courts Of Justice Act

NOTICE WHETHER ACTION UNDER RULE 76

(Court file no.)

ONTARIO
SUPERIOR COURT OF JUSTICE

BETWEEN:

(name)

Plaintiff

and

(name)

Defendant

NOTICE WHETHER ACTION UNDER RULE 76

The plaintiff states that this action and any related proceedings are:

(select one of the following:)

( ) continuing under Rule 76

( ) continuing under Rule 77 — fast track

( ) continuing under Rule 77 — standard track

( ) continuing as an ordinary procedure.

(Name, address and telephone and fax numbers of lawyer or plaintiff)

[O. Reg. 533/95, s. 11; O. Reg. 652/00, s. 7; O. Reg. 284/01, s. 36]

Form 76B

Courts of Justice Act

SIMPLIFIED PROCEDURE MOTION FORM

Court File No. ....

ONTARIO
SUPERIOR COURT OF JUSTICE

BETWEEN:

(name)

Plaintiff

and

(name)

Defendant

SIMPLIFIED PROCEDURE MOTION FORM

JURISDICTION   ( ) Judge
                            ( ) Master
                            ( ) Registrar

THIS FORM IS FILED BY *(Check appropriate boxes to identify the party filing this form as a moving/responding party on this motion AND to identify this party as plaintiff, defendant, etc. in the action)*

[ ] moving party
[ ] plaintiff

....

[ ] responding party
[ ] defendant

....

[ ] Other — specify kind of party and name

....

MOTION MADE

[ ] on consent of all parties
[ ] without notice

[ ] on notice to all parties and unopposed
[ ] on notice to all parties and expected to be opposed

Notice of this motion was served on (date): ....

by means of:

....

METHOD OF HEARING REQUESTED

[ ] by attendance
[ ] in writing only, no attendance
[ ] by fax
[ ] by telephone conference under rule 1.08
[ ] by video conference under rule 1.08

Date, time and place for conference call, telephone call or appearances

| .... | .... | .... |
| *(date)* | *(time)* | *(place)* |

ORDER SOUGHT BY THIS PARTY *(Responding party is presumed to request dismissal of motion and costs)*

[ ] Extension of time — until *(give specific date)*: ....
[ ] serve claim
[ ] file or deliver statement of defence
[ ] Other relief — be specific

....
....

MATERIAL RELIED ON BY THIS PARTY

[ ] this form
[ ] pleadings
[ ] affidavits — specify
[ ] other — specify

....
....

GROUNDS IN SUPPORT OF/IN OPPOSITION TO MOTION (INCLUDING RULE AND STATUTORY PROVISIONS RELIED ON)

....
....

CERTIFICATION BY LAWYER

I certify that the above information is correct, to the best of my knowledge. Signature of lawyer *(If no lawyer, party must sign)*

....

Date

....

THIS PARTY'S LAWYER *(If no lawyer, give party's name, address for service, telephone and fax number)*	OTHER LAWYER *(If no lawyer, give other party's name, address for service, telephone and fax number.)*
Name and firm:	Name and firm:
Address:	Address:
Telephone: Fax:	Telephone: Fax:

THIS PARTY'S LAWYER
(If no lawyer, give party's name,

OTHER LAWYER *(If no lawyer, give other party's name, address for service, address for service, telephone and fax number)*   *telephone and fax number.)*

Name and firm: Name and firm:

Address: Address:

Telephone: Fax: Telephone: Fax:

DISPOSITION

[ ] order to go as asked
[ ] adjourned to
[ ] order refused
[ ] order to go as follows:

....
....

Hearing method ....
Hearing duration ....…..min.

Heard in: [ ] courtroom   [ ] office

[ ] Successful party MUST prepare formal order for signature
[ ] No copy of disposition to be sent to parties
[ ] Other directions — specify

....
....

Date .... Name........................ Signature...........................
                    Judge/Master/
                    Registrar

[O. Reg. 284/01, s. 36]

Appendix 9

Form 76C

Courts of Justice Act

NOTICE OF READINESS FOR PRE-TRIAL CONFERENCE

(Court file no.)

ONTARIO
SUPERIOR COURT OF JUSTICE

BETWEEN:

(name)

Plaintiff

and

(name)

Defendant

NOTICE OF READINESS FOR PRE-TRIAL CONFERENCE

The *(identify party)* is ready for a pre-trial conference and is setting this action down for trial. A pre-trial conference in the action will proceed as scheduled and the trial will proceed when the action is reached on the trial list, unless the court orders otherwise.

CERTIFICATE

I CERTIFY that there was a settlement discussion under rule 76.08.

Date   *(Signature)*

(Name, address and telephone and fax numbers of lawyer or party giving notice)

TO   *(Name and address of lawyer or party receiving notice)*

[O. Reg. 284/01, s. 36]

Form 76D

Courts of Justice Act

TRIAL MANAGEMENT CHECKLIST

(Court file no.)

ONTARIO
SUPERIOR COURT OF JUSTICE

BETWEEN:

(name)

Plaintiff

and

(name)

Defendant

(Insert name of party filing this form)

TRIAL MANAGEMENT CHECKLIST

Trial Lawyer — Plaintiff (s):

Trial Lawyer — Defendant (s):

Filed by Plaintiff
Filed by Defendant
Filed by Subsequent Party

1. Issues Outstanding

    (a) liability: ....

    (b) damages: ....

    (c) other:
    ....

2. Names of Plaintiff's Witnesses
   ....

3. Names of Defendant's Witnesses
   ....

4. Admissions

....

Are the parties prepared to admit any facts for the purposes of the trial or summary trial?   yes ☐   no ☐

5. Document Brief

Will there be a document brief?   yes ☐   no ☐

6. Request to Admit

Will there be a request to admit?   yes ☐   no ☐

If so, have the parties agreed to a timetable?   yes ☐   no ☐

7. Expert's Reports

Are any expert's reports anticipated?   yes ☐   no ☐

8. Amendments to Pleadings

Are any amendments likely to be sought?   yes ☐   no ☐

9. Mode of Trial

Have the parties agreed to a summary trial?   yes ☐   no ☐

Have the parties agreed to an ordinary trial?   yes ☐   no ☐

If the parties have not agreed about the mode of trial, what mode of trial is being requested by the party filing this checklist?

....

10. Factum of Law

Will the parties be submitting factums of law?   yes ☐   no ☐

[O. Reg. 284/01, s. 36]

APPENDIX 10

Court Fees

(July 31, 2002)

SMALL CLAIMS COURT — CLERKS' FEES

1. Filing of a claim by an infrequent claimant	$50.00
2. Filing of a claim by a frequent claimant[1]	145.00
3. Filing of a defendant's claim	50.00
4. Filing a notice of motion (except a notice of motion under the *Wages Act*[2] — no fee)	40.00
5. Filing a defence	25.00
6. Issuing a summons to a witness	10.00
7. Receiving for enforcement a process from the Ontario Court (Provincial Division) or an order of judgment as provided by statute	25.00
8. Issuing a certificate of judgment	10.00
9. Issuing a writ of delivery, a writ of seizure and sale or a notice of examination	35.00
10. Issuing a notice of garnishment	50.00
11. Preparing and filing a consolidation order	75.00
12. Forwarding a court file to Divisional Court for appeal	20.00
13. Issuing a certified copy of a judgment or other document, per page	2.00
14. Transmitting a document other than by first class mail	Cost of Transmission
15. For the inspection of a court file,	
(i) By a solicitor or party in the proceeding	No charge
(ii) By a person who has entered into an agreement with the Attorney General for the bulk inspection of court files, per file	1.00
(iii) By any other person per file	10.00

---

[1] A frequent claimant is defined as a claimant who has filed 10 or more claims in the same office between September 2, 1997 and December 31, 1997.

    For subsequent years, a frequent claimant is someone who files a claim on or after January 1, in any calendar year, and who has filed 10 or more claims in the same office in the relevant calendar year. O. Reg. 214/97 under the *Administration of Justice Act*, R.S.O. 1990, c. A.6 (amending O. Reg. 432/93).

[2] R.S.O. 1990, c. W.1.

16. Making a photocopy of a document not requiring certification, per page — 1.00
17. Preparing records of orders, per name — 2.00
18. In an application under the *Repair and Storage Liens Act*,[3]
    (i) On the filing of,
        A. an application — 100.00
        B. a notice of objection — 35.00
        C. a waiver of further claim and a receipt — No charge
    (ii) On the issuing of,
        A. an initial certificate — 35.00
        B. a final certificate — 35.00
        C. a writ of seizure — 35.00
19. Fixing of a date for trial by an infrequent claimant — 100.00
20. Fixing of a date for trial by a frequent claimant — 130.00
21. Entering of a default judgment by an infrequent claimant — 35.00
22. Entering of a default judgment by a frequent claimant — 50.00

SIMPLIFIED PROCEDURE FEES

Issue Claim/Notice of Action/Notice of Application/Third Party Notice	$157.00
Notice of Intent to Defend	125.00
Statement of Defence and Counterclaim	157.00
Statement of Defence (if intent not filed)	125.00
Jury Notice	90.00
Default Judgment	90.00
Writ of Execution	48.00
Notice of Garnishment	100.00
Trial Record (setting down for trial)	293.00
Notice of Motion	110.00
Notice of Return of Motion	110.00
Ex parte and Consent Motions	110.00
Appointment re: Assessment of Partial Indemnity Costs	90.00
Appointment re: Assessment of Substantial Indemnity Costs	65.00
Appointment with Registrar to settle an Order	90.00
Bulk Sale Affidavit	65.00
Swearing of Affidavits	11.00
Request to retrieve a Civil file from storage	53.00
Inspection of Court File (not a party to the action)	28.00
Making up/Forwarding Documents/Exhibits	65.00
Making copies for Certification, per page	3.50
Making copies, per page	2.00
Summons to Witness	19.00
Request to Redeem/Request for Sale	90.00

---

[3] R.S.O. 1990, c. R.25.

APPENDIX 11

Costs Grid*

PART I — COSTS GRID

Where students-at-law or law clerks have provided services of a nature that the Law Society of Upper Canada authorizes them to provide, the fees for those services may be assessed and allowed under this costs grid.

Where counsel has special expertise, his or her hourly rate classification may be varied accordingly.

1. Fees other than Counsel Fee		
Hourly rates for pleadings, mediation under Rule 24.1 or Rule 75.1, financial statements, discovery of documents, drawing and settling issues on special case, setting down for trial, pre-motion conference, examination, pre-trial conference, settlement conference, notice or offer, preparation for hearing, attendance at assignment court, order, issuing or renewing a writ of execution or notice of garnishment, seizure under writ of execution, seizure and sale under writ of execution, notice of garnishment, or for any other procedure authorized by the *Rules of Civil Procedure* and not provided for elsewhere in the costs grid.		
	Partial Indemnity Scale	Substantial Indemnity Scale
Law Clerks	Up to $80.00 per hour	Up to $125.00 per hour
Students-at-law	Up to $60.00 per hour	Up to $90.00 per hour
Lawyer (less than 10 years)	Up to $225.00 per hour	Up to $300.00 per hour
Lawyer (10 years or more but less than 20 years)	Up to $300.00 per hour	Up to $400.00 per hour
Lawyer (20 years and over)	Up to $350.00 per hour	Up to $450.00 per hour

---

* Part I of Tariff A — Solicitors' Fees and Disbursements Allowable Under Rule 58.05, *Rules of Civil Procedure*, R.R.O. 1990, Reg. 194 [am. O. Reg. 533/95, s. 12; O. Reg. 453/98, s. 3; O. Reg. 290/99, s. 6; O. Reg. 652/00, s. 8; O. Reg. 244/01, s. 5; O. Reg. 284/01, s. 38].

2. Counsel Fee — Motion or Application		
	Partial Indemnity Scale	Substantial Indemnity Scale
0.25 hour	Up to $400.00	Up to $800.00
1.00 hour	Up to $1,000.00	Up to $1,500.00
2.00 hours (half day)	Up to $1,400.00	Up to $2,400.00
1 day	Up to $2,100.00	Up to $3,500.00
3. Counsel Fee — Trial or Reference		
	Partial Indemnity Scale	Substantial Indemnity Scale
Half Day	Up to $1,500.00	Up to $2,500.00
Day	Up to $2,300.00	Up to $4,000.00
Week	Up to $9,500.00	Up to $17,500.00
4. Counsel Fee — Appeal		
	Partial Indemnity Scale	Substantial Indemnity Scale
1.00 hour	Up to $1,000.00	Up to $1,500.00
2.00 hours (half day)	Up to $1,250.00	Up to $2,000.00
1 day	Up to $2,000.00	Up to $4,000.00

Index

A

Abandoned action
    dismissal as, 37, 197
Adjournments. *See* Trial
Alternative dispute resolution
    forms re mediation. *See* Simplified procedure court forms
    mandatory mediation, 48
    private mediation, 47
Appeal
    interlocutory orders, of, 60-62
    judgment, of. *See* Appealing judgment
    summary judgment, of, 43
Appealing judgment
    appeal book, 109
    appeal hearing, 113
    appeal route, 107
    books of authorities, 111
    certificate of perfection, 112
    conduct of, chart re, 117, 121
    decision to appeal, considerations, 105
    Divisional Court, to, 127
    evidence
        certificate of, 108
        compendium of, 111-12
    factums, 110
    motion for new trial (small claims court), 105-06
    notice of appeal, 107
    perfecting appeal, 109-13
    procedure, 107
    summary trial, 86
    transcripts, ordering, 109

C

Children's Lawyer, 13
Claim
    forms re. *See* Simplified procedure court forms; Small Claims Court forms
    generally. *See* Pleadings
    third party. *See* Third party claims
Client interview
    costs and retainer, 6
    counsel's opinion, 6
    first, 5
    professional relationship, elements of, 6-7
Consolidation of proceedings, 98, 128, 187-89
Contempt hearing, 190-91, 253
Costs
    client interview, explanation of, 6
    court discretion re, 132
    Crown's, 132
    generally. *See* Trial
    interlocutory motions, on, 60
    limit on, 127
    sanctions, as, 19-20
    simplified procedure rules re, 208-12
    Small Claims Court rules, 175-78
Counsel
    opinion of case, 6
    representation by, 126
Courts of Justice Act (Small Claims Court)
    appeal to Divisional Court, 127
    composition of court, 125
    consolidation of proceedings, 128
    constitution of, 123
    continuation of, 123
    costs
        court discretion re, 132
        Crown's, 132
        limit on, 127
    evidence in, 126
    installment orders, 127
    interest awards, 127-32
    judges of, 123, 125
        deputy judges, 125, 128
    jurisdiction
        court, of, 123
        judges, of, 123
    representation by counsel or agent, 126
    summary hearings, 125
    transfer from Superior Court of Justice, 125

D

Default judgment
    simplified procedure action, 37-39
    small claims, 35, 158-61, 230
Defence. *See* Pleadings
Disclosure. *See* Simplified procedure, rules of
Discovery of documents
    oral, 55
    simplified procedure, 54
        affidavit of documents, 54
        limitations on, 198
    small claims court, 53
Dismissal
    abandoned action, as, 37, 197
    registrar, by, 200
    summary judgment motion, 42
Documents
    affidavit of, 197, 277
    discovery of. *See* Discovery of documents
    evidence preparation and, 71, 74
    service of, 146-53

E

Enforcing judgment
  collection, 91
  costs of, 103
  Highway Traffic Act provisions, 102
  simplified procedure, 99-102
    examination of debtor, 99
    garnishment, 101-02
    writ of delivery, 99-100
    writ of seizure and sale, 100-01
      personal property, 100
      sale of land, 101
  Small Claims Court, 91-98
    consolidation orders, 98
    examination of debtor, 92-94
    garnishment, 96-97
    jurisdiction, 91-92
    writ of delivery of personal property, 94
    writ of seizure and sale, 95-96
      personal property, 95
      sale of land, 96
Evidence
  affidavit of, 58
  appeal, on, 108, 112
  preparation of. *See* Preparation for trial
  Small Claims Court rules re, 126, 173-75
  summary judgment requirements, 40
Examination
  debtor, of, 92-94, 99, 189-91
  medical, 57
  notice of, 251
  trial, at, 81-82

F

Fees, 289-91
Forms. *See* Simplified procedure court forms; Small Claims Court forms
Forum of action, 142-45

G

Garnishment
  forms, 242, 245
  proceedings, 96-97, 101-02, 182-87

I

Interest
  awards, 127-32
  post-judgment, 87
  pre-judgment, 86
Interlocutory motions
  generally, 58
  simplified procedure, 60-63
    interlocutory orders, appeals of, 61
    judge's order, 62
    master's order, 61
    motions, 60
  small claims court, 58-60
    affidavit evidence, 58
    appeal, 60
    costs on, 60

J

Judges. *See* Courts of Justice Act
Judgment
  appeal of. *See* Appealing judgment
  certificate of, 237
  default. *See* Default judgment
  enforcing. *See* Enforcing judgment
  generally. *See* Trial
  setting aside/varying, 169
  summary. *See* Summary judgment
Jurisdiction
  enforcement, re, 91-92
  monetary
    simplified procedure rules, under, 3, 17
    Small Claims Court, of, 2, 16, 123, 142-45
  territorial
    simplified procedure rules, under, 21
    Small Claims Court, of, 21, 123
  transfers between courts, 21-22

L

Limitation periods, 9-11
  notice requirements, 10
  procedural limits, 11-12
  substantive limits, 10-11
Litigation
  alternatives to, 9
  delay, 1
  expense of, 1
  limitation periods. *See* Limitation periods
  parties. *See* Parties
Litigation guardian, 12-14

M

Mediation. *See* Alternative dispute resolution
Medical examinations
  simplified procedure, 57
  small claims court, 57
Minors. *See* Litigation guardian
Motions
  interlocutory. *See* Interlocutory motions
  new trial, for, 105-06, 171-73
  simplified procedure rules re, 199
  Small Claims Court rules re, 168
  summary judgment, for, 40-42

O

Orders
  appeal of interlocutory orders, 60-62
  consolidation order, 98, 187-89
  enforcement of, 179-91

P

Particulars, demand for
  simplified procedure, 55
  small claims court, 55
Parties
  corporations, 15
  disability, under, 12-15
  partnerships, 15
  sole proprietors, 16
Pleadings
  amendment of, 33, 161-62
  drafting guidelines, 23
  Small Claims Court, in, 24-28
    claim
      affidavit of service, 25
      contents, 24
      issuing, 24
      rules re, 145-46, 155-58
      serving, 25
    defence, 26, 153-55
    defendant's claim, 26-27
      defence to, 28
  simplified procedure rules, under, 28-33
    counterclaim, 30
    crossclaim, 31
    jury notice, 33
    reply, 32-33
    statement of claim
      issuing, 28
      rule re, 195
      serving, 29
    statement of defence, 29-30
    third party claim, 31-32
  striking
    simplified procedure, 39
    small claims, 36
Preparation for trial
  evidence, preparation of
    simplified procedure
      documents, 74
      expert witness, 75
      generally, 73
      witnesses, 74
    small claims court
      documents, 71
      generally, 70
      site visit, 73
      witnesses, 72
  file organization, 69
  theory of case, 70
  trial brief, 69

Pre-trial conferences
  generally, 63
  notice of readiness for, 205, 285
  request for, 231
  simplified procedure
    conference procedure, 65
    readiness for, 65
    setting action down for trial, 66
  small claims court, 162-65
    conference procedure, 64
    notice of trial, 65
    request for, 63
Public Guardian and Trustee, 13

R

Referee, 192
Request to admit
  simplified procedure, 56
  small claims court, 56

S

Seizure and sale. *See* Enforcing judgment
Settlement
  alternative dispute resolution. *See* Alternative dispute resolution
  concluding settlement, 50-51
    simplified procedure, under, 51
    small claims, 51
  conferences
    private settlement meetings, 46
    simplified procedure rule, 46
  discussion, 204
  offers to settle, *see also* Small Claims Court Rules
    cost consequences of, 49-50
      simplified procedure, under, 50
      small claims, 50
    generally, 49
  party under disability, where, 15
  preparation for, 46
  pre-trial, 78
  rationale of, 45
Simplified procedure, rules of
  abandonment, effect of, 197
  affidavit of documents, 197
  appeal from judgment
    conduct of, chart re, 121
    generally. *See* Appealing judgment
  application of, 193
  availability of, 193
  certificate of readiness for trial, 205
  conduct of action, chart re, 119-20
  continuing action under, 19, 196
  costs. *See* Costs
  disclosure
    documentary, 204
    failure re, 198

Simplified procedure, rules of — *cont'd*
  discovery, limitations on, 198
  dismissal by registrar, 200
  fees, court, 290
  intention of, 3
  lawyer's certificate, 198
  mandatory, when, 193-95
  monetary jurisdiction, 3
  motions, 199
  notice of action, 195
  notice of readiness for pre-trial conference, 205
  optional, when, 195
  origins of, 3
  pre-trial conference, 205-06
  settlement discussion, 204
  solicitor's fees and disbursements, tariff costs grid, 291
  statement of claim, 195
  summary judgment, 201-04
  summary trial, 207
  trial list, placing action on, 206
  witnesses, list of potential, 197
Simplified procedure court forms
  affidavit of documents (30A), 277
  certificate of non-compliance — mediation (24.1D), 264
  counterclaim (27A), 266
  crossclaim (28A), 269
  defence to counterclaim (27C), 267
  defence to crossclaim (28B), 270
  notice by assigned mediator (24.1B), 260
  notice of intent to defend (18B), 258
  notice of name of mediator and date of session (24.1A), 259
  notice of readiness for pre-trial conference (76C), 285
  notice where action under rule 76 (76A), 280
  reply (25A), 265
  reply to defence to counterclaim (27D), 268
  reply to defence to crossclaim (28C), 271
  reply to third party defence (29C), 276
  simplified procedure motion form (76B), 281
  statement of claim — notice of action (14D), 256
  statement of defence (18A), 257
  statement of issues — mediation (24.1C), 262
  third party claim (29A), 272
  third party defence (29B), 275
  trial management checklist (76D), 286
Small Claims Court, *see also* Courts of Justice Act
  appeal from judgment
    conduct of, chart re, 117
    generally. *See* Appealing judgment
  conduct of action, chart, 115
  costs. *See* Costs
  fees, 289
  history of, 2
  monetary jurisdictions in, 2
  "people's court", as, 3
  rules. *See* Small Claims Court Rules
  summary procedure of, purpose of, 3
Small Claims Court forms
  affidavit (15B), 233
  affidavit of service (8B), 223
  certificate of judgment (20A), 237
  certificate of service (8A), 222
  consent to act as defendant's litigation guardian (4B), 218
  consent to act as plaintiff's litigation guardian (4A), 216
  defence (9A), 226
  defendant's claim (10A), 229
  garnishee's statement (20F), 245
  general heading (1A), 214
  notice of contempt hearing (20I), 253
  notice of default judgment (11A), 230
  notice of examination (20H), 251
  notice of garnishment (20E), 242
  notice of motion (15A), 232
  notice of trial (16A), 234
  notice to alleged partner (5A), 220
  notice to co-owner of debt (20G), 248
  order as to terms of payment (9C), 228
  plaintiff's claim (7A), 221
  request for hearing (9B), 227
  request for pre-trial conference (13A), 231
  summons to witness (18A), 235
  warrant for arrest of defaulting witness (18B), 236
  warrant of committal (20J), 254
  writ of delivery (20B), 238
  writ of seizure and sale of land (20D), 241
  writ of seizure and sale of personal property (20C), 239
Small Claims Court Rules
  amendment of pleadings, 161-62
  citation, 133
  claim
    defendant's, 155-58
    plaintiff's, 145-46
  commencement of proceedings, 145-46
  compliance with, 136
  consolidation order, 187-89
  contempt hearing, 190-91
  costs, 175-78
  default proceedings, 158-61
  defence, 153-55
  definitions, 134
  disability, parties under, 137-40
  documents in proceedings, general heading of, 136
  evidence, 173-75

Small Claims Court Rules — *cont'd*
  examination of debtor, 189-91
  forms, 136
  forum of action, 142-45
  garnishment proceedings, 182-87
  general principle re interpretation of, 135
  inspection of property, 170
  jurisdiction, 142-45
  litigation guardian, 138-40
  matters not provided for, 135
  motion for new trial, 171-73
  motions, 168
  orders, enforcement of, 179-91
  orders on terms, 136
  partnerships, 140-42
  pre-trial conferences, 162-65
  referee, role of, 192
  seizure or sale of property, 180-82
  service of documents, 146-53
  settlement
    offers, generally, 165-68
    person under disability, 140
  sole proprietorships, 142
  striking out pleadings, 162
  time, 137
  trial
    adjournment, 170
    evidence at, 173-75
    failure to attend, 169
    notice of, 169
    setting aside/varying judgment, 169
  witnesses, 173-75
Summary hearing, 125
Summary judgment, 201-04
  appeal of, 43
  dismissal of motion for, 42
  evidentiary requirements, 40
  hearing of motion, 41
  motion record, 40
  notice of motion for, 40
  rules re, 201-04
  test for, 41-42
Summary trial
  appeal of judgment, 86
  conduct of, 85
  generally, 84
  rules re, 207
  trial record, 84

T

Third party claims
  form, 272
  simplified procedure rules, under, 18, 31-32
Transfer
  courts, between, 21-22
  Superior Court of Justice, from, 125
Trial
  adjournments
    simplified procedure, 78-79
    small claims court, 78, 170
  closing arguments, 83
  conduct of, 77-89
  costs
    generally, 87
    simplified procedure, 88
    small claims court, 87
  courtroom custom and etiquette, 80
  cross-examination, 81-82
  direct examination, 81
  judgment
    generally, 86
    post-judgment interest, 87
    pre-judgment interest, 86
  objections, 83
  opening statements, 80-81
  parties, failure of, to attend, 79
  planning and preparation, 77
  preparation. *See* Preparation for trial
  settlement, pre-trial, 78
  summary trial. *See* Summary trial
  witnesses, failure of, to attend, 79
Trial brief, 69
Trial list, 206
Trial management, 286

W

Witnesses
  expert, 75
  failure to attend, 79
  list of potential, 197
  preparation, 72, 74
  Small Claims Court rules re, 173-75
  summons to, 235
Writs. *See* Enforcing judgment